REUNITED

# REUNITED

FAMILY SEPARATION AND CENTRAL AMERICAN
YOUTH MIGRATION

**Ernesto Castañeda and Daniel Jenks**

*Russell Sage Foundation*  NEW YORK

THE RUSSELL SAGE FOUNDATION

The Russell Sage Foundation, one of the oldest of America's general purpose foundations, was established in 1907 by Mrs. Margaret Olivia Sage for "the improvement of social and living conditions in the United States." The foundation seeks to fulfill this mandate by fostering the development and dissemination of knowledge about the country's political, social, and economic problems. While the foundation endeavors to assure the accuracy and objectivity of each book it publishes, the conclusions and interpretations in Russell Sage Foundation publications are those of the authors and not of the foundation, its trustees, or its staff. Publication by Russell Sage, therefore, does not imply foundation endorsement.

BOARD OF TRUSTEES
*Jennifer Lee, Chair*

| | | | |
|---|---|---|---|
| Marianne Bertrand | Jason Furman | David Leonhardt | Jennifer Richeson |
| Sheldon Danziger | Michael Jones-Correa | Earl Lewis | Thomas J. Sugrue |
| James N. Druckman | David Laibson | Hazel Rose Markus | Celeste Watkins-Hayes |

DOI: https://doi.org/10.7758/dvxg2393

LIBRARY OF CONGRESS
CATALOGING-IN-PUBLICATION DATA
Names: Castañeda, Ernesto, author. | Jenks, Daniel, author.
Title: Reunited : family separation and Central American youth migration / Ernesto Castañeda and Daniel Jenks.
Description: New York : Russell Sage Foundation, [2024] | Includes bibliographical references and index. | Summary: "Reunited focuses on Central American youth who migrate without their parents to the United States, particularly to the suburbs of Washington, DC, and how they reunite with family members. The book explains the circumstances of these migrants' arrival and puts their experiences in socio-historical context. The authors discuss Central American migration to the country and DC region and the methods used to collect data; provide a brief recent history of El Salvador, Guatemala, and Honduras to explain why people have migrated from this region to the United States; explore the motives for migration; recount the journey from Central America to the U.S. border; present data investigating how family reunification unfolds as well as data involving trauma, PTSD, and depression; delve into how migrant youth fare in schools; and suggest how country-, state-, and local-level policy can help or hinder youth integration and family reunification"—Provided by publisher.
Identifiers: LCCN 2023050630 (print) | LCCN 2023050631 (ebook) | ISBN 9780871544995 (paperback) | ISBN 9781610449137 (ebook)
Subjects: LCSH: Immigrant youth—Washington (D.C.) | Immigrant youth—Central America. | Family reunification—Washington (D.C.) | Family reunification—Central America.
Classification: LCC JV6940 .C37 2024 (print) | LCC JV6940 (ebook) | DDC 305.23089/68/7280753—dc23/eng/20240212
LC record available at https://lccn.loc.gov/2023050630
LC ebook record available at https://lccn.loc.gov/2023050631

Copyright © 2024 by Russell Sage Foundation. All rights reserved. Printed in the United States of America. No part of this publication may be reproduced, stored in a retrieval system, or transmitted in any form or by any means, electronic, mechanical, photocopying, recording, or otherwise, without the prior written permission of the publisher. Permission is not granted for large language model training. Reproduction by the United States Government in whole or in part is permitted for any purpose.

The paper used in this publication meets the minimum requirements of American National Standard for Information Sciences—Permanence of Paper for Printed Library Materials. ANSI Z39.48-1992.

Text design by Matthew T. Avery. Front matter DOI: https://doi.org/10.7758/dvxg2393.6362

RUSSELL SAGE FOUNDATION
112 East 64th Street,
New York, New York 10065
10 9 8 7 6 5 4 3 2 1

*To Alexander and Ernesto III,*
*To John, Jennifer, and Leah Jenks,*
*And to migrant minors looking for peace and family*

# CONTENTS

LIST OF ILLUSTRATIONS *ix*
GLOSSARY *xi*
ABOUT THE AUTHORS *xvii*
PREFACE *xix*
ACKNOWLEDGMENTS *xxxi*

Introduction *1*

*Chapter 1* What We Know and What We Set Out to Find *34*

*Chapter 2* A Brief History of El Salvador, Honduras, and Guatemala: Historical Contexts and Drivers of Migration *53*

*Chapter 3* Reasons to Emigrate *77*

*Chapter 4* Central Americans and Their Passage through Mexico to the United States *102*

*Chapter 5* Legal Uncertainty, Family Reunification, and Learning a New Life *118*

*Chapter 6* Mental Health and Immigration: Symptoms of PTSD and Depression *140*

*Chapter 7* Immigrant Integration into School Environments *171*

*Chapter 8* Family-Propelled Migration and Immigrant Integration *185*

APPENDIX: NOTES ON METHODS AND INSTRUMENTS *211*
NOTES *229*
REFERENCES *243*
INDEX *269*

# ILLUSTRATIONS

### Figures

*Figure 1.1* Southwest Border Apprehensions by Country of Origin, Fiscal Years 2014–2018  *40*

*Figure 1.2* Unaccompanied Children Released to Sponsors, by State, Fiscal Years 2014–2018  *42*

*Figure 1.3* Unaccompanied Children Released to Sponsors in the D.C. Area, Fiscal Years 2014–2018  *43*

*Figure 1.4* Unaccompanied Children Released to Sponsors in the D.C. Area, by Year  *43*

*Figure 1.5* Total Number of Unaccompanied Children Placed with Sponsors, 2015–2019  *44*

*Figure 6.1* Respondents' Self-Reported Mental Health before and after Migration  *159*

### Tables

*Table 1.1* Demographic Characteristics of Immigrant Minors  *48*

*Table 1.2* Demographic Characteristics of Immigrant Minor Respondents  *50*

*Table 6.1* Sources of Respondents' Mental Health Worries and Stressors before and after Migration  *162*

*Table 6.2* PHQ-8 Scoring Guide to Severity of Depression Symptoms  *163*

*Table 6.3* Respondents' Symptoms of Depression as Determined by the PHQ-8  *164*

*Table 6.4* Respondents' Symptoms of PTSD as Measured on the Child PTSD Symptom Scale  *165*

*Table 7.1* Respondents' Relationships with School Staff at Their D.C. Area School  *172*

*Table 7.2* Respondents' Relationships with Peers in the D.C. Area  *173*

*Table 8.1* Challenges and Facilitators to Integration  *186*

# GLOSSARY

**adverse childhood experiences (ACEs):** Experiences suffered during childhood that may have long-term negative effects, such as experiencing or witnessing violence, abuse, neglect, poverty, homelessness, racism, incarceration, illness, or other traumatic events. ACEs are common, and research has found correlations between more adverse childhood experiences and greater health risks, depression, substance abuse, poor academic achievement, and time out of work later in life.

**La Bestia:** A freight train line from the Guatemala-Mexico border to Central Mexico that migrants board to travel north. Also known as "The Train of Death." Migrants ride on the rooftops of the trains, risking loss of limbs or even life if they fall from the train while it is in motion. Robberies and violence are also common aboard the trains.

**Central America:** The portion of the Americas that extends from Guatemala to Panama, from the south of Mexico to the north of Colombia. In this book, we mainly refer to northern Central America: El Salvador, Honduras, and Guatemala. Security officials call these countries the Northern Triangle because they are the primary sources of immigration to the United States, in contrast to Belize, Costa Rica, and Panama. In recent years, Nicaragua has also seen an uptick in emigration. People in the Americas outside of the United States refer to the continent as "America" and consider Mexico part of North America.

*coyote:* The Spanish word for a guide who takes people to their destination. Traditionally distinguished from a smuggler or a human trafficker. Coyotes used to be trusted community members with a reputation to protect if they were to continue their business. With intensifying criminalization of border crossing, the business of transporting asylum seekers and irregular migrants to the U.S.-Mexico border or across it has become more expensive, more anonymous, and increasingly dominated by integrated cartels and organized crime.

**English for Speakers of Other Languages (ESOL):** Language training programs for speakers of other languages offered in schools or community centers.

**family-propelled migration:** Migration motivated by the desire to be with biological parents after years of living apart as a transnational family. An individual in location A with close family members living in location B is likelier to move from A to B than somebody without close family members in B. This concept is similar to "chain migration" and "social networks" but limited to the context of family reunification, whether through official or informal channels.

**Flores Settlement Agreement:** A 1997 court settlement that set federal policies and standards for the detention, release, and treatment of minors in the custody of the Office of Refugee Resettlement by prioritizing them for release to the custody of their families and requiring those in federal custody to be placed in the least restrictive setting.

*hielera:* The Spanish word for "icebox" or "freezer." Refers to cells, cages, or rooms where the government keeps immigrants at very low temperatures with aluminum blankets and without warm clothing.

**immigrant:** A person moving into a new country. See *migrant*.

**integration:** The process that gives immigrants and their families the opportunity to thrive in their new homes in a particular social and policy context. Integration is the opposite of exclusion. We use "integration" as synonymous with incorporation into U.S. jobs, schools, neighborhoods, and institutions. We also take an intercultural approach based on the assumption that the outcomes and opportunities afforded to immigrants and refugees should be the same as those enjoyed by natives and should not require that they assimilate into the local culture and lose important cultural practices and identities.

**interculturalism:** The goal of diverse cultures coexisting, with no culture or language being given preference over another, in order to promote exchange, innovation, and cultural richness.

**Latin:** The gender-neutral term we use instead of "Latin/o/a/e/x" and interchangeably with "Hispanic." "Latin people" as used here encompasses Central American immigrants, their families, and their children born in the United States, along with Mexicans, Puerto Ricans, Cubans, and others with origins in Latin America and the Caribbean, regardless of skin color, language spoken, or place of birth. We also prefer to use "Latin" as an adjective and not as a noun to underline that being Latin is not the defining feature of a person or a group of people.

**migrant:** A person who moves from their place of residence to another a relatively long distance away. "Migrants" includes families moving within a political unit, such as "internal migrants," or internally displaced people, as well as those moving across nation-state borders as "international migrants." There are also "transnational" and "circular migrants," who move back and forth often, and "return migrants," who move back to their place of birth or last residence after living abroad for some time. Around half of all emigrants eventually return.

The state and polemicists put a lot of emphasis on these distinctions between types of migrants. Analytically speaking, however, there is not much point in differentiating between internal and international migrants or between documented and undocumented migrants. A lack of documents creates a lot of hurdles for people, but immigration status is created by restrictionist policies and through decrees, legislation, and amnesties, and it can be transformed by these means. Immigration status is not related to the morality or objective deservingness of an individual or family, though it is connected to race, class, gender, age, and geopolitics. The differences between "economic" migrants, political asylum seekers, and refugees are blurrier in real life than in statute definitions. Therefore, we use the term "migrants" to encompass all these experiences and legal and discursive categories.

**migrant protection protocols (MPPs):** Instituted on January 25, 2019, the Migrant Protection Protocols, better known as the "Remain in Mexico" program, mandate that migrants who crossed from one or more countries through Mexico on their way to the United States could be sent back to Mexico as their claims worked their way through the immigration system.

**Office of Refugee Resettlement (ORR):** A part of the U.S. Department of Health and Human Services, the ORR is in charge of providing shelter and care to adult and minor refugees while they are settled with families or in the community.

**social networks/social capital:** People's ties and connections. Does not refer to social media services and apps.

**special immigrant juvenile (SIJ):** A minor who is eligible for permanent residency (a green card) but cannot be reunified with their parents or return to their home country because of alleged abuse, neglect, or abandonment by their parents.

**sponsor:** An adult, often a parent or relative of minors who arrive at the border, who becomes the legal guardian of those minors in the United States. In this book, we often use the term "sponsor" even when talking about biological parents because, legally and in the eyes of the state, any such adult is a sponsor. This matters because individuals who act as sponsors are legally responsible for the children; also, by stepping up in this way, they may risk deportation by sharing their information with the federal government. Indeed, some sponsors are undocumented and may be deported, sometimes accompanied by U.S. citizen children who are going to the country where their parents were born. Therefore, undocumented biological parents may not become their children's official sponsor, and extended family or friends will do so on their behalf.

**structural family separation:** Separations of nuclear and extended families due to labor demand for adults and immigration laws that do not allow working-class people from the Global South to bring their children and spouses with them or whose salaries in the Global North are so low that they cannot support their family.

**Title 42:** A Trump administration policy that barred entry to migrants and asylum seekers at the U.S.-Mexico border during the COVID-19 pandemic and allowed their expulsion. The policy ended on May 11, 2023.

**Trafficking Victims Protection Reauthorization Act (TVPRA):** A law passed in 2008 that strengthens federal trafficking laws and adds provisions that govern the rights of unaccompanied children who enter the United States.

**trauma:** The adverse interpretation and mental health effects of experiencing a highly distressing event. Experiencing a highly distressing event does not always cause trauma. An individual may have symptoms of post-traumatic stress disorder (PTSD) if this experience negatively impacts their daily life and mental health.

**T visa:** A visa that allows victims of trafficking to enter the United States.

**unaccompanied alien child/children (UAC):** U.S. government classification for children who arrive at the border or another port of entry without proper documentation or the legal status to be in the United States. They are also known as unaccompanied children (UC) or unaccompanied alien minors (UAM). While technically UAC must be minors (younger than eighteen) and traveling with no close relative, underage immigrants who travel accompanied by a trusted coyote or a distant family member whom they barely know also face the experience of traveling without the support and reassurance of a loved one. This designation matters for the likelihood that a migrant child will be allowed to stay in the United States, but as we show in this book, there are few sociological differences between UACs and "accompanied minors" in terms of reasons for migration and family dynamics after family reunification.

**unaccompanied refugee minor (URM):** An eligible displaced minor who is selected for resettlement in the United States but who has no predetermined adult relative or acquaintance who will commit to their long-term care. There are special programs to welcome them and integrate them into the United States.

**U.S. Customs and Border Protection (CBP):** The immigration enforcement arm of the U.S. Department of Homeland Security (DHS).

**U visa:** A visa for victims of serious crimes.

# ABOUT THE AUTHORS

ERNESTO CASTAÑEDA is director of the Center for Latin American and Latino Studies and the Immigration Lab at American University.

DANIEL JENKS works in policy research in Washington, D.C., and as an adjunct instructor in the Department of Sociology at American University.

# PREFACE

In this book, we show the multifaceted ways in which family separation is not limited to forced separation by authorities at an international border. More specifically, we document how Central American youth in the D.C. area experience structural separation and subsequent reunifications and show how the dynamics that cumulatively cause young Central Americans to migrate are not very different for many other migrants.

Families are often separated years before a child ends up at the border. Separation can start with a parent's "choice" to migrate without their children. This choice is made within a set of constrained options in a global context that limits family migration for people from the Global South. After years of separation enforced by exclusionary border and visa controls, parents and/or children may decide to reunite, even if they face a risky trip and low odds of success. Other families are forced apart later on. They may arrive and get settled, but later the father is deported. Such family separations should be discussed alongside other discussions of family separation due to immigration policies. Reducing the set of difficult choices that families make to survive to a single event at the border does them a disservice and oversimplifies migration dynamics. This book is largely the story of organic family reunification despite the many miles, dangers, and legal obstacles.

In this preface, we recount the experiences of four young migrants who illustrate many of the situations, histories, challenges, and successes that we describe in the following pages. They do not represent specific typologies. We summarize their experiences to introduce some of the people we will follow across the book and provide short profiles to round out those aspects of youth migration and family separation we explore. We reproduce their own words later in the book.

The protagonists described here suffered from many of the same structural issues that others face in Central America: poverty, the legacy of the dependency of Central American countries on the United States, governments that cannot provide adequate public services, and threats from gangs, to name a few. They all migrated to and settled with family in the Washington, D.C., region. In some ways, many of those whose stories are recounted in this book are the "lucky" ones, in that they left intending to arrive in the D.C. region and actually made it, having beaten the odds—always against them—that they would be prevented from reuniting with their families and from studying or working in the United States. Some people die along the way, many are detained in Mexico and deported, and many others are detained at the U.S.-Mexico border and deported. These outcomes have become even more common with programs such as "Remain in Mexico," Title 42, and Title 8, which prevent many people arriving at the border from staying or even applying for asylum.

Others with fewer economic resources are unable to pay a *coyote* or the transportation costs and have to ride atop freight trains, and many who do so have fallen and died or lost a limb. Many others are stopped along the way by Mexican authorities and returned to Mexico, or they are not allowed into the United States by immigration authorities because they are traveling with family members or because their asylum claims are not deemed credible. Thus, they are seen as not deserving of consideration for legal immigration status.

The ones already living here have to pass a credible fear interview and be allowed to wait for a court date inside the United States to ask for asylum, refuge, or family reunification. They are given into the custody of any parents and family members who come forward; such persons are not always present. Others risk deportation as soon as they are in the United States, and some may already have been placed in deportation procedures. The protagonists in this book were lucky in the sense that they were not special and simply by happenstance were able to scale many of the barriers that block many others.

As has happened for centuries, immigration by individuals often leads to family migration and the creation of kinship and coethnic networks in U.S. cities. Nonetheless, making immigration easier would not prompt all Central Americans to leave the region; more legal pathways reflecting the reality on the ground would simply mean safer passage for migrants and a more equitable system. Furthermore, being in a position to receive people who are willing and able to become part of the American economy and political project makes the United States the lucky one. Their arrival would neither spell the end of the United States nor drastically change the country's racial composition, as those talking about "the great replacement" posit.[1] Instead, immigration allows for the continuation of the U.S. democratic experiment and culture, promotes a growing economy, and increases innovation, creativity, and scientific discoveries. More solid work permits would help ensure stronger rights for all workers who pay their way in labor and taxes. Most importantly, new immigration from Central America would ensure the safety of those who are emigrating to escape threats on their lives and families. Even in non-life-threatening cases, children and young adults who were separated from their families in a global system of racial capitalism should be able to make safe passage to reunify with their caregivers.

Many of the migrants interviewed for this book were escaping difficult home lives and situations within their country. The following vignettes include references to physical, sexual, and emotional abuse of minors and the mention of suicidal ideation.

## Maria

Maria was seventeen years old when she was interviewed for this project. She had lived in Montgomery County, Maryland, for a year after migrating from Honduras. Maria and many other migrants said that they ultimately decided to migrate because of the constant threat of violence from gangs. Gang violence had deeply affected Maria and her family. Before she was born, her sister, then six years old, was kidnapped. Her family organized community members and worked with local police until her sister was found over a week later, alone and naked, wandering in the nearby brush, somehow unharmed. Maria explained that, while she had never been targeted by the local gangs in the same way that her sister was, the constant threat drove her to leave Honduras when she was sixteen.

In Honduras, Maria had lived with her grandmother. They made their living by running a small bakery and receiving remittances from her mother and siblings already living in the United States. Maria was eager to join them, escaping the violence in her community and living a better life up north. For Maria, this meant crossing El Salvador and Guatemala to reach Mexico's northern border. It took her a month to move from Honduras to Maryland.

However, Maria's struggles did not end when she reunited with her family. It was difficult for her to get used to her new life in the United States. She felt like her community in the United States was not the same as back home, and she did not feel supported. She did not like the new church she attended in Maryland. Overwhelmed by her new life, she felt the need to drink to cope with the transition.

Despite these challenges, Maria was glad to have educational and career opportunities she had not had before. She told us that she wanted to become a nurse and learn English. Nonetheless, life still was not easy. Maria seemed to feel obligated to be grateful to be in the United States, to have new opportunities, and to be reunited with her family. However, aspiring to live the American dream did not make her completely happy. Even though she had wanted to leave Honduras, she often missed it. Maria's new country had brought new struggles to navigate.

Maria said that school had been difficult for her. She struggled with English but was pleasantly surprised to meet other Hispanic students. As time passed, her classmates became her new friends and a support system helping her stay motivated in her studies. Eventually, Maria was able to join her school's soccer team. Things started to look up.

Since coming to the United States, Maria had been meeting with a lawyer and attending court dates to determine her legal status. She told us that she was finally granted permission by the federal government to stay in the United States. Maria's new legal status removed a massive burden from her shoulders. Graduating from high school and eventually attending university to study nursing now felt within reach. She had started meeting with her school's guidance counselor to explore the possibilities for college. They had discussed opportunities to receive scholarships and attend university as a Latin student who earned good grades and got involved in extracurricular activities.[2]

## Sebastián

When we spoke with Sebastián, a nineteen-year-old Salvadoran, he was living with his uncle in Montgomery County, Maryland. Having migrated when he was only fifteen, he described being mistreated from a young age by his parents, particularly by his father. As a child, Sebastián did not see this treatment as abnormal or abusive. He described instances of his father hitting him until he was bruised and bleeding. On top of the physical abuse, Sebastian experienced emotional abuse as well. His father would berate him with insults such as, "You are useless," and, "You never do anything right." Reflecting on those experiences, he stated his belief that it is within a parent's right to punish their children when they misbehave, but that the extreme punishment in his own family affected him significantly. Sebastián added that he used to be very depressed and even had considered suicide from time to time.

His father used to live in the United States but was deported after several years. Sebastián's uncle was a permanent resident in the United States, and in his frequent travels between the United States and El Salvador, he had encouraged Sebastián to come north for more opportunities. Feeling exhausted from the constant gang violence in his home environment, Sebastián gained his parents' consent to go north.

Rather than being carefully planned, Sebastián's trip north was ultimately decided on the spur of the moment. His uncle paid for the trip, including the coyote who guided him north. Sebastián crossed through El Salvador and Guatemala with relative ease; he encountered his first difficulties with Mexican federal border patrol agents at Mexico's southern border with Guatemala. Mexican agents can sometimes be paid off for allowing migrants to cross, so Sebastián and his party paid the agents and made it into Mexico. Crossing Mexico is arguably one of the hardest legs of the journey, given the distance that needs to be traveled and the anti-Central American sentiments in Mexico. However, they made it to the U.S. border without any major issues.

Arriving at the border, Sebastián crossed into the United States outside of an official port of entry and stayed at a safe house for two months, waiting to be passed into an area away from the border. He did not have enough money to pay for the second part of his trip and awaited funds from family members. However, before the funds arrived, U.S. Customs and Border Protection (CBP) found the safe house and detained him for two days in a large, communal, cold room in a detention center, a type of place that migrants call the *hielera*—the icebox. He was then moved to a different facility for a month and a half before he could contact his uncle and access the paperwork required to be released into the custody of his uncle.

All in all, Sebastián's journey cost his uncle around $5,000. The rate was reduced from $8,000 owing to the coyote's failure to get him through the border without being caught by CBP. Sebastián spent over three months at the U.S.-Mexico border waiting. When he was finally released from CBP custody, he said that he looked like a completely different person, bruised and having suffered significant weight loss.

Sebastián still struggled once he was settled in the United States. After release from CBP, he went to North Carolina to live with a different uncle, one who was a U.S. citizen and would be looked at more favorably by the federal authorities than the first uncle who paid for the trip. Sebastián struggled with the new environment, school, and the need to speak English all the time. His relatives in North Carolina were not patient with him and critiqued his grades and work ethic. During this time, Sebastián struggled with depression and missed his family in El Salvador. After a year, he moved to Montgomery County to live with the first uncle.

Despite the ups and downs he had experienced during his time in the United States, Sebastián reported that he was much happier at his new high school, enjoyed a variety of extracurricular activities, and had many friends who were also from El Salvador. He planned to attend a university and to become an English teacher for new migrants.

Violence often motivates young people to leave El Salvador—violence from the civil war in the 1980s to the violence of the country's nationwide struggle with MS-13 and other gangs. However, it is essential to understand that violence is not pervasive across all of Central America and that violence is not limited to that region. For example, Sebastián never witnessed a shooting in El Salvador, but he did see an African American man being killed in front of him in the D.C. area when he was coming out of a restaurant. Some might argue that simply leaving El Salvador and coming to the United States makes everything better for a young person, but this is not the case. Besides the difficulties of acculturation, they are met with challenges at the contextual level; witnessing a murder, for example, is a traumatizing experience that would be difficult for a young person to process anywhere. In this book, we hope to show some of the environments that are conducive to positive integration.

## Alexander

Alexander was seventeen years old when he left El Salvador. Like many Central American migrants, Alexander fled his home country because of gang violence. His town was under gang control, and he and his family were victims of violence, threats, and extortion by the 18th Street Gang.

In El Salvador, Alexander lived with his grandmother, siblings, and cousins. Even without the daily pressures from gangs, life there was difficult enough for Alexander and his family. They struggled to make ends meet, even with the financial support that his mother sent from abroad. His father had always been out of the picture. His family had to pay off the gangs in exchange for their safety, sometimes with no money left over to buy food. Alexander and his cousins worked when they could. When they were not at school, they would find work at their local cemetery digging graves. Alexander reported that they sometimes had the harrowing job of digging graves for their own friends who were killed by gangs. They gave all the money they made to their grandmother to buy food and pay off the gangs.

Gangs commonly recruit members by using extortion and violence toward young men. Teenagers are beaten up and targeted, and often this treatment stops only when they finally agree to join the gang. Alexander's family was constantly called and harassed by the local gang with demands that they pay the gang in exchange for being left alone in their home. Some of those who join no longer live with the constant fear of being targeted and have relatively more freedom of mobility.[3] In an environment where powerful violent groups are the key to safety, joining can be tempting, or simply becomes necessary for survival. Alexander briefly considered joining the local gang, after watching former friends stop worrying about being preyed on constantly after they joined. However, these friends became targeted by rival gangs and police forces. Ultimately, Alexander decided against joining a gang, a decision that some are unable to make because of the threat of violence is imminent. Alexander was lucky in that he could afford to leave.

In the United States, Alexander's mother and stepfather were successful in obtaining visas for him and his siblings, and they were able to fly to the United States. Flying with papers is a much easier path to the United States than traveling by land. Most family members of Central American workers in the United States are denied visas. Thus, compared to many other Central American migrants, Alexander and his family arrived here easily.

Alexander's mother had been in the United States for almost thirteen years before she could successfully apply for visas and save enough money to pay for her children's airfare. Alexander had been under his grandmother's care since he was five years old. The last time he saw his grandmother was just a few months before we interviewed him. He had returned to El Salvador right before she passed away. Because Alexander had lived apart from his mother for many years, his grandmother was more of a mother to him. Being in the United States with his mother was difficult because he did not see her as a mother but more as a close friend. This is not to say that he had a bad relationship with his mother or did not respect her, but that he saw his grandmother as the maternal figure who raised him. He described as mostly positive the relationship he and his siblings had with their parents, who had always looked after them.

Alexander's story is a fortunate one despite the difficulties he experienced. Many migrants have to cross through more of Central America and Mexico before finally reaching the United States at the southern border, where they may be detained for any period of time. The journey is long, treacherous, and expensive, and some have to make multiple attempts before finally arriving on the other side of the border. Alexander's relationship with his parents was also relatively strong, as they were very patient and understood that their absence had created a disconnect in their relationship with their children. Having been under the care of grandparents or relatives for almost their entire lives, many youth migrants find it very difficult to navigate their reunited family life in the United States, especially life with their parents, who may hardly be known to them. Stepparents can also complicate the transition; some are dismissive of their spouse's children, as was the case for Alexander.

It is unclear what the situation would have been like for Alexander's family if their visas were never granted. Alexander would have had to join the 18th Street Gang or risk his and his family's lives by refusing to do so. While life in the United States was not entirely what he had expected, he knew that he was safe in his new home in Prince George's County, Maryland. That was a priceless feeling.

## Elizabeth

Sixteen-year-old Elizabeth had lived in Prince George's County, Maryland, for less than a year. Before migrating, she had lived with various family members in Guatemala. Her mother migrated to the United States when she was eight months old, and Elizabeth was left in the care of her aunt and uncle, and later with her older brother. Her father was never in the picture. She faced significant hardships from a young age. When she lived with her aunt and uncle, they were abusive, often hitting her and her brothers. Elizabeth said that they would never hit their own kids for doing the same things that she and her brothers were being punished for. They felt less valued. Eventually, one of her brothers joined MS-13 and moved out of the house.

He was not the first person Elizabeth knew who joined MS-13. In school, she had friends who eventually decided to join the gangs too. Her old friends and other members of the gangs pressured her to join. They would tempt her by saying that she would always be protected and have money if she joined. However, she refused to join on multiple occasions. Eventually, what may have initially come across as friendly invitations became threats. The gangs had a practice of sending out armed members in groups of three to try to round up women to join their gang, threatening to kill them if they did not. Elizabeth said she had witnessed firsthand four or five murders of random people in the streets during her time living in Guatemala. What was most striking from her account was how common it was. On those four or five occasions, she was walking through her neighborhood and saw gang members suddenly fire at someone and then quickly leave. Elizabeth would keep walking afterward to get to her destination as if nothing had happened.

Elizabeth's desire to meet her mother in the United States had increased by the time she felt truly and fully that she was no longer safe in Guatemala, both from the general surroundings and gang violence and from the violence against her by those who were taking care of her. In addition to the verbal abuse by the aunt and uncle she lived with, her uncle sexually assaulted her at the age of twelve. She left her aunt and uncle's house to live with a cousin and her husband. Her cousin worked as a waitress, and her cousin's husband was a factory worker. Her brother migrated north at that time. Elizabeth lived more comfortably in her cousin's house, as they only wanted her to go to school and focus on her studies, but then her cousin's husband assaulted her, too.

Elizabeth had come to feel that she could no longer stay in Guatemala. She explained that the constant violence she witnessed where she lived and the types of abuse she endured prompted her to migrate north and find her mother, with whom she rarely talked on the phone more than once a month. Despite essentially having no relationship with her mother, she still felt that living in the United States would be better than what she had gone through in Guatemala. The uncle who abused her was against her going to the United States, fearing that Elizabeth would share with her mother what had happened and her mother would stop sending them money. Elizabeth was able to get financial support from her godmother to make the journey north through Mexico. She decided not to let her cousin know about her plans because she did not want to worry her when she left.

Her godmother advised her to get to the U.S. southern border, turn herself in, and give immigration authorities her mother's phone number to call her to claim her. Elizabeth left alone. She found three young Central American men in central Mexico who traveled with her and helped her get to the United States safely. Her journey to the border, through Guatemala and to Mexico's northern border, took around twenty-four days. She said she found her way to the United States by following her phone's GPS. After she arrived at the border, she was detained in a facility for migrant children in Phoenix, Arizona, for around three months. After eventually being granted custody, her mother paid for her airfare, and Elizabeth arrived in the D.C. area on a Valentine's Day, February 14.

Family reunification is not a single event that happens when an individual crosses a border. Instead, it is a process that can be as complicated and rocky as it is beautiful and rewarding. For Elizabeth, being reunited with her estranged mother after many years apart was not easy, and life in her family was new and different. Elizabeth said that she felt like her mother wanted to be with her stepfather rather than with her, and that her mother blamed all her problems on Elizabeth and her brother. Even so, she felt okay with this relationship at the end of the day because she had gone through most of her life without a mother. Despite some familial tension and strain, she was happier in the United States, which she attributed to having more educational opportunities and being safer than she had been in Guatemala. She attended high school in Hyattsville, Maryland, was going to therapy, and said that she ultimately wanted to attend a military academy or a university to study industrial engineering.

# ACKNOWLEDGMENTS

The narratives in this book come from the "Household Contexts and School Integration of Resettled Migrant Youth" project, administered by the Center for Latin American and Latino Studies (CLALS) at American University in Washington, D.C. A 2016–2017 Faculty Research Support Grant from the Provost's Office at American University provided the co-principal investigators, Ernesto Castañeda, Eric Hershberg, and Noemi Enchautegui-de-Jesús, with funds to conduct this project. We thank former provosts Scott Bass and Peter Starr for institutional support. We thank Eric Hershberg and Dennis Stinchcomb for their leadership administering this project within CLALS and for providing support beyond the original grant. We thank Kim Blankenship and the Center on Health, Risk, and Society for providing funds to hire research assistants. Gay Young and the Department of Sociology at American University also supported the project.

We provide demographic specifics here for the interviewers, given that their identities and positionality may have impacted the answers given. Noemi Enchautegui-de-Jesús (Puerto Rican) helped design the study and carry out some of the interviews. The bilingual team that conducted the interviews included Aída Romero (born in Honduras), Catie Prechtel (born in the United States), Dennis Stinchcomb (United States), Natali Collazos (Colombian-Cuban-American), Cynthia Cristobal (Mexican-American), Maria de Luna (Mexican-American), and Ines Luengo de Krom (born in Guatemala). We thank them and the other research assistants who helped to transcribe, enter, and code the interviews. Cristian Mendoza Gómez (Mexican-American) provided vital support in drafting the narratives presented at the beginning of each chapter and in selecting and translating the quotes used throughout the book.

Neither of us is Central American by nationality. However, we both have been living in D.C. more than eight years, including the period when we were finishing this book, and we are both active participants and advocates in our local communities. One of us is an immigrant and the other is the child of an immigrant, and we have done our best to represent the voices and experiences of the people we learned from through interviews and fieldwork. We also asked a dozen Central American colleagues and students to read the draft text and alert us to any issues they found.

Giovanna Calderon, who has direct experience working with unaccompanied minors applying for legal relief in the United States, helped us with the policy section in chapter 8. Alec Singer and other members of the Immigration Lab helped research the historical background of the sending countries presented in chapter 2. Part of chapter 4 was published in Spanish in *Ética, política, y migración*, edited by Luis Rubén Díaz Cepeda, Roberto Sánchez Benítez, and Amy Reed-Sandoval. Cristian Mendoza Gómez, Fernanda Pérez, and Fernando Rocha helped write the Spanish version of the chapter. Cynthia Cristobal helped draft a previous version of chapter 6 that was published in *Children and Youths' Migration in a Global Landscape*, a volume in Emerald Books' Sociological Studies of Children and Youth Emerald series. We thank editors Derrace Garfield McCallum, Adrienne Lee Atterberry, Siqi Tu, and Amy Lutz for feedback on a previous version of the chapter. A previous version of chapter 7 was published in *Trauma Care* with coauthors Jessica Chaikof, Carina Cione, SteVon Felton, Isabella Goris, Lesley Buck, and Eric Hershberg. We collectively hold the copyright for all three papers and reproduce here some of the ideas presented in them with permission.

We also thank audiences at the Immigration Seminar Series, Department of Sociology, CUNY Graduate Center; ProBar legal group working with immigrant children and youth; and panels at academic conferences such as the American Sociological Society (ASA), the Eastern Sociological Society (ESS), and the Latinx studies conference in D.C. We especially thank Dennis Stinchcomb, Noemi Enchauteguide-Jesús, Aida Romero, and Eric Hershberg at CLALS for their crucial contributions to this project in leading the data gathering and initial analyses. We appreciate the close reading and feedback provided by Rene Flores, Yossi Harpaz, Ali R. Chaudhary, Eric Macias, Karen Perez Torres, Lesley Buck, SteVon Felton, Jessica Chaikof, Isabella Goris, Sarah Schech, Claire Whitman, Alec Singer, Alex Nelson, Sandra Castro, Ted Everett, Harry Ehlers, Michelle Newton-Francis, Carlos Coleman, Jonathan Klassen, Abigail Carl-Klassen, John Jenks, and Jennifer Jenks. Special thanks to Carina Cione for their close reading, honest feedback, coauthorship in other projects, and support at CLALS. All errors and shortcomings remain our own.

We thank Suzanne Nichols, Sheldon Danzinger, Aixa Cintrón-Vélez, and the board of trustees of the Russell Sage Foundation for their support in publishing this book. We thank five anonymous reviewers for their questions and feedback at the proposal, manuscript, and revision stages. Cynthia Buck did a phenomenal job copyediting the manuscript in a careful and expert manner. We also thank the journalists who cover this beat and the many scholars who have researched Central American migration, migrant children and youth, and international migration in general and upon whose work we build.

*Ernesto Castañeda:* I thank Lesley Buck, my sons' teachers and coaches, and my parents, Ernesto Castañeda Merino and Ma. Elena Tinoco in Mexico, who made it possible for me to put the finishing touches on this book in the summer of 2023 by taking care of their grandchildren while I stepped away for a few hours to write every day. I had to be away from my children during evenings, weekends, and some days during vacation while working on this book and other academic projects and tasks. They resented it and openly voiced their discontent. Nonetheless, we are fortunate that we did not have to be apart for years on end and could wake up in the same household, do the morning routines together, and share dinner and other meals at the same table. We could also talk in person daily and on special days, and together we could swim, play soccer, and watch movies and series—unlike many migrant families divided by political borders.

*Daniel Jenks:* I have so many people to thank for their support who directly or indirectly made it possible for me to coauthor this book. First, thanks to my parents for always pushing me and encouraging me to do my best work, write clearly, and do good in the world. Thanks to Leah for the help and guidance over the years, both on and off this project. Thank you to my grandparents for your wisdom and support.

Thanks to Jordan for being a constant sounding board and being there for me during the entire process. Thanks to my grad school cohort—SteVon, Jessica, and Bella—for great discussions about this topic and others and for your support and friendship. Thanks to current and former American University professors Nicole Angotti, Angela Luvara, Bill Davies, Glenn Moomau, Juliana Martínez, and many others for encouraging my intellectual development and pushing me to improve my analytical and writing skill sets over the last eight years.

# INTRODUCTION

A May 28, 2014, story in *Roll Call* titled "Alone, Illegal, and Underage: The Child Migrant Crisis" informed readers that "a trickle of children crossing the Rio Grande" on the U.S. southern border had become "a veritable flood." There were

> so many kids, in fact, that the issue has triggered a crisis, as Secretary of Homeland Security Jeh Johnson had to issue an emergency alert. . . . The phenomenon has completely overwhelmed federal resources in a matter of weeks, turning Border Patrol offices into day cares and military barracks into youth dormitories. The Health and Human Services Department struggles to keep up with the demands for its foster care, often leaving the kids stuck in detention facilities designed for adults.[1]

Despite the tone of surprise and use of sensationalizing words and phrases like "crisis" and "veritable flood"—well documented as dangerous and inciteful ways in which migrants were described in much of the news coverage—the arrival of Central Americans at the U.S. southern border around 2014 was not happening for the first time.[2] Far from it. Throughout U.S. history, newspaper stories and congressional speeches have produced a negative discourse about the accommodation of minorities and immigrants—minors or not—in the economy, in schools, and on the streets.[3] Immigrant children, accompanied or not, have always been a part of U.S. history, and the forces compelling other groups to migrate are often no different than those that cause the migration of young people from Central America.[4] There are important structural reasons that explain why children would migrate without

https://doi.org/10.7758/dvxg2393.8141

a parent. After relatively recent international efforts to protect migrant children and prevent child trafficking created the legal figure of the "unaccompanied minor," some countries did enact further protections and rights, but elsewhere the term just became a new label for the stigmatized "Other." At the same time, responsibility for the plight of unaccompanied minor migrants was shifted to supposed traffickers, and the social conditions in the countries of origin, while anti-immigrant policies in the countries of arrival and passage continued.

The migration of children has a long history. Images of crowded nineteenth-century cities, "orphan trains," or the Kindertransport are dramatic historical examples of unaccompanied youth migrants. Thousands of orphaned children wandered the streets of New York in the 1850s. In the early 1900s, poor living and working conditions left many immigrant children parentless. These orphans were often rounded up and placed in prisons with adults. Sometimes children were "placed out" on orphan trains and sent westward to rural communities with families who would take them in to work on their land.[5] There was also the dramatic case of the Kindertransport during the Holocaust: to save them from genocide, Jewish children from eastern Europe were transported to England and other places to be placed with adoptive parents.[6] These are still important examples to consider when thinking about today's world, where men, women, and children must escape situations where their lives are at risk in places like Latin America, Afghanistan, and Ukraine.

This book is about young Central American migrants and their families' experiences before, during, and after migration to the United States, particularly to the D.C. suburbs. The trend of increasing numbers of minors from El Salvador, Honduras, and Guatemala arriving at the U.S.-Mexico border without a parent began to be observed in the 2010s. Many Central American minors came in through legal family reunification or outside ports of entry. But because many others were turning themselves in to immigration authorities or were easily found by the Border Patrol, the official numbers of non-Mexican minors encountered at the border seemed to be increasing.

Under current U.S. and international law, the United States, like most countries, is responsible for protecting the well-being of what the government called "unaccompanied alien children" (UACs) and now often called "unaccompanied minors" (UAM) from non-neighboring countries. For these reasons, Central American minors have become very visible and receive much media and political attention. Nevertheless, while the situation may have looked unprecedented when it arose, structurally it was predictable. Since the U.S. interventions in the civil wars of the 1980s, a common survival and economic strategy used by Central Americans has been migration. U.S. immigration and asylum law almost always prevented parents from bringing their children with them, causing family separation. Only eventually, for reasons we explore, are families reunified. The process and experience of reunification, then, is shaped by the structural contexts of the sending country, the transit countries, and the country of arrival. We argue that young Central Americans have recently migrated to the D.C. area owing to these processes of structural family separation, as we explain more fully in the coming pages.

This book explains the circumstances and predictability of the arrival of so-called unaccompanied migrant youth. It gives primacy to the experiences of migrants themselves and puts those experiences in a sociohistorical context. In this introduction, we discuss basic facts about migration to the United States from Central America, provide an essential background understanding about migration and integration as a concept, and explain the core arguments presented in this book.

Before we look into why Central Americans leave the region and the challenges and opportunities they face once they reach the United States, it is essential to understand migration in general. In the first three chapters, we summarize some core concepts of migration social science theory, present a framework for analyzing and understanding the stories and integration of these youth and families, and provide the sociopolitical context of migration from Central America to the United States. The overall experiences and processes are similar to those of other immigrant groups in the United States and elsewhere. Thus, we start with a general overview of migration theory that will not only help the nonspecialist reader understand how the social sciences approach international migration but also frame our arguments and takeaways throughout the book for the specialist and nonspecialist alike.

## Why Do People Migrate?

There is no universally agreed-upon general theory of migration. Instead, there are several "middle-range" theories that explain common processes and patterns but fail to address the phenomenon as a whole.[7]

For example, both macro- and microeconomic studies have explained migration with theories that do not hold up in empirical tests when applied to actual population moves, findings from ethnographic fieldwork, and, most importantly, the lived experiences of migrants.

Similarly, "push and pull" accounts—that is, ex post facto explanations of why a certain population moves to a certain place—do not explain why other groups within and outside of the area under discussion are not also pulled or pushed to migrate. This is illustrated by the oft-cited push factors of poverty and unemployment. If these were such significant push factors, more of the world's population would emigrate, but we know that in the last decades a bit more than 3 percent but less than 4 percent of the world population has migrated across international borders.[8] While poverty and unemployment play a role, Central Americans and others emigrate for more complex reasons than simply relative poverty.

As we elaborate later in this chapter and in chapter 1, migration is often caused by war, conquest, forced displacement, political exile, geopolitics, climate change, natural disasters, or genocide. There are guest worker programs, refugee resettlement programs, and social networks that help connect migrants to a specific destination, but these supports are not always available, and resettlement and worker programs are not always administered in an egalitarian manner. Migration decisions do not happen in a vacuum. Immigration pathways are determined by a multitude of factors, including labor recruiters and international commercial ties, state regulations and migratory policies, professional licensing and credentialing requirements, humanitarian nongovernmental organizations helping people at risk relocate across borders, churches, tax advisers, travel and recruiting agencies, guides, and family and preexisting migrant networks.[9]

## What Is "Structural Integration" and Why Focus on Belonging?

Of equal concern to the question of why people migrate is what happens after they do. If sacrifices are made, as they often are, does the migrant find these sacrifices to have been "worth it"? Is the migrant happy? What about their family? Do they have friends, a job, a community to be a part of? Are they at risk of harassment, discrimination, or even hate crimes?

Throughout this book, we use the lens of "structural integration," a concept that engages with all of these questions and more. Until somewhere around the turn of the twenty-first century, the term "immigration" was understood among sociologists largely in relation to what was called "assimilation"—how immigrants were faring in their country of arrival and how their life chances and outcomes compared to those of locals—and their questions centered on how similar the migrant group had become to the local population. Debates over how to theorize and summarize this process in the contemporary United States have gone on for decades. Scholars familiar with the immigration history of Italians, Irish, Polish, and other southern and eastern Europeans saw them as eventually assimilating into a slowly changing "mainstream" White culture.[10] This idea of assimilation as the process of immigrants eventually becoming like the descendants of older White Protestant Anglo-Saxon settlers, colonizers, and earlier immigrants became the traditional approach. Indeed, the Protestant English, Germanic, and Scandinavian groups were the reference group for the early scholars trying to theorize about the implications of immigration into cities at the turn of the twentieth century. These theories were represented in the academic literature by the Chicago School of Sociology of the early 1900s.

The proponents of the assimilation hypothesis took race partly into account in discussing certain European non-Anglo-Saxon Protestants, primarily Catholic and Jewish immigrants, who were initially perceived as unassimilable cultural and political threats to the United States in public panics against them and even as non-White by xenophobic politicians.[11] Of course, in analyzing the discourse about immigration, race, and assimilation, it is vital to understand first that race is a socially constructed category with a moving goalpost.[12] It is also essential to understand that the classical and dated idea that immigrants must assimilate is a largely racist and xenophobic proposal in itself; most immigration scholars today prefer to consider ideas around integration, multiculturalism, or interculturalism, allowing for a more organic process of settlement rather than forcing immigrants to forget immediately about their culture.

After two or three generations, and with the relative decline of southern and eastern Europeans as a proportion of new immigrants, they became seen in the United States as de facto White. Even today, when some of these originally European groups feel and express a "symbolic ethnicity"—exemplified, for example, by the identity performed by Irish Americans on Saint Patrick's Day—they face no stigmatization or negative consequences in daily life, such as discrimination, harassment, or racialized violence.[13] Some of their descendants are part of the elite, some belong to the middle class, and some, like other Americans, are working-class. The question is whether this model would apply to more recent immigrants, mainly those from Latin America and Asia. The answer, of course, is messy, unclear, and changeable depending on local contexts, sociopolitical environments, and global events.

In contrast to symbolic ethnicity, others, especially many Asian and Latin people, experience a "durable ethnicity."[14] They may be treated as newcomers even if they were born in the United States and experience stigmatization, discrimination, xenophobia, and hate crimes owing to their perceived ethnicity.[15] Furthermore, in the popular imagination, Black immigrants are often subsumed into the African American population descended from enslaved people. They may feel distant from mainstream African American culture, however, and experience a durable ethnicity in being differentiated by others from the majority native population.[16] Still, they will be racialized as Black with possible effects on their social mobility.

Proponents of a "new assimilation" theory posit that contemporary non-White immigrants will follow a path similar to that of earlier European immigrants. Key to the new assimilation theory is the argument that assimilation itself is still relevant for today's immigrants.[17] Although they recognize the complex struggles that non-White immigrants face owing to racial stratification in the United States, they propose that the demographic and institutional changes following the civil rights movement have been sufficient to create an environment in which assimilation into the mainstream happens by the third or fourth generation.[18]

Nevertheless, a linear—or even a two-way—assimilation model fails to account for the historical and contemporary barriers that Black Americans, Black immigrants, Indigenous peoples, and other racialized and excluded groups face in being allowed to integrate structurally into schools, jobs, and neighborhoods and to avoid the perils of discrimination and structural racism. In contrast to the new assimilation theory, the "segmented assimilation" theory emerged to explain the disadvantages experienced by contemporary non-White immigrants into the second generation. This theory, advanced by Alejandro Portes, Min Zhou, Rubén Rumbaut, Alex Stepick, Patricia Fernández-Kelly, and many others, argues that while highly educated and more White-passing immigrants may assimilate into the middle and upper classes, Black immigrants and racialized, undocumented Latin immigrants find themselves being assimilated into the "underclass" of marginalized people of color, with impacts on the integration outcomes of their children.[19] Under this approach, disparities and factors such as the education level and income of the first immigrant generation can predict the assimilation outcomes of their children. Some individual exceptions aside, the segmented assimilation approach also proposes that those assimilation patterns occur at the ethnic group level, given that people from particular places tend to come from similar situations and to be perceived through group or categorical stereotypes.[20]

We take an intercultural approach that assumes no culture is inherently superior to another.[21] The outcomes and opportunities afforded to immigrants and refugees should be similar to those enjoyed by natives with no requirement that they lose important cultural practices and identities. This is why we use the term "structural integration" rather than "assimilation," as in many cases (though not all) assimilation implies loss of language, culture, practices, and identity over time.[22] Contrary to "Americanization" or "assimilation," the terms "integration" and "interculturalism" do not connote the suppression of a native culture or language. In this book, we conceptually build on previous work by Castañeda focused not only on objective indicators of economic, political, and social integration but also on subjective feelings of integration—often called "belonging"—in the U.S. and European literature on immigration.[23] In previous work, Castañeda and others focus on the concept of belonging as feeling at home in a particular place and identifying with a new location, which most often is an urban area.[24]

Whether the integration of recent immigrants is similar to previous arrivals of immigrants or is more enduringly racialized depends on the context of reception, that is, the particular history and geography of where immigrants work and live after arrival.[25] Some studies of immigrants in New York City and other large cities in the Northeast support the new assimilation theory.[26] For instance, Richard Alba, Philip Kasinitz, and Mary Waters found in the New York Second Generation Study that second-generation immigrants benefited from the post–civil rights era programs that supported racial minorities and became successful and prominent New Yorkers without having to change and adopt mainstream behavior wholesale. Instead, they became part of the mainstream while maintaining aspects of a symbolic and durable ethnicity.[27]

The outcomes also vary by immigrant generation and are not homogeneous within a national group, much less among the pan-ethnic categories such as Latino or Asian.[28] Outcomes also may vary in different parts of the country; the experience of a Latin immigrant in New York City, Miami, or El Paso will differ from the experience of immigrants in Whiter areas, but also from each other owing to different state and local policies, programs, and safety nets that shape the context of integration in these cities.

Although some studies may support new assimilation theory, studies of Latin people and other groups in many parts of the United States find that they encounter more barriers to integration compared to their White or New Yorker counterparts, leading to generations of exclusion.[29] Given that Latin people have been racialized in different ways in the United States since the annexation of Texas, New Mexico, Arizona, California, Colorado, and parts of Oklahoma and Wyoming after the invasion of Mexico in the 1840s, much evidence supports downward assimilation—that is, the argument that racialization, legal systems, and categorical inequality can make it more difficult for certain groups to integrate structurally.[30]

Related to the discussion of assimilation and integration is "selective acculturation"—the theory propounded by other scholars that immigrant families and individuals can pick and choose which elements to retain from their immigrant culture and how to integrate on their own terms. Multiple research programs conclude that, when allowed by the context of reception, this practical approach produces the best objective and subjective outcomes in terms of structural integration, success, well-being, and mental health.[31] Rather than following a prescriptive path forced from outside, settlement happens in a practical and personalized manner that better prepares individuals and families to deal with their new cultural, labor, and legal environments. Key to selective acculturation is true religious freedom, cultural humility, and policies and practices in places of arrival that support interculturalism—the cohabitation of people of diverse backgrounds as equals.[32]

In summary, both theories of integration in the literature and research on paths to integration suggest that relatively wealthy and highly educated individuals and their children and grandchildren are likely to integrate, as proposed by the new assimilation theory. Those who are part of a united and organized community can access middle-class lifestyles. Racialized immigrants with less education or lower-paying jobs may integrate into the urban "underclass," as proposed by the segmented assimilation theory, though we should not overemphasize the existence of a clearly delineated "underclass."[33] Nonetheless, a segmented integration approach is compatible with the argument of theories of categorical inequality, social stratification, and racial capitalism that argue that inequality is more easily maintained when differences in wealth and health are justified as deserved owing to supposedly natural attributes of distinct racial/ethnic groups. Given that these processes unfold over long periods of time, it is difficult to say with certainty how the recently arrived Central American children and youth will fare over the long term in the Washington, D.C., area. Nevertheless, by focusing on structural integration, selective acculturation, and belonging, we can explore the experiences and thoughts of those affected by family separation, as recounted in their own words. How children and youth understand and interact with the world at an early stage can reveal what their experiences of family separation, traumatic or violent incidents, and identity formation as a migrant say about the effect of the context of reception, among other factors.

### Violence, Family Separation, Trauma, and Integration

If structural or individual violence often precedes migration, then it is important to understand the role of politics, policy, violence, and trauma in the social processes of integration. Politicians and news pundits often speak about the dangers posed by migrants from Central America—Donald Trump's 2016 campaign, presidency, and immigration policy being a clear exemplar—but we found the opposite to be true. Rather than being crime perpetrators, Central American immigrants are often victims themselves of impunity, state violence, and organized crime, and many migrate in order to flee violence. Fleeing violence and trauma has been a core driver of migration from Central America since the civil wars in the 1980s, which we contextualize in chapter 2.

Far from posing a violent threat to anyone around them, many migrants from Central America who participated in this study had fled gang or state-sponsored violence. They were searching for a calmer life, and the United States represented a place of safety for many of them. Carlos, age thirteen, mentioned that he felt much safer in the United States and could perform better in school. Gang activity in his country of birth had made it hard for him to study, move around, or take advantage of opportunities that many in the United States take for granted, like playing soccer with his friends. After reuniting with his father, Carlos could visualize both short- and long-term goals as being within reach. In the short term, he wanted to join a soccer team. In the long term, he wanted to become a lawyer. These goals were hard for him to imagine himself reaching in Central America against a backdrop of gang violence, with his father thousands of miles away.

The violence in their communities, the trauma of the journey north, and detention by U.S. Customs and Border Protection (CBP) are experiences that those who have not had them can hardly imagine. Many minors can only be reunited with their biological parent after they endure those harrowing experiences. Carlos's ability to visualize his goals and speak about achieving them showed that he was integrating well into the community where he lived and that he felt like he belonged there. He saw himself participating in life where he was and imagining life in the future, wherever it would be.

To counter dehumanizing rhetoric, point up the inhumaneness of immigration policy, and address the outrage surrounding family separations at the border, this book aims to humanize young people's lived experiences. Some aspects of the migration experience from Central America and of youth migration are well documented and understood throughout the academic community and by some of the public.[34] There is more to learn, however, from looking at the experiences of a set of minors as they went from living in Central America to migrating and integrating into the United States.

### Theoretical Contributions

We begin the book by briefly recounting the stories of five young immigrants. As researchers, we identify common themes throughout the book, but of course, even though many of the other minors we reference had similar or overlapping experiences, we also acknowledge the full agency of these young people and the uniqueness of their experience. The young people we interviewed had been placed with sponsors already in the United States, but it is critical to note that some of them may have since been denied asylum, deported, or placed in deportation proceedings by the federal government.

The main contribution of this book is to show how young Central American migrants who had recently arrived in the D.C. area transitioned from escaping what we call structural family separation to crafting a road for integration and belonging. This book also fills a gap in the literature regarding family-driven migration and immigrant youth integration in the D.C. school and community contexts. Much has been written about immigrant youth and families, as well as about smaller subsets of youth such as Dreamers,[35] the school experiences of immigrant youth,[36] and the migration experiences of adults.[37] However, few have researched the lives of young Central American immigrants and the social dynamics within their families, schools, and communities in the Washington metropolitan area in recent years. Examining these dynamics together gives us a broad perspective on integration, one focused on how migrants feel and think rather than solely on how others view them or on structural integration. To do this, we analyze the rich data from interviews we conducted with young immigrants, their parents, teachers, and local professionals who work with immigrant youth to understand the impact of the family as a factor in emigration and immigrant integration. In attempting to tell a sociological story, we include a brief overview of each sending country's history, a description of the journey north, and an account of immigrants' challenges after arriving and being allowed to reside in the United States (although sometimes only temporarily). We build on three interconnected areas of migration theory:

1. Several authors have shown how having family members and social ties abroad facilitates migration. In what we call "family-propelled migration," many children and young adults are able to flee Central America because family members have already migrated to the United States. This was the case for the great majority of our respondents. Despite the generalized violence in parts of northern Central America, those who do not have family

in the United States have a harder time financing and making the journey. They are more likely to be unsuccessful in trying to migrate and to attempt the perilous journey again.

2. If migration is propelled in one way by a desire or need for family reunification, then the family separation that preceded it is structural. Our second contribution is showing that, by limiting the social mobility of unskilled workers from the so-called Global South to work in the Global North with permits and their ability to bring their families with them safely or soon after moving abroad, international migration laws systematically cause the physical separation of the members of a transnational family.[38] We call this process "structural family separation" to underline that global economic inequality and restrictive immigration policies separate families against their wishes. We set the stage for this argument in chapter 2 and elaborate it throughout other chapters and in the conclusion. Relatedly, we question how we can speak of immigrant and human rights or about refugee and immigrant integration if we do not conceive of family unity as a right.

3. We touch on the importance for children and young adults of being in understanding and supportive surroundings in the early years after they immigrate in order for their integration trajectory to be successful and speedy. Our respondents had found a home and knew how to make sense of the Washington metropolitan area, even if they would have felt less at ease in other parts of the United States. We build on the integration literature by explaining how and why this is the case for children and young adults in reunited families, who will surely interact with the world in different ways than older family members.

If immigrants are hindered from becoming integrated into American society, they may experience more discrimination and be given fewer opportunities, and thus becoming more limited financially, civically, and socially and suffering worse physical and mental health. They and their children will face more challenges, which may be largely ignored by the larger public. That is why investigating immigrant integration outcomes, both immediately after arrival and a couple of years later, is important. This book focuses on the spheres in which integration largely happens in the U.S. context: at schools, in workplaces, and in neighborhoods and urban areas where immigrants and their families spend time.[39] The main takeaways from our research show that despite important challenges, Central American immigrants find jobs promptly, their children attend school and learn English, and these families become integral parts of the communities where they live.

Integration does not happen in a vacuum. It is shaped by the context of reception but also by the emotional state of the immigrants themselves, and it is a relational phenomenon, as shown for example, in the discussion later in the book about school dynamics. Immigrants' subjective assessments, which are influenced by laws, social relations, and objective factors such as poverty rates, housing access, etc., will impact mental health. In turn, mental health may impact how proactive immigrants are in engaging with their places of worship, schools, and communities as most Central Americans do in the DMV (D.C., Maryland, and Virginia) area or whether they will withdraw to the private sphere of their living quarters, as, for example, many North Africans do in the Parisian metropolitan area.[40]

Given the policy and media interest in unaccompanied minors, it is particularly important to listen to their experiences. A crucial point that our work makes is that migration does not start or end at the border. To any immigrant, this is not news, but it is to the many native-born people who view migration as a border-specific event because of the increasing politicization of the southern border and the fearmongering about immigrants before, during, and after Trump's presidency.[41] However necessary it is, media coverage that focuses on speeches and policy ups and downs can be misleading and disorienting for anyone trying to understand overall trends. This book strives to understand the migration phenomenon through a human lens that brings the perspectives of Central American youth into focus. Their stories are both more dramatic and urgent than is depicted in political debates and more mundane within the context of history and the human experience. Furthermore, political and social debates about new immigrants are not exogenous to the process we discuss; the book highlights the policy context that led to respondents' migration experiences.

By building on other recent literature that discusses, describes, and engages with youth migration from Central America and focuses on youths' agency, we show the importance of immigrant youths' interface with their host society and their role as agents who direct their own survival and success within a structure stacked against them.⁴²

## Implications for Social and Immigration Policy

This book tackles one of the biggest immigration controversies during the Trump and Biden administrations: minors arriving at the U.S.-Mexico border without a parent or legal guardian. In also addressing family separation, we examine a key topic in immigrant integration scholarship. The experience of "unaccompanied minors" cannot be understood without considering the larger context of immigrant family separation, including the emigration of only some family members and anti-immigrant laws put in place by both political parties. Families can sometimes be reunited under legal auspices; this is the desired path, of course, but one that may take too long and depends on the ability of immigrants to regularize their status if undocumented or on a liminal status such as temporary protective status (TPS) or DACA (Deferred Action for Childhood Arrivals).⁴³ Otherwise, immigrants must place their trust in third parties or coyotes to bring their children to them. In dire circumstances, children decide on their own to leave and may attempt to cross countries on foot or use freight train routes.

Immigration from Mexico to the United States has been declining since the 2008 economic recession.⁴⁴ Central American immigration has increased since then, however, and unaccompanied Central American immigrant minors have been arriving in the United States in increasing numbers since the start of the 2010s. The current number of unaccompanied minors is small compared to the overall number of contemporary and historical immigrants. They became visible partly because there was a well-documented and discussed increase in minors crossing the border in 2014.

Mexican migration has been around zero or net-negative since 2008 because there are more Mexican people who leave or are deported than Mexican people entering the United States.⁴⁵ Furthermore, as geographer Rebecca Torres and her coauthors write, "Historically, until recently, Mexican youth have formed the largest group of unaccompanied minors attempting to move across the U.S.-Mexico border. However, structural political, socio-legal, and everyday institutional violence lead to their neglect, disregard, and exclusion from rights and protections in both the U.S. and Mexico."[46] Most Mexican children and youth are treated this way because they can more easily be sent back from the United States to Mexico, a partner and contiguous country. Central American minors are not as easily deported owing to international commitments to protect migrant children.

The United States treats unaccompanied minors from countries other than Mexico and Canada, which share land borders with the United States, with special care.[47] Since 2014, the largest shares of unaccompanied minors have come from three countries in northern Central America: El Salvador, Guatemala, and Honduras. Unaccompanied minors and, later, Central American migrant caravans played an outsized role in U.S. immigration politics at the end of the Obama administration.[48] Utilizing them to create the false optics of an out-of-control border, anti-immigrant advocates pushed for greater restrictions, securitization, and militarization of the border and for continuing to build the border wall.[49] These policies have had real effects on the mental and physical health of migrants and families, often putting them in greater and continued danger in the United States, as they make their way through Mexico, and in their own home countries (see chapter 6). The unfair linking of Central Americans to gang membership was a convenient lightning rod for Trump's campaigns and anti-immigrant speeches in which he implicated and framed the youth fleeing gang violence as gang-involved themselves.

The Trump administration intentionally separated families arriving together at the border to dissuade them from asking for asylum and to punish unsanctioned immigrants with his so-called zero-tolerance policy (see chapter 9). The painful images and sounds of crying toddlers and children being torn away from their parents by Border Patrol agents that the media captured in 2018 created a lot of empathy and compassion for these minors and their families. Trump's cruel and highly visible anti-immigrant policies, including forced family separation at the border, intensified much of the anti-Trump sentiment, and protests and marches against these policies took place nationwide. After the outcry, Trump signed an executive order to end his administration's family separation policies at the border. Nevertheless, many of those families are still separated because no reliable records were kept that could be used to reunite them.[50]

Furthermore, with "Remain in Mexico" and then with Title 42—under the guise of public health guidance during the COVID-19 pandemic—families seeking asylum were made to wait in Mexico for many months before their petitions were processed. According to Human Rights Watch, as of November 2019, over fifty-six thousand asylum seekers had been sent back to Mexico while their claims were processed, and sixteen thousand of them were youth. As of August 2018, over one million people were sent back under Title 42, which officially ended on May 11, 2023.

Central American migration and the longing of children and parents to reunite is part of a longer history that is nearly as heartrending and just as important as forced separations at the border. Anti-immigrant policies that separate families predate Trump and continue to this day in the United States and abroad. In-depth interviews and life histories are the best sources for understanding how the main actors experience these separations. We pay particular attention here to a part of the story that is rarely told in the media: the process of family reunification. Many assume that once minors are back in the arms of a parent or relative, the problem is over. In reality, "picking up the pieces" can be tricky and complicated. The guilt and resentment that long-term separation may produce among parents and children takes time and intentionality to overcome.

Furthermore, for most Central American and mixed-status families, legal violence further circumscribes the parent-child decision to reunite.[51] Besides the many cumbersome and expensive immigration procedures (see chapter 5), immigrant children and youth are reunited with families that they have not lived with in years and that sometimes include new siblings, stepparents, or stepsiblings. They are also expected to attend schools in a foreign language in a place they do not know. The many split-second changes experienced by these minors under trying circumstances can have long-term psychological effects, and some show signs and symptoms of post-traumatic stress disorder (PTSD) and depression, as discussed in chapter 6. Through all this, however, many of these youth manifest resilience, aspirations, and early signs of success.

Although many social workers, teachers, and community organization leaders who interact with minors in reunited families may be well-meaning, they often lack the knowledge to help them adapt to their new homes. Many of the community practitioners and school program managers stressed the importance and, at times, the difficulty of bringing in staff who speak the language of new students from Central America; speaking the same native language as new students is especially important for those who deeply understand the experiences and needs of these children and youth. At the same time, we found many great programs and organizations designed to support immigrant youth and their families.

## The Long History of Forced Family Separation

For most of human history, family units have usually migrated together. They may have been looking for better lands to hunt or to cultivate, or they may have had to move to escape war, violence, or famine. The contemporary nation-state system—with its increasingly fortified political borders and an international "remote control" system of passports and visas—treats migration mainly as something to discourage.[52] Most contemporary migration legal systems conceive of immigrants— especially those from poorer nations—as solitary individuals rather than as members of families. Part of the problem started with guest worker programs, whose sole purpose was providing temporary labor in the host country. These programs and those who designed them viewed foreign-born people as vehicles for labor rather than as individuals with agency, families, goals, and emotional needs. One such program was the Mexican Farm Labor Program, more commonly known as the Bracero Program (1942–1964), which brought essential labor to the United States from Mexico during and after World War II. Some argue that the term "bracero" is derived from the Spanish word *brazo* ("arm").[53] In the United States, Mexican and Filipino labor fulfilled the needs in agriculture, mining, and railroad construction on the West Coast after passage of the Chinese Exclusion Act of 1882 and the Gentlemen's Agreement reached with Japan in 1907.[54] Along with the women who entered the labor force, immigrants were essential in filling industrial jobs while soldiers fought abroad in the world wars.

Another example of a nation-state encouraging the arrival of workers from outside its borders is West Germany in the 1950s, where labor was needed to rebuild and fuel the booming economy following the end of World War II and the Marshall Plan bankrolling of the nation's reconstruction. To this end, West Germany made bilateral agreements with Italy (1955), Spain and Greece (1960), Turkey (1961),

Morocco (1963), Portugal (1964), Tunisia (1965), and Yugoslavia (1968).[55] Infamously, the Swiss novelist Max Frisch wrote disapprovingly about guest workers (*Gastarbeiter*) and their families: "We wanted a labour force, but human beings came." To this, the fiction writer Terry Hayes adds, "What nobody had foreseen was that those workers would bring their mosques, their holy book, and huge swathes of their culture with them."[56] Unfortunately, in the past and to this day, the concern of many about assimilation is motivated more by racism and xenophobia than by cultural humility and a preference for multiculturalism. The guest worker policies were designed to bring prime-age workers to the country, without paying for their upraising and education, while their families stayed in the country of origin; this system amounted to yet another way in which many less wealthy nations and former colonies subsidized wealthier nations. Furthermore, after becoming skilled at their jobs in the United States, workers were supposed to return to their countries of origin when it came time to retire and live out their old age.

Guest workers in Germany organized against the rigid division between workers and family members in German immigration policies, which disallowed family reunification. Nonetheless, after the right to family reunification was won in 1973, the German government continued to use those policies to dissuade the families of guest workers from reunifying.[57] Germany made it difficult for them and even their German-born children to become citizens; finally, legal changes were made in 2000 that allowed the children of foreign-born parents to naturalize.[58] Still, the children and grandchildren of Turkish immigrants born and raised in Germany face challenges being accepted as fully German because of the ongoing equation of nation with blood.[59] French-Algerian sociologist Abdelmalek Sayad wrote at length about the pain brought to many Algerians by working and living in France without their family members. In the postwar period, the French state, like Germany, fought a long battle in the legislative and legal systems to block, delay, and dissuade family reunification for immigrants.[60] It is these types of experiences of family separation and durable ethnicity that shape integration and feelings of belonging.

After the 2015 *Kerry v. Din* Supreme Court decision regarding marriages between citizens and foreigners, sociologist Jane Lilly López wrote, "In matters of citizenship and immigration, the state deals with individuals, not families."[61] The 1952 Immigration and Nationality

Act (INA) and subsequent legislation changed the U.S. immigration authority's conception of family reunification to one that adheres to "the fundamental American value of individualism." That is, the family reunification process in the United States "prioritizes autonomy and self-sufficiency over community and social interdependence, a notion that runs counter to cultural and social norms in countries across the globe. In practice, it contributes to the long-term separation of millions of American families, with multigenerational repercussions."[62] Both formal and informal immigration systems have prioritized labor over individual rights to a family.

As Marcelo Suárez-Orozco writes, in broad terms, "Labor migration begat family reunification, which in turn begat the rise of the second generation now transforming Europe, North America, and Australia."[63] Suárez-Orozco is not saying that guest worker programs do not work. They do; these programs have provided countries with crucial labor force and population growth to recover and reconstruct after wars, economic crises, and local population decline. Suárez-Orozco is also not saying that most guest workers settle in. Indeed, half or more return to their former homes. Historically, family reunification for guest workers in the United States, Europe, and the Arabian Peninsula has been bureaucratically slow, cumbersome, and openly discouraged. Nevertheless, as the academic literature and immigrant novels show, "the fundamental unit of migration is the family."[64]

Of course, Suárez-Orozco also does not mean to imply that refugee and immigrant families do not exist or that fixing the family glitch around immigration law is the panacea. Many migrants who go to wealthy nations to work in offices and universities are coming from other wealthy nations, and they often have no problem bringing their families. However, the immigration systems set up by these wealthy nations are what sociologist David FitzGerald refers to as a "remote control" that allows wealthy democracies to pick and choose who gets to come.[65]

The experiences of children who migrate internally for labor purposes can be particularly cruel. For example, adults from southern Mexico, many of them Indigenous, work in agricultural fields in the United States while their minor children work in large agricultural fields in northern Mexico.[66] Some Guatemalan families and unaccompanied minors travel to southern Mexico to work in agriculture.[67]

In Turkey, Kurdish families that move seasonally to work in agriculture, forestation, or charcoal production are hired as a family unit of labor and paid at the end of the season; if children and the elderly in a family slow the pace of work, adults in the family must compensate for failing to make quotas.[68] More commonly, however, so-called low-skilled labor migrants experience structural family separation with parents migrating and children staying behind, as we explain in the following section.

The painful experience of family separation is not unique to Latin people in the United States; also affected are other groups in the United States as well as people who work irregularly in other countries or are employed through guest worker programs, like the extensive work abroad programs organized by the government of the Philippines. *New York Times* journalist and author Jason DeParle writes that during the reunification after many years apart of an extended family he observed closely, "the kids had to learn English. The parents had to learn to parent."[69] He adds that "they weren't just learning to live together in a new country; they were learning to live together" and the parents were learning how "to be parents again."[70] Sociologist Paolo Boccagni writes about these tensions in families divided between Bolivia and Italy, and sociologist Cinzia Solari writes about Ukrainian mothers and grandmothers who move to Italy and the United States to care for older adults while becoming breadwinners for their extended families.[71]

### Migration as a Household Survival Strategy in a Sea of Imperfect Information and Impossible Choices

Migration in response to economic desperation can be seen as an act of individual personal resolve and determination, especially when the migrant is a "pioneer," that is, the first one in their family or community to emigrate. Nonetheless, the decision to emigrate is most often made as a household strategy within a conductive social context that may include an already developed translocal community.[72] Sociologist Douglas Massey and his coauthors point out in their "cumulative causation of migration" theory that "once the number of network connections reaches a critical threshold, migration becomes self-perpetuating because each act of movement creates the social structure necessary to sustain it."[73] In other words, after the practice of migrating diffuses via social ties and chain migration—through processes elaborated on by other social scientists such as Charles Tilly—it becomes a more popular household strategy to increase earnings.[74] The birth of a child, financial emergencies, and sickness may lead a household to consider migration to obtain needed capital because few resources are available in the home society to meet these challenges. In towns with an emigration tradition, the social context makes the decision easier, almost natural.[75]

Unaccompanied migration is not a new phenomenon. An estimated 48,000 unaccompanied minors from Mexico and Central America entered the United States in 2001, 75 percent of whom intended to rejoin their mothers.[76] In fiscal year 2022, 152,057 unaccompanied minors were encountered at the southern border; 27,994 of them were from Mexico, 16,432 were from El Salvador, 60,780 from Guatemala, 37,374 from Honduras, and 9,478 from other countries, according to official data.[77] This contrasts with 2,963 accompanied minors, 560,646 people in family units, and 1,663,278 encounters with single adults (many individuals probably counted multiple times).[78]

As the migration experience spreads in a town, the migration stream becomes more diverse in terms of age and socioeconomic origin. As women, children, and older adults make the journey north to join their family members, thousands of Mexican children traveling alone are captured yearly by U.S. authorities and sent to shelters at the Mexican border.[79] Many of these children set out to find their parents abroad and may have started their trip without the consent or knowledge of their families. Sometimes internally migrating parents bring their children to work in the fields or factories for low wages. Some children have been abandoned by their parents, who have migrated to the United States or to northern states within Mexico, where they live in dire conditions and receive wages too low to leave them enough money to remit. Some Indigenous parents have no choice but to leave their kids in commercial towns to beg, fend for themselves, or go into shelters for migrant Indigenous children supported by the Instituto Nacional Indigenista, which are underfunded and in poor condition.[80] But these are exceptional circumstances; in most cases, parents left their kids with a trusted adult and have been sending remittances to cover their material needs.

In the streets of Morocco in 2007, Castañeda found many children whose parents were abroad and who were fending for themselves. They could not wait to go to Europe, where they would work and reunite with their parents. There were many stories of children hiding under trucks in places like Tangiers in order to enter boats and containers heading for Europe, although many of them died in the attempt.[81]

## Changing Gender Roles

In many places, migration has become a gendered rite of passage. For example, for decades in parts of Mexico and Algeria, a commonly held belief was that only "real men" migrated, making migration a core part of how masculinity was defined in those places during much of the twentieth century.[82] Thus, dependence on remittances as a financial household strategy has implications beyond the economic realm, affecting social roles and emotional processes such as identity and gender formation. For example, remitting fathers affect the model of masculinity that the remittance-receiving sons will tend to reproduce. Once care providers and heads of households, fathers become only remitters and long-distance breadwinners, with possibly negative effects on the mental health of male migrants.[83] Migration thus disturbs family and gender roles, because those left behind have to try to make up for the unpaid house labor and decision-making from those who have emigrated.[84]

While the migrant father's primary role is to act as a breadwinner, more emotional labor is often expected from the mother, even when she remits. Gender roles are sometimes changed by migration, but sometimes they are reinforced. Studies have observed that sometimes wives follow their migrating husbands, but other times women promote not only their own migration but that of their husbands and the whole family.

## Remittances: Psychological Aspects

León and Rebeca Grinberg were among the first to study the shock and adjustment process undergone by migrants. Departure, prolonged separation from one's place of origin and loved ones, uncertainty about the conditions in the receiving country, and the risks and dangers of the migration journey can all deliver a shock to a migrant's psyche, with accompanying feelings of anxiety, depression, and mourning:

Migration is not an isolated traumatic experience that manifests itself at the moment of departure-separation from the place of origin, or that of arrival in the new, unfamiliar place where the individual will settle down. Migration would fall into the category of the so-called "cumulative" and "tension" traumas, with reactions not always spectacular, but with profound and lasting effects.... This risk is experienced more intensely if important situations of privation and separation have been suffered during childhood.[85]

Childhood experiences have a determining role in our character and identity. The child left behind may face feelings of abandonment, loss of identity, and loneliness. Their emotional needs are often taken care of by grandmothers, fathers, aunts, uncles, and others. However, the migration of minors or the caretakers may produce another experience of separation for which the youth may blame themselves unconsciously.

Migration is a personal crisis, even for adults, in the sense that it is an often abrupt change in one's circumstances. Salman Akhtar describes migration as threatening an individual's sense of identity.[86] Several factors determine whether a migrant will fall victim to these emotional consequences.[87] The meaning given to migration—as sacrifice or as abandonment—is critical in determining how the family manages the emotional consequences of the migration, either coping or prolonging the trauma.

In discussing the possible effects of migration on migrants' mental health, we do not mean to imply that all migrants face paralyzing emotional pain. An individual's response to trauma depends on character, maturity, life experience, past responses to trauma, and the quality of parenting received. However, migrants coping with the new distance from loved ones and overcoming the trauma of migration face many additional hurdles, including finding a job, looking for a new place to live, remitting, and negotiating a new language and culture.

## The Children Left Behind

Castañeda went to the Mixteca region of Guerrero, Mexico, in 2004 to study the impact of remittances sent by immigrants from the region working in New York City. What stood out most was the number of children whose parents living in New York City were asking about them and longing for their physical presence. With family separation and the formation of transnational households, we see the phenomenon of "teleparenting," or parenting at a distance.[88] Although smartphones, Zoom, and similar online services help create a sense of simultaneity, the sharing of information is not complete.

Dual-earning parents are forced to leave their children home alone, take older children out of school to care for the younger children, or take their children with them to the workplace. Many of the adults left at home who are caring for the young are also engaged in the local workforce. In their efforts to keep their small businesses afloat, grandparents, aunts, and uncles may have the children left behind help in the family restaurant or store. In these families, the remittances sent to children do not always enable more hours or years of study for them. Moreover, these children often raise each other, and infants and toddlers are at risk of receiving an inadequate social and emotional environment in which to grow as economic pressures bring more and more family members into the workforce.[89] This is also the case for U.S. households, especially during the recent pandemic years. Given the lack of affordable childcare in the United States, the children of working-class non-immigrants are typically left with grandparents, aunts, uncles, or godparents, whom they may come to regard as their "real parents." But in transnational households, if the biological parents decide to reunite with their children left behind, the reunion may be bittersweet for the children as they suffer a second separation from a main caregiver.

Studies of the psychological impacts of such separations have shown a positive correlation between the disruption of attachment in early childhood and proneness to develop conflictual and unsatisfying interpersonal relations in adulthood.[90]

## Caveats and Reasons to Avoid Negative Judgments of Transnational Families

How detrimental the migration of a member is to a family depends on how well the family can adapt and recover. Many transnational families are flexible and resilient; although they differ from the nuclear family model in family structure, they are not detrimental to society but have been formed as a response to a particular situation. In some households, grandparents successfully take on parenting roles. Emerging psychological research on child development points to the important role of grandparents in building resilience in children, especially when they are working cooperatively with the biological parents. The success of transnational family models appears to depend on context and specific factors, such as the responsiveness of substitute caregivers, the quality of the previous relationships between parents and children, the ability to maintain social and emotional ties with migrating parents, and overall community support. When the family reunites on either side of the border after years of separation, the emotional bonds may be successfully repaired given adequate circumstances and emotional attunement.[91]

Families are social institutions that have existed in many ways and modalities throughout history. It is important to note here that although there can be negative side effects from family separation, we are not making a case for the traditional nuclear family; rather, we are arguing against families being forced to separate because of political instability, poverty, and immigration policies. Families come in all shapes and sizes; the key to their well-being is their ability to choose their arrangements, not forced into a certain configuration by migration policies. As Carola Suárez-Orozco and her colleagues remind us, "In communities where child fostering is widely practiced, no stigma is attached to its occurrence."[92] Separated families are also not without historical precedents: in previous decades, they were common among Polish, Jewish, Italian, and Chinese immigrants to the United States.[93] Rhacel Salazar Parreñas mentions that illiberal regimes in Asia and the Gulf region have guest worker programs that encourage family separation.[94] The same happens in "liberal" regimes. For example, the previously mentioned Bracero Program mandated divided families since it provided Mexican men with temporary visas for agricultural work in the United States without making any provisions for family unity.

Temporal workers with visas can live with their families for some months each year, avoiding prolonged family separations. For internal migrants, like Mayans who work in Cancun, remittances can represent an economic advancement without taking a complete toll on social relations and parenting because the ease of travel enables visits, at least on weekends.[95] However, the effects of these short-distance migrations cannot be generalized to international migration, especially not for undocumented workers. With no other way to meet the family's needs besides migration, many parents and children are separated by international borders for years at a time.

## Implications of Recent Laws for Family Reunification

In the spring of 2018, the Trump administration implemented what they called a "zero tolerance" immigration policy, which included a pilot program in El Paso, later expanded to other border sectors, that authorized the separation of minors from their migrant parents. The purpose was to dissuade more Latin American and Caribbean families from arriving at the border, even those applying for asylum. Many quickly denounced the cruelty of such a policy of explicit family separation at the border. While this practice took it a step further, the pairing of labor migration and family separation has a long history in practice and in immigration law as a result of the criminalization of undocumented and, indirectly, documented migration since the 1980s. Immigration reforms have since included larger budgets for policing, detention, and deportation. Laws that are supposed to tackle the real problem of human trafficking define human trafficking so broadly that sometimes they criminalize migrants' extended family members, trusted community members, and minors who are forced to work as coyotes in the final journey to cross the border.[96] Legal conceptions intended to prioritize the "best interest of the child"[97] are often used to blame and criminalize immigrant parents and withdraw custody.[98]

Sometimes children arrive unaccompanied by direct family members, but most of these minors are arriving with extended family members or other trusted people. Some children are made "unaccompanied" by the state when the state separates them from family members it deports while allowing the minors to stay. U visas (suspected abuse), T visas (trafficking), or special immigrant juvenile (SIJ) status for abused, neglected, and abandoned children provide unaccompanied children with protection from deportation and a path to citizenship. Nevertheless, in granting U visas, T visas, and SIJ status, the state often severs ties and separates families, supposedly in the name of protecting vulnerable, worthy, or deserving victims.[99] Constructing these qualities in the law and in the courtroom requires a delicate dance and performance by many actors: judges, lawyers, nonprofits, expert witnesses, doctors, and journalists.[100] The results help a few but end up further rationalizing the exclusion of many people displaced from their homes by violence and relative poverty and of those who prefer family reunification. Exempted under certain forms of legal relief, individuals are separated from their families forever. They cannot later apply for family reunification or return parental rights from the state to the biological parents.[101] Those applying for asylum are not permitted to visit their country of birth, not even to see a dying parent, nor cross the border to go to a dentist or other establishment next to the border bridge. Asylum applicants must apply mainly on an individual basis. They must successfully ask for permission to enter the country to claim asylum based on being a member of an explicitly persecuted "social group" (always open to legal interpretation). Many get a legal status on the basis of protection from violent, neglectful or abandoning family members, but in doing so they must legally terminate those family relationships.[102] The state deported parents without their children even before Trump became president, and the practice is not unique to the United States.

Thus, we question the use of the term "unaccompanied." The category may be meaningful to the state, but there is no ontological or theoretical reason to have these conversations solely around the concept of the "unaccompanied," and we do not use it as the major way to frame the migrants whose experience is addressed in this book.

## Moments of Joy

We have focused this introduction on the harmful effects of family separation caused by restrictive immigration policies. Nonetheless, collective joy and healing can accompany family reunification through either legal channels or the agency of family members who make it across the border.

In the concluding chapter of her book *Sacrificing Families*, Leisy Abrego asks the crucial question of whether family separation to increase family income is worth the sacrifice, pain, and constant struggle to fit in. After deeply interrogating this question in the context of her research on transnational Salvadoran families, she concludes that the answer is deeply personal for the individuals who experience it. However, the increasingly hostile policy environment toward immigrants makes the decision much harder and more dangerous, and the results more precarious. As we do, she argues that family separation is built into immigration policies.[103]

What happens after reunification is arguably just as important as the separation. Although family reunification has its challenges, it is important to mention its positive emotions. For many families, the reunification is what made the separation "worth it."

In the following excerpt, a Guatemalan mother recounts her feelings after her daughter joined her in the United States:

> My daughter, she made a great sacrifice to be here with me. She tried crossing three times. The first two they deported her back to El Salvador. She spent one birthday detained in Mexico. I told her over the phone, "Do not worry, my girl, I will throw you a party and make you a cake when you are here with me." And I did. She invited her friends from school. She had a good time. It is my happiness to see her laugh. I am a single mother; she is my only child. All I do, I do for her. She is my priority.

Jesus, who migrated when he was ten years old, answered some of our questions:

> INTERVIEWER: What did you feel when you knew you were going to see your mom and dad?
>
> JESUS: Well, happiness, and sadness for leaving my sister.
>
> INTERVIEWER: How do you think your relationship with your dad changed before and now?
>
> JESUS: It was like seeing a new person. I did not remember what he looked like. I could only see him in photos.

Despite leaving his sister, Jesus gained a father who would now be an integral part of his daily life and with whom he would start a new relationship, with all its potential for building self-esteem and self-love.

Several parents observed that their children's well-being improved upon reunification. A father from Honduras recounted that his son "has seemingly been calmer. . . . Since he came here at an older age, he could see what the situation was back home compared to here. He is seemingly calmer, more relaxed here." Another father from El Salvador, living in Prince George's County, Maryland, explained the entire process of youth migrant acculturation very well when talking about his children:

> The hardest part is when someone who has recently arrived in this country has to get adapted to life here. That has affected them a lot. To leave their mom and see how the situation was there is what has affected them the most. But with time, little by little, they've been adapting to life here. In the first place, like I said, they didn't know me. So when I went to wait for them in Baltimore, they didn't know me then. For them, I was a distant person; they heard me mentioned, they saw me in pictures, but not in person. Getting accustomed to living with me was one of the hardest things because honestly, to move from being with someone that you've been with your whole life [their mother] to a new place with someone they had not met in person [their father] . . . was a big change. But with time you adjust, and they've been adapting and adapting, bit by bit. As the days [pass] they are getting used to the new life. We have lived here since they came; we have not moved from one apartment to another.

We asked this father whether he felt that his children were having difficulty in school. He replied:

> Up until now, they haven't had any difficulty, as they've done their part and haven't had any conflicts with other people. They've always moved forward . . . they are my trophies. So I give thanks to God for the intelligence that He has given them. I admire them a lot, because to move from one place to another and keep moving forward is not easy. They are motivated, and it's God who gives them the strength. I am proud of them, and they are the best gift I've been given. Even though I didn't have them when they were little, they're with me now.

As this father explained, reintegration into family and a new context is not easy, but it can happen slowly with love, patience, and community support. It is important to remember that, alongside the challenges, families can and do experience a great deal of growth, joy, and happiness. Regardless of where they were born, the family members we interviewed, once they were reunited in the Washington, D.C., metropolitan area, had the same worries as many of the other residents of the area, but also the same joys to be experienced in sports, work, loved ones, music, movies, food, learning, and friendship.

## The Contributions of This Book to the Collective Conversation

We have three main goals in this book. The first and most important is to communicate the stories of Central American youth and families living in the D.C. area. These stories provide important data about an often misconstrued group. Between reports from the border, exposés about MS-13, and warnings not to come to the United States, there is a need for more nuance and clarity about who Central American migrants are. In attempting to provide this, we hope to make a clearer argument about immigration, beginning with the fact that there is no one single type of Central American immigrant; whether a Salvadoran teenager or a Guatemalan mother, everyone comes with their own background, circumstances, experiences, and motivations. This is what makes the act and process of immigration so compelling. We also find it important to share stories of joy and success and to show that migrants are not simply victims of violence, poverty, or other unfavorable circumstances but individuals who, like anyone else, deserve respect and empathy.

Our second goal is to highlight the role of imperialism, interventionism, and global capitalism in the so-called root causes of migration from countries such as El Salvador, Honduras, and Guatemala. Much of the destabilization, poverty, and corruption that individuals in these countries deal with is connected to historical injustices. This historical context and argument are explained briefly in chapter 2.

Our third goal is to provide context on the topic of immigrant integration, with a focus on children, adolescents, and families and the roles of school and community programming. We also stress the importance of federal immigration policy and the social safety net (including at the state and local levels) in helping or hindering the integration process. We argue, as many others have done, that more empathetic immigration policies would aid the integration process and, by helping immigrants feel more at home in their new communities, strengthen those communities overall. We also believe that a social safety net that is not means-tested could help the integration process. Welcoming programs and more education about the realities of immigration can help prevent inaccurate, racist, and xenophobic narratives about immigrants from forming in the mainstream. The bulk of this argument appears in the last chapter, but data supporting it appear throughout.

Many immigration policies have clearly intended effects, but it is important to understand that even when they achieve their main goals, they may simultaneously exacerbate the problem they claim to be trying to fix, or they may have unintended consequences that are antithetical to the purpose of the policy. In chapter 8, we discuss a number of these and include a time line of policies regarding unaccompanied children and Central American immigrants. Many hard-liners on immigration posit that we should let fewer people in, and that immigrants are a problem, especially poor ones. The policies created by hard-liners often result in discrimination, violence, and hostile environments for immigrants. For instance, the mass shooter at a Walmart in El Paso, Texas, in 2018 was motivated by his belief in conspiracy theories such as the Great Replacement to kill anyone he perceived as Hispanic.[104] Other policies have allowed law enforcement to profile Hispanic-appearing people as likely to be undocumented.

How should immigration policy respond to its historically harmful effects? The data we present in this book lead us to several conclusions (discussed at length in chapter 8):

1. The United States needs more humane, compassionate, and efficient asylum and family reunification policies.
2. Social policy programs such as ESL classes, family counseling, and food and education assistance can improve the integration process. Labor protections for all working people, immigrant and non-immigrant alike, strengthen communities and help migrant families integrate, reunify, and become a part of their community.
3. Immigrant exclusion, xenophobia, and racism predate the Trump administration and have continued afterwards.

We contribute to the overall literature on immigration by discussing family reunification and the integration process for Central American youth during the first years of the Trump era, a topic on which we are some of the first to report. We focus on youths' lives in Central America and the contexts that shaped their decision to leave, their migration journeys (including time in CBP detention), their legal challenges once they arrived in the United States, their home lives, their relationships with sponsors and family dynamics after reunification, their mental health, and their social lives in schools. In this extensive overview, we hope to sketch the big picture of youth migration. In the concluding chapter, we bring all of these ideas together while discussing the implications of our findings for policy and immigrant integration programs.

## Road Map for the Book

Chapter 1 discusses Central American migration to the United States and to the D.C. region. Here we also explain where our data come from, the methods we used to collect them, and the structure of the rest of the book.

Chapter 2 recounts a brief recent history of El Salvador, Guatemala, and Honduras to inform readers' understanding of why these countries look the way they do today and why longtime migration to the United States from the region continues to this day. The history of Central America is a long history of interventionism and exploitation that destabilized states and encouraged war for geopolitical and economic reasons that would benefit some groups in the United States. This history is also connected to modern immigration policy toward the region and partly explains why immigration from the region looks the way it does today. For this reason, we also discuss remittances—what they are, their role in migration, and their limitations. The chapter aims to quickly get the reader up to speed on some of the larger issues in the region's history that are relevant to a discussion of contemporary migration.

Chapter 3 takes a deep dive into individuals' motives for migrating, incorporating the theory presented in the earlier pages into an answer to the question of why people migrate. It includes a host of quotes, descriptions, and analyses from youth themselves on why, how, and who made their decision to leave.

Chapter 4 recounts young migrants' journey from Central America to the U.S. border, including detailed descriptions and analyses of what they endured and what they hoped for during that time.

Chapter 5 presents rich data detailing the characteristics of family reunification and investigating how it unfolds. We present these data alongside discussions of legal barriers and of the holistic nature of family reunification and structural integration.

Using mental health scales, chapter 6 engages qualitative data from the study involving trauma, PTSD, and depression. Then chapter 7 delves into how respondents fare in schools—what they like about their educational experience, what they struggle with, and where they excel.

Concluding the book, chapter 8 discusses all of the data in the context of policy and makes suggestions for modifying policy at the federal, state, and local levels to help rather than hinder youth integration and family reunification.

CHAPTER ONE

# WHAT WE KNOW AND WHAT WE SET OUT TO FIND

Although there was incredible public outcry during the Trump administration's forced family separations at the U.S. border with Mexico, we argue in this book that both distress-based and labor-based migration by members of transnational households were responsible for these separations in the first place. Family separations started long before Trump took office and have continued since he left.

Previous U.S. interventionism and the global economic system have driven low wages and lack of opportunity in Central America, alongside a demand for cheap labor in the United States. Parents feel that they must go north to work without their children, not knowing when they will see them next. Often the separation lasts for years, and eventual reunification may be bittersweet, scary, and challenging, even as family members feel the relief of being together again. A significant contribution of this book is showing how integration works for youth in the first few years after their arrival ends a long separation.

We argue that the migration of unaccompanied Central American children, even though it reemerges as an "issue" in the news every few months, is not a new phenomenon. Importantly, the data presented in this book highlight (1) the predictability of these migrations and the misplaced alarmism around them, (2) the predictable trauma many young migrants experience on the journey northward owing to U.S. immigration laws and policies, and relatedly (3) youths' experiences during long-term separation from their families affect them deeply both before and after reunification and also impact the context of integration within the family, school, and community at large.

https://doi.org/10.7758/dvxg2393.9735

The uproar that followed the first separation of families at the border by the Trump administration was a response to an admittedly cruel and shortsighted immigration policy, but these policies did not start during the Trump administration, nor did they end when Trump left office. Economic global systems that distribute wealth unequally among populations create what we call "structural family separation." It begins when, as Jorge Duran, Douglas Massey, and others have shown, able-bodied individuals feel compelled to leave their community and family after a "hook" has connected labor recruitment from the Global North with the poverty and excess labor in the Global South (rural Mexico, the Philippines, Algeria, Morocco, El Salvador, and so on).[1] Social networks continue to perpetuate migration, but initially, this labor supply is mainly fueled by able-bodied men and women of working age, not by other members of nuclear families, for several reasons.[2] First, many of these workers are undocumented and thus cannot use legal channels for family migration or prompt family reunification. Second, not only is raising a family in the Global North very costly, but doing so defeats the strategy of sending remittances in a strong currency that will go a long way in the Global South toward sustaining a family.[3] Finally, family reunification in the Global North is challenging economically for those in agriculture, construction, health care, childcare, restaurants, and the overall service sector because the pay is too low to sustain a family.

Therefore, as sociologist Michael Burawoy writes, long-distance family separation due to economic inequality creates a system that rewards labor extraction and profit in the Global North and family and social reproduction in the Global South.[4] The developing world subsidizes many of the luxuries of the middle and upper classes in global cities with hourglass social structures by providing cheap labor on demand.[5] But these workers are also easily deportable during economic crises, as we saw in the United States after the 2008 financial crisis and with the mass deportations of the Obama administration. Furthermore, in another example of neocolonial extraction, the developing world pays for the birth, upbringing, feeding, education, health maintenance, and retirement of an important proportion of the workforce in global cities such as New York, London, Paris, and, increasingly, Washington, D.C. Thus, the common picture drawn by Castañeda's fieldwork in Mexico and by the work of Joanna Dreby, Gabrielle Oliveira, and others of immigrants who live and work abroad who want to be able to visit their families and children—who might join them later, if at all—but are made to stay away for years on end by restrictive policies.[6]

Acknowledging critiques of purely "structural" explanations of migration, we want to be clear that we are not arguing that the people we write about have no agency or that they are not making their own tough decisions about whether to migrate. Instead, we aim to shed light on the incongruency between the public response when Trump separated families and the lack of response to the implementation of policies with similar effects both before and after the Trump administration.

This chapter presents the studies on which the rest of the book is built: the work of Cecilia Menjívar, Leisy Abrego, Sarah Mahler, Joanna Dreby, Rhacel Salazar Parreñas, Lesley Buck, Leah Schmalzbauer, and many others who have written about Central American migration or children and youth migration. The findings reported in this book confirm and connect the takeaways of much of their research.

## Why Leave?

The decision to emigrate is not necessarily a long-held plan or desire. Sometimes changes on the ground push a person to migrate unexpectedly.[7] Sociologist Leah Schmalzbauer's work on Honduran transnational families and children left behind is illuminating: she found that, in the first several years of the 2000s, the children she interviewed who had parents in the United States had no intention of leaving Honduras. Several changes in the Honduran sending context since then—for example, more persistent and widespread gang violence and a coup d'état—have had an impact on "individual" migration decisions.

Having gained unprecedented access to the U.S. Department of Health and Human Services' Office of Refugee Resettlement (ORR) shelters, anthropologist Susan Terrio, in her book *Whose Child Am I?*, recounts the conditions under which children and youth are held in U.S. government custody.[8] Sociologist Stephanie Canizales talks about unaccompanied youths' entry into the labor force in Los Angeles.[9]

Rebecca Hamlin discusses how arbitrarily states designate some people on the move as migrants, asylum seekers, or refugees. These state-centered designations do not reflect sociological realities and are often determined by local and international political considerations.[10] Refugees are often artificially depicted as "in need of protection," whereas migrants are usually thought of as voluntarily on the move and motivated by economic concerns. Hamlin recalls some of the ways in which U.S. and European asylum policies, politics, media, and public opinion have shaped and changed how these designations are made. Such binary thinking, which distinguishes between "deserving" and "underserving" people, has many drawbacks; for instance, it underlies extreme border control measures, like those that make the journey from Central America to the United States so dangerous. The acceptance rate for the asylum claims of those coming from Central America and Haiti in the 1980s was only 2 percent, despite their clear humanitarian need. Hamlin argues that the distinction between migrants and refugees reinforces the idea in public discourse that those who are *actually* in need comprise a tiny fraction of those on the move.

Chiara Galli, who interviewed lawyers and unaccompanied minors in Los Angeles, describes the limited avenues available to minor asylum seekers, whose lawyers, in order for these minors to satisfy the narrow legal requirements for being granted asylum, must construct recognizable portraits of suffering that match protections in the law. She finds that lawyers tend to represent mainly those migrants whom they think have a higher probability of being granted asylum—to the further neglect of the needs of other immigrants.[11] The same conditions in the Washington, D.C., region and nationwide have been documented by Dennis Stinchcomb and the staff of the Center for Latin American and Latino Studies.[12] Sociologist Emily Ruehs-Navarro writes about how lawyers and nonprofit workers who help unaccompanied minors shape their narratives and determine how they enter the United States.[13] The legal process takes center stage for the many people who closely follow the efforts of migrant youth seeking asylum and resettlement. We recognize that the legal-bureaucratic process is very important and helps shape outcomes, but we also maintain that this tiny part of a person's history has little to nothing to do with why they migrated or the dynamics of their physical reunification with their families.

## Latin America Youth Migration and Barriers to Family Reunification

As we discussed in the previous chapter, the term "transnational families" describes several types of family units: one or both parents have left their children in their country of origin in order to work abroad;[14] the family reunified in another country at a different time;[15] or the parents have created a home in two other countries if they can travel despite living across international borders.[16] The sociologist Joanna Dreby, who interviewed 141 people who were members of Mexican transnational families, details how children felt after one of their parents migrated.[17] She finds that the children exerted their agency and feelings over their situation differently based on age. The younger children reported disappointment, "emotional withholding," and a desire for their parents to return. The adolescents reported distress and resentment and asked their parents for more resources or pressured them to finance their migration. Mexican transnational families who experienced separation owing to constrained choices included both those who migrated for economic prosperity and those who had been involuntarily separated by deportation.[18] The children whose transnational family situation resulted from constrained choices often resented their parents, especially if they believed that their parents' migration had been unsuccessful. On the other hand, the children who were part of involuntarily separated transnational families owing to violence or persecution experienced anxiety but were understanding of the family situation.

Sociologist Leisy Abrego interviewed youth in El Salvador whose parents had gone to the United States.[19] When she asked them about the possibility of reuniting with their parents in the United States, responses varied based on their emotional state and their family's financial circumstances. The youth with financial and emotional struggles were unclear about their future in the United States. Those with better finances expressed a desire to stay in El Salvador.

Another struggle faced by transnational families is the varying citizenship status of the family members and the state's legal interpretation of the family's position. In her ethnography on Mexican migrants from transnational families, anthropologist Deborah Boehm discusses U.S. citizens who have undocumented parents or caregivers and undocumented minors who, having grown up, attended school, and made friends in the United States, are de facto members of their community but are still considered out of place by the government.[20]

Not knowing whether they can stay in the United States because of their legal status generates a lot of psychological uncertainty and a feeling of "living in limbo."[21] Also subject to this uncertainty are unaccompanied children who eventually become citizens and permanent residents, attend public schools, and use public spaces but whose parents or primary caregivers do not. Children and parents with different legal statuses can encounter additional barriers to reunification.

The experiences of reunification, legal limbo, and precarious documentation statuses all trouble the concept of "home," which becomes a nonstatic place full of new or changing people and surroundings. This is the case, for instance, for members of transnational households, for working-class immigrant families who relocate often for seasonal agricultural work, and for families who have been evicted multiple times because of rising rental prices alongside stagnating and often illegally low wages.

## Contextualizing the Numbers

From 2012 to 2021, around 360,000 minors were referred to the Office of Refugee Resettlement by the U.S. Department of Homeland Security (DHS).[22] According to government figures, in fiscal year 2021, around "72% of all children referred were over 14 years of age, and 66% were boys."[23] Approximately 47 percent were from Guatemala, 13 percent from El Salvador, 32 percent from Honduras, and 8 percent from other countries. (Figure 1.1 shows the countries of origin of unaccompanied minors and family units encountered by authorities at the border.) These numbers may continue to grow, as there is no easy solution to the increased violence and economic and political instability in their countries of birth; there will continue to be many youth migrating to join family members who are long settled in the United States. Also, if labor demands are not met by Central Americans, they may be met by people from South America or other parts of the world.

Many recently arrived immigrant children and teens face structural barriers to integration into communities in the United States.[24] Such obstacles can include the experience of migration-related family separation, inconsistent or interrupted schooling in their home country, language barriers in their new schools, and inconsistent application of federal resettlement policies.

In 1980, around 354,000 Central American immigrants were living in the United States; by 2019, there were at least 3,782,000. Given Central America's political turmoil and violence in the 1980s, many D.C.-based activists, church leaders, and diplomats who had spent time in Central

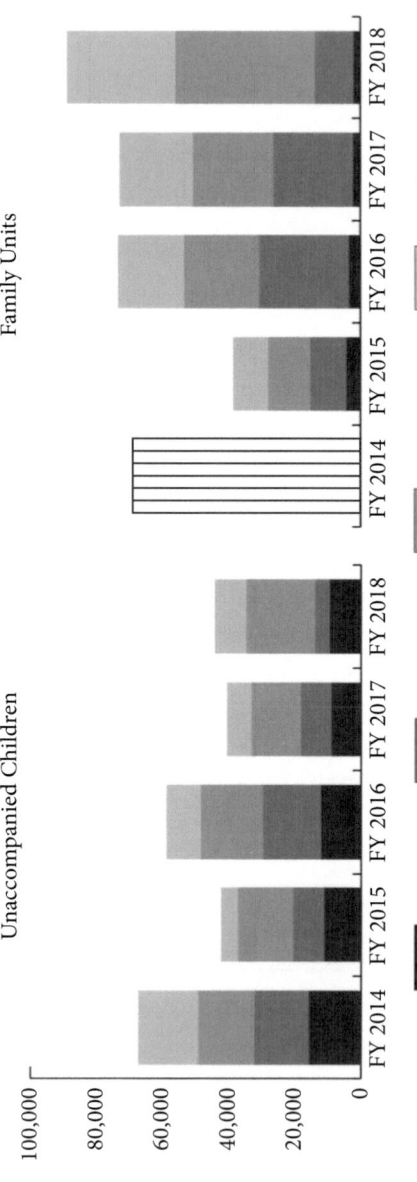

**Figure 1.1** *Southwest Border Apprehensions by Country of Origin, Fiscal Years 2014–2018*

*Source*: Stinchcomb and Berger Cardoso 2018, 2, reproduced with permission from CLALS.
*Data source*: U.S. Customs and Border Protection 2016, 2018.
*Note*: Data for fiscal year 2018 is through August 31. Country-of-origin data for family unit apprehensions in fiscal year 2014 is unavailable.

America helped people settle in the D.C. metropolitan region. Washington, D.C., San Francisco, and Los Angeles became important sanctuary cities for people who were escaping persecution and lacked immigration papers. With the birth of the sanctuary movement in the United States, nonprofit organizations and activist networks formed to welcome Central American immigrants and to advocate for government recognition of Central Americans as refugees who had needed to escape real threats in the countries, including natural disasters. This support network eventually led to the creation of temporary protective status (TPS), which was granted to many Central Americans.[25] As it receives busloads of asylum seekers from Latin America to Washington, D.C., the network remains important today.

With its rich history as a location for immigrant populations, especially those from Central America, the Washington, D.C., metropolitan area provides an ideal location for studying the family reunification of Central Americans. Since the 1980s, the D.C. region has grown to have the highest concentration of Central Americans of all the major metropolitan regions in the United States and is home to a rich and developed Salvadoran culinary and cultural scene. During this time of growth, D.C. has been an ideal destination for migrants. Central American immigrants comprise at least 4.9 percent of the D.C. metro area's population compared to 4.3 percent in Los Angeles, 4.2 percent in Miami, 3.6 percent in Houston, and 2 percent in New York.[26] Youth also frequently arrive in the area after being released from ORR custody.

Figure 1.2 shows the primary destination places of Central American unaccompanied minors during this period. As can be seen, D.C., Maryland, and Virginia collectively constitute the most prominent destination (see also figure 1.3). We stopped graphing the data in 2018 because our interviewees arrived within this time frame. Note that the government used the term "unaccompanied alien child(ren)" (UAC) to describe this population. In presenting these graphs, we use "UAC" to reflect the data pool on which we relied, but we will not routinely use that term throughout the rest of the book.

In the 1980s, diplomats, aid workers, and activists helped people settle in the District. For instance, the D.C. neighborhoods of Mount Pleasant, Columbia Heights, and Adams Morgan became immigrant enclaves for Salvadorans fleeing the civil war, which lasted for over twelve years.[27] According to the Office of Refugee Resettlement, from

**Figure 1.2** *Unaccompanied Children Released to Sponsors, by State, Fiscal Years 2014–2018*

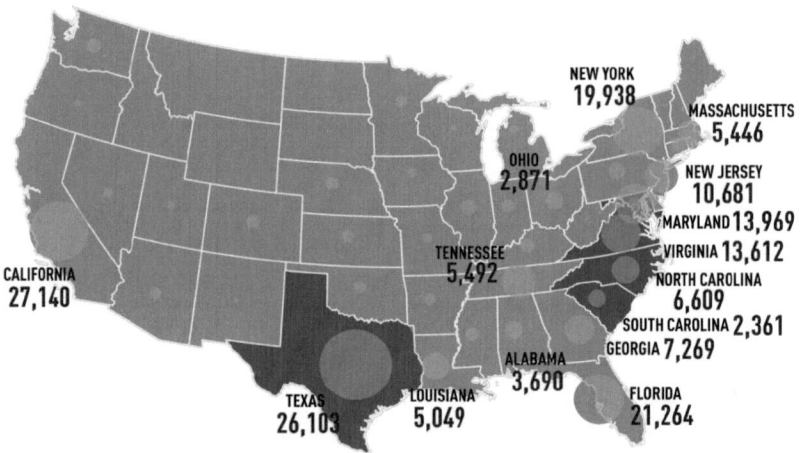

*Source:* Stinchcomb and Berger Cardoso 2018, reproduced with permission from CLALS.
*Data source:* Office of Refugee Resettlement (ORR) 2024b.
*Note:* Data for fiscal year 2018 is through July 31. Placement data include UACs of all nationalities; UACs from El Salvador, Guatemala, and Honduras accounted for between 91 and 95 percent of all annual placements between fiscal year 2014 and fiscal year 2017 (ORR 2024a).

the start of fiscal year 2014 until April 2018, more than 26,500 UACs were released to sponsors in Maryland and Virginia—more than in any other region of the country. At the time of our interviews, most minors were resettled after arrival in the D.C. suburbs and exurbs close to D.C. proper but not within the city limits (see figures 1.4 and 1.5), partly because of the gentrification and increasing cost of living in the District. However, its formerly Latin-majority neighborhoods have remained centers of immigrant knowledge, influence, social networks, and services.[28] Although these places have changed and new Central American migrants no longer settle in neighborhoods like Mount Pleasant and Adams Morgan, the interpersonal social networks established there continue to echo throughout the region, especially in Montgomery and Prince George's Counties in Maryland and in Fairfax, Virginia, which are common places of arrival for new Central American migrants, both adult and minor.

**Figure 1.3** *Unaccompanied Children Released to Sponsors in the D.C. Area, Fiscal Years 2014–2018*

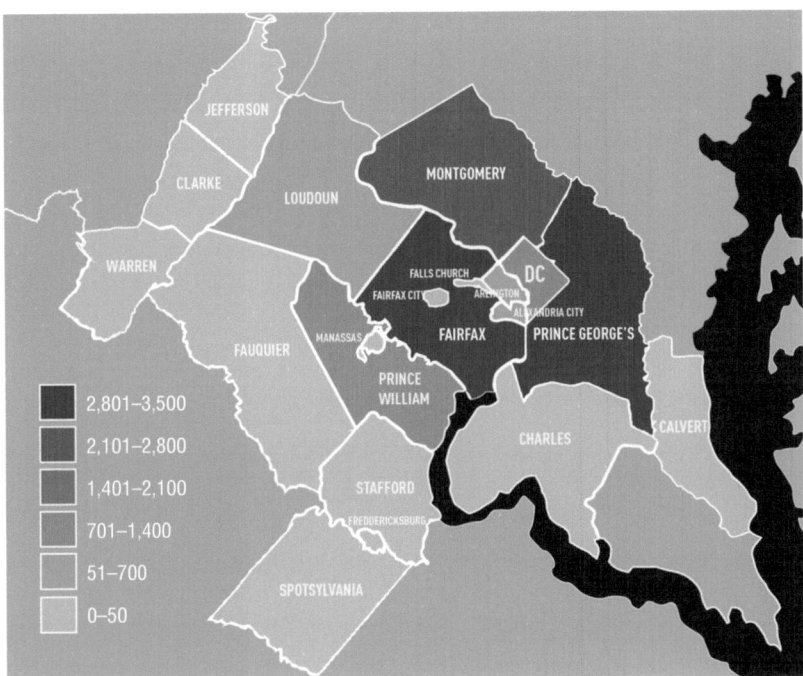

*Source:* Office of Refugee Resettlement (ORR) 2024b.
*Note:* Data for fiscal year 2018 is through April 30. Placement data include UACs of all nationalities; UACs from the NTCA accounted for between 91 and 95 percent of all annual placements between fiscal year 2014 and fiscal year 2017 (ORR 2024a).

**Figure 1.4** *Unaccompanied Children Released to Sponsors in the D.C. Area, by Year*

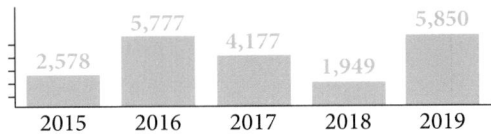

*Source:* Castañeda and Jenks 2021b.

**Figure 1.5** *Total Number of Unaccompanied Children Placed with Sponsors, 2015–2019*

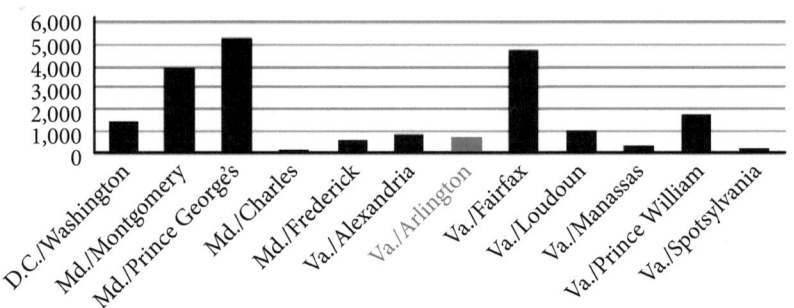

*Source:* Castañeda and Jenks 2021b.

Understanding minors' experiences on their journey north can tell us much about their financial standing and stability; for instance, if they were not used to having enough money to pay for food, or if they were not always able to go to school, their educational needs will look different. If they never had trouble going to school but were separated from their parents in the United States, family reunification may be the main challenge they face.

Washington, D.C., and the surrounding area have the highest concentration of Central Americans in the United States. The region is home to the largest Salvadoran population in the country, a relatively small Mexican population, and a large community of Hondurans and Guatemalans. Across the larger metropolitan region, several immigrant-owned businesses, such as grocery stores, restaurants, and financial transfer firms, cater to the needs of immigrants from Central America. These establishments can be found not only in D.C. proper but also in Fairfax County and Arlington in Virginia and in Montgomery and Prince George's County in Maryland, where many Central Americans live.

## The Study

Unaccompanied minors from Central America have been a frequent topic of discussion in the news since at least the so-called border crisis of 2014, but with few exceptions, their own voices are rarely heard.[29]

These exceptions include a few journalistic accounts,[30] some first-person accounts,[31] interviews with detainees,[32] considerations of the art they have produced during detention,[33] interviews mainly with advocates, and great studies of deported Central American youth and children.[34] Children, like anyone else, have the ability to make decisions within a range of options, and they have their own way of processing and understanding their experiences and conditions.[35] One of the best ways to understand their mental health outside of a clinical setting is through interviewing and assessing them directly. In 2017, our team interviewed fifty-eight recently arrived Central American youth, forty-one of their sponsors, and a group of twenty-three social services practitioners and school resource providers who were experts on these issues because of their continued interaction with migrant children and their families.

This book derives from the study "Household Contexts and School Integration of Resettled Migrant Youth," co-led by sociologist Ernesto Castañeda, community psychologist Noemi Enchautegui-de-Jesús, and political scientist Eric Hershberg. This research was sponsored by American University's Provost Office and administered at the Center for Latin American and Latino Studies (CLALS). Castañeda led the study and interview questionnaire design, selected the instruments, and supervised training and data collection with input from Enchautegui and Hershberg. The research team interviewed recently arrived teenagers and young adults ($N = 58$), including a few siblings, and in all but four cases, we also interviewed the sponsor, who was often a parent or extended family member ($N = 41$). We also interviewed social services practitioners and school officials from the area surrounding Washington, D.C. ($N = 23$). Eleven of the service providers worked for their county public school system, often specializing in international students, integration, and English for Speakers of Other Languages (ESOL) programs for students and their families. The rest worked for nonprofit organizations that worked with immigrants. We used these complementary interviews to contextualize and triangulate the accounts provided in the book, but our overall focus is centered on the words of the young immigrants and the service providers.

Verbal informed consent was given, but no written records of identifying information or contact information were kept in order to protect participants. Unaccompanied minors and recently arrived immigrant youth are a vulnerable and hard-to-reach subpopulation. Therefore, we used several sampling methods, including recruitment through after-school programs, advocacy and legal services, nonprofit agencies, and snowball sampling. The research ethics board of American University approved the study (IRB-2016-227). All researchers and data collectors were certified in human subject ethics training and trained in trauma-informed interviewing. The principal investigators had previous experience working with undocumented, homeless, disabled, and vulnerable populations.[36] We made it clear to respondents that we were not working for the government and were not lawyers or journalists. All the PIs and research assistants spoke Spanish fluently. Most of the interviewers were Latin and some were Central American. Many interviewers were immigrants or children of immigrants, and most were women. The interviewing team included undergraduate and master's level students, two university staff members, and a professor, all of whom spoke Spanish and were professional, friendly, and approachable. Establishing rapport with the interviewees was relatively easy, and it was possible to gain a certain level of trust and confidence.[37]

All participants were paid US$25 for their participation. The interviews with youth and sponsors were all conducted in Spanish; most interviews with school officials and community workers were in English. The interviews were wide-ranging and lasted between an hour and two and a half hours. Immigrants responded to questions about their lives and experiences in their home countries and in the United States, about their schooling and their migration journey, and about their experience with the U.S. immigration system. Some answers were open-ended, whereas others were responses to simple yes-or-no questions; some were scale-ranked. The youth survey on which this book is focused included both open- and closed-ended questions, as well as two mental health symptom scales.[38] Respondents filled out a Patient Health Questionnaire (PHQ-9), which screens for depression, as well as the Child PTSD Symptoms Scale based on the DSM-IV mental health manual (instruments at the end of this book).[39]

This is a mixed-methods study. That is, we use different approaches to collection and analysis of data in order to increase confidence in the findings.[40] We designed this to be a mixed-methods study using closed-ended quantifiable questions and open-ended questions that would elicit narrative responses. The purpose was to triangulate the qualitative and quantitative responses collected simultaneously from the same respondents at the same point in time. This work of analytical sociology utilizes data from a hard-to-reach population presenting their understandings in their own words. We share many stories of the youth and aim to contextualize these stories with other available data about immigrant integration, social services, and public policy.[41]

All interviews with youth were conducted in Spanish; recorded, transcribed, and entered into Qualtrics to analyze responses to the same question; and coded in NVivo, using spelled-out coding trees to bring together themes described by participants at any point during the interviews. We analyzed quantitative variables on SPSS, thus allowing for the triangulation of both qualitative data and descriptive quantitative statistics. The narrative sections selected as representing important trends and cases were translated for use in English-language publications after the coding and analyses were done. This ensured that the text remained faithful to its original meaning.

## SAMPLE DEMOGRAPHICS

Thirty-seven youth respondents were from El Salvador, sixteen were from Honduras, and five were from Guatemala (see table 1.1). Ages at the time of migration ranged from eight to twenty; only two participants reported being older than eighteen (nineteen and twenty). We decided to include them because their experiences were very similar to those of fourteen- and sixteen-year-olds, who sometimes already saw themselves as being of working age.[42] The average age at the time of the interview was sixteen. Their ages at the time of the interview ranged from ten to twenty-two, and at the time of migration ranged from eight to twenty. When interviewed, twenty-two participants resided in Prince George's County, Maryland, twenty-four in Montgomery County, Maryland, and twelve in Fairfax County, Virginia—all core jurisdictions in the Washington, D.C., metropolitan area.

We note several other variables: accompaniment and documentation status. At the time of their arrival at the border, thirty-four youth migrants were unaccompanied, and twenty-four were accompanied. We argue that, sociologically, and in the discussion of early integration experiences, this distinction is unclear and often unimportant given the similar conditions before migration. If a child migrated with their

**Table 1.1** *Demographic Characteristics of Immigrant Minors*

|  | N | Percent |
|---|---|---|
| Gender | 58 | |
|   Male | 31 | 53.45 |
|   Female | 26 | 44.83 |
|   Nonbinary | 1 | 1.72 |
| U.S. legal citizenship status at time of arrival | | |
|   Documented | 9 | 15.52 |
|   Undocumented | 49 | 84.48 |
| Country of origin | | |
|   El Salvador | 37 | 63.79 |
|   Honduras | 16 | 27.59 |
|   Guatemala | 5 | 8.63 |
| Jurisdiction within a D.C. metropolitan county | | |
|   Prince George's County | 22 | 37.93 |
|   Montgomery County | 24 | 41.38 |
|   Fairfax County | 12 | 20.69 |
| Accompaniment status at border | | |
|   Accompanied | 34 | 58.62 |
|   Unaccompanied | 24 | 41.38 |

*Source:* Authors' compilation.
*Note:* The average age of minors at the time of arrival was fourteen; at the time of the interview, the average age was sixteen.

mother, for instance, but still had to spend two months on foot traveling through Mexico and was then separated from their mother at the border, they are not necessarily better off than a child who traveled alone to meet their mother already in the United States.

Another very important sociological distinction that is instrumental in the physical, psychological, and economic futures of these minors is whether they arrived with or without legal papers. Yet documented minors are often placed in the same category as undocumented minors by schoolmates and the U.S.-born generally. In our study, nine respondents arrived with documentation, and forty-nine were undocumented. Two people arrived in 2013, ten during 2014, four in 2015, ten in 2016, and six in 2017, the year of the interviews. Although many had family members who were well established in the United States, our participants had arrived in the United States recently. Thus, they described integration experiences from those first years and months after migration.

Furthermore, we interviewed twenty-three professionals who often interacted with Central American youth arrivals: fourteen individuals who worked in schools or in school district offices, seven who worked at community-based organizations or clinics, and two who worked for a local government jurisdiction. They included teachers, counselors, and program directors in Washington, D.C. and in Fairfax, Montgomery, and Prince George's Counties. Most of these interviews were conducted between December 2016 and December 2017. Table 1.2 provides demographic information only for the interviewed minors.

We have organized, translated, and analyzed the interviews to shed light on the process and challenges of the integration of immigrant youth in the Washington, D.C., area. We use the interviews to contextualize the theoretical discussions and to provide tangible narratives of the experiences of youth. Additionally, the study combines and compares multiple viewpoints: what local and school officials say about working with unaccompanied Central American youth; the direct words of the youth and their sponsors; and finally, a theoretical framework with which to understand the integration experiences of the youth.

## LIMITATIONS

This book is an academic recounting and contextualizing of the experiences of family separation, family reunification, and immigrant integration. Although we draw from our respondents' personal experiences, the book is nothing like a memoir or even a conventional ethnography. We use various sociological methods to analyze how young people understand their experiences of immigration, new homes, and reunited families. By contrast, *Solito* by Javier Zamora and *Unforgetting* by Roberto Lovato are memoirs about specific and different experiences of migranthood.[43] Valeria Luiselli's books *Tell Me How It Ends* and *Lost Children Archive* use poetic prose to narrate an experience of longing to be reunited with parents and children, suffering the pain of the trip, and swimming in an ocean of uncertainty.[44]

**Table 1.2** *Demographic Characteristics of Immigrant Minor Respondents*

| Alias | Gender | Unaccompanied? | Age at Migration | Age at Interview | Country of Origin |
|---|---|---|---|---|---|
| Daniela | Female | Y | 16 | 18 | El Salvador |
| Dominick | Male | Y | 12 | 14 | El Salvador |
| Alberto | Male | Y | 14 | 16 | El Salvador |
| Diana | Female | N | 13 | 16 | El Salvador |
| Carlos | Male | Y | 15 | 15 | El Salvador |
| Juan | Male | N | 18 | 18 | El Salvador |
| David | Male | N | 13 | 14 | El Salvador |
| Sofia | Female | N | 15 | 16 | El Salvador |
| Nina | Female | Y | 15 | 15 | Guatemala |
| Valentina | Female | N | 16 | 16 | El Salvador |
| Luis | Male | Y | 17 | 19 | El Salvador |
| Samantha | Female | N | 13 | 15 | Honduras |
| Alison | Female | Y | 12 | 14 | El Salvador |
| Ana Cristina | Female | Y | 14 | 17 | Honduras |
| David | Male | Y | 11 | 13 | Honduras |
| Beatriz | Female | Y | 12 | 13 | El Salvador |
| Jose | Male | Y | 17 | 17 | El Salvador |
| Sarah | Female | Y | 15 | 18 | Honduras |
| Jorge | Male | Y | 13 | 16 | Honduras |
| Maria | Female | Y | 16 | 17 | Honduras |
| Isabela | Female | Y | 17 | 17 | El Salvador |
| Fernanda | Female | N | 13 | 15 | El Salvador |
| Camila | Female | Y | 13 | 17 | El Salvador |
| Jesus | Male | Y | 10 | 13 | El Salvador |
| Mario | Male | Y | 13 | 14 | El Salvador |
| Manuel | Male | N | 15 | 16 | El Salvador |
| Nelson | Male | N | 11 | 12 | Guatemala |
| Monica | Female | Y | 15 | 15 | Guatemala |
| Alexander | Male | N | 17 | 20 | El Salvador |
| Antonio | Male | N | 16 | 19 | El Salvador |
| Flor | Female | N | 14 | 17 | El Salvador |
| Elizabeth | Female | Y | 16 | 16 | Guatemala |
| Sarita | Female | Y | 12 | 13 | Honduras |
| Usmani | Male | Y | 16 | 16 | Honduras |
| Sebastián | Male | Y | 15 | 18 | El Salvador |
| Jessica | Female | N | 19 | 19 | El Salvador |
| Gabriela | Female | N | 14 | 18 | El Salvador |
| Deisy | Female | N | 10 | 13 | El Salvador |
| Oscar | Male | N | 16 | 19 | El Salvador |
| Isaac | Male | N | 12 | 16 | El Salvador |

**Table 1.2** (continued)

| Alias | Gender | Unaccompanied? | Age at Migration | Age at Interview | Country of Origin |
|---|---|---|---|---|---|
| Jisel | Female | Y | 15 | 18 | Honduras |
| Juana | Female | N | 14 | 16 | Honduras |
| Francisco | Male | N | 11 | 13 | Honduras |
| Jason | Male | N | 8 | 10 | Honduras |
| Delia | Female | Y | 17 | 17 | El Salvador |
| Rosemary | Female | N | 20 | 20 | El Salvador |
| Dylan | Male | Y | 15 | 18 | Honduras |
| Gloria | Female | Y | 16 | 19 | El Salvador |
| Johny | Male | Y | 13 | 16 | El Salvador |
| Juan Carlos | Male | Y | 17 | 18 | Honduras |
| Ruben | Male | N | 16 | 18 | Honduras |
| Melissa | Female | Y | 13 | 14 | Honduras |
| Carmen | Female | Y | 13 | 15 | El Salvador |
| Avery | Nonbinary | Y | 17 | 19 | El Salvador |
| Miguel | Male | N | 12 | 13 | El Salvador |
| Walter | Male | N | 19 | 21 | El Salvador |
| Angel | Male | Y | 10 | 12 | El Salvador |
| Barbie | Female | Y | 10 | 12 | El Salvador |

*Source:* Authors' compilation.

The study respondents were not chosen from a probability random sample because this is a vulnerable and hard-to-reach population. There is no equivalent of a census, phonebook, or neighborhood to create a randomizing sample strategy from such a population; thus, our recruitment strategy utilized nonprofit organizations, law offices, and snowball sampling. We also found respondents through schools, especially in Montgomery County. Because the recruitment strategy included schools, we lack stories from those who dropped out of school, some to work full-time, and who might have reported different experiences, owing to being embedded in the community in ways other than school. For the same reasons we did not interview many Guatemalans—especially indigenous ones. Thus, although we do discuss the struggles of minors who were not in school, we had access to migrants who had been relatively successful in integrating into their community because they had time to study, spoke Spanish, and were connected to nonprofits, services, and programs.

Another consideration is that the bulk of the interviews were conducted during the first six months of 2017—a period before the Trump administration had enacted many of its immigration policies and practices, before they took effect, and before the general public became aware of them. The 2016 election and the Trump administration's enacted immigration policies and directives have since changed the conversation about Latin immigrants, Central America, and intercultural and community violence in several ways. Even so, these data provide a strong benchmark for how youth fared before 2016.

Finally, as has been widely noted, legal papers are a key determinant of whether an immigrant will integrate well. Only a small proportion (15 percent) of youth respondents were documented, although it is important to note that most unaccompanied minors turn themselves in to immigration authorities at the border and ask for asylum and family reunification based on their status as minors. This study addresses only the experiences of those who were not sent back after turning themselves in to CBP. The study cannot measure long-term integration outcomes, but it contributes to the literature by documenting the hurdles to integration in the few years after arrival.

Some details are particular to the journey of each respondent, but they all had shared the experience of coming, usually unaccompanied, to the United States at significant risk to themselves and sometimes their families. There are indeed common experiences among this group, but each of their stories brings new understanding and nuance to the situations that we see playing out at the nation's southern border, on the news, and in our communities and schools. Many of those who were interviewed for this project had been exposed to trauma from a young age. Most had been separated from their parents, who came to the United States to work. Many had dealt with threats from both gangs and police in their home communities.

Finally, since the Cold War, U.S. foreign policy has played a significant role in Central America. Among the grave consequences of U.S. involvement in that part of the world (described in the next chapter) are the dire living and working conditions that have made so many youths and families willing to risk their lives for the chance of a safer and more stable life in the United States.

CHAPTER TWO

# A BRIEF HISTORY OF EL SALVADOR, HONDURAS, AND GUATEMALA: HISTORICAL CONTEXTS AND DRIVERS OF MIGRATION

In this chapter, we provide a brief history of Central America—including the history of U.S. interventionism in the region—to place the individual lives and experiences presented later in the book in a larger, sociohistorical context.[1] After a very brief discussion of the relevant history of each country and the region, we expand the discussion to cover the history and social contexts of remittances. This topic is strongly related to the history presented in the first part of the chapter owing to the impact of global forces and international relations on the region's economic interconnections with the economy of the Global North, including the impact on migration and family separation. Readers who are well versed in the region's history and current sociopolitical landscapes—including the reasons why unauthorized migration increased during the 1980s, MS-13 developed, and remittances became socially important in the migration landscape—may decide to skip this chapter. In the coming chapters, we discuss respondents' motives for migration, how they felt when leaving, and their experiences and lives in their sending communities.

The migration of Central Americans to the United States did not begin when unaccompanied minors arrived in 2014, nor did it begin when the Trump administration highlighted and misrepresented them. Over the last century, much of Central America has faced political turmoil, instability, and, more recently, the growth of organized crime. These social forces have influenced some people to migrate to the

United States as a last resort for finding safety and work that will ensure they can provide for their families.

Those who think of Central American countries as failed states often lack a key nuance in their analysis: U.S. foreign policy, interventionism, and imperialism have played a pivotal role in the long-term issues plaguing Central American countries that, in turn, have produced emigration. This role is related to the concept of "Manifest Destiny" and the building of the Panama Canal, the support of fruit companies over democratic rule in the region, and the waging of ideology-driven proxy wars in the region during the Cold War. Although small countries that depend on the export of one product and are filled with political turmoil and violence are often derided as "banana republics," in reality these conditions are the outcome of U.S. actions in Central American countries. Corruption and laziness do not underlie laggard economic development but rather the concentration of wealth and extractive exploitation by local elites and foreign companies.[2] U.S. migration policy also played a pivotal role in the development and growth of MS-13, a transnational gang with roots in Los Angeles, racism, and police abuse. These conditions came to a head in El Salvador, Honduras, Nicaragua, and Guatemala in the 1980s and 1990s, when individuals and families started migrating in search of safety and work.[3] When all of these countries moved to the export of coffee and fruits as sources of income, haciendas and large agricultural operations sprang up, leading to the concentration of land in the hands of the local elite and foreign companies such as the United Fruit Company. Roosevelt's "Good Neighbor Policy" in the 1930s encouraged trade and was respectful of the sovereignty of countries in the Americas. Democratic practices began to grow organically from the bottom up, but eventually "too much democracy" led to both workers and the government challenging the dominance of elites and transnational corporations. Subsequently, "United Fruit discovered that it was much more profitable to do business with a dictator than with a democratic president."[4]

Under more repressive regimes, many farmers in these countries were displaced from good lands and onto less productive ones. As it became harder to engage in small-scale commercial agriculture, or even self-subsistence, these citizens had another reason to migrate.[5]

## The Precolonial and Colonial Periods

Many Indigenous groups once lived in what is contemporary El Salvador, Guatemala, and Honduras. This area, particularly Guatemala, northern El Salvador, Honduras, and southern Mexico, was dominated by the cities and chiefdoms of the Mayan civilization at their height between AD 250 and 900. By the time of Spanish arrival, the Mayans were already on a relative decline. They often acted more as city-states than as a unified empire or federation. There were local differences among the Mayan peoples across the area, with local identities and languages that became differentiated over time, although they shared a religion. So, the term "Maya" is itself a pan-ethnicity.[6] Furthermore, another group, the Nahuatl-speaking people, arrived in El Salvador and became established there.

A few Spanish colonists founded San Salvador in today's El Salvador in 1525, in addition to the cities of San Pedro Sula in Honduras in 1536 and Antigua, Guatemala, in 1543.[7] The area was not as densely populated as central Mexico, and besides Honduras, it did not have the gold and silver mines found in Mexico and South America, so it was not a central focus of the Spanish crown. The area was called the Captaincy General of Guatemala and was governed by the Vice-Royalty of New Spain, with headquarters in Mexico City. When Mexico became independent in 1821, the Captaincy became the independent United Provinces of Central America. This entity was part of the short-lived First Mexican Empire (1822–1823). What became present-day Honduras, Guatemala, and El Salvador pulled apart in 1842.

The area had around six million Indigenous inhabitants at the time of European arrival but only six hundred thousand by the time of independence (a tenth of the original population), owing to pandemics, war, and being worked to death or starved through the *encomienda* system of semi-slavery during the colonial period.[8] Even after independence from Spain, Indigenous people in Nicaragua were subjected to slavery. Police chiefs received payments from *hacendados*, especially foreign ones, for capturing Indians by searching their "homes to carry them off, tied up, to the hacienda, where they would have to work for an indefinite period of time."[9]

Soon after Latin America became independent from Spain and the United States of America became independent from England, U.S. president James Monroe warned European powers not to claim any of the new countries and reserved for the United States the prerogative to interfere in the Americas. What is now called the Monroe Doctrine designated the Americas and the Caribbean as spheres of influence for the United States, setting up decades of neocolonial relations and the growth of the U.S. empire.

## El Salvador: Indigo, Coffee, and Fourteen Families

Lacking easily mineable gold and silver, Spanish colonists in El Salvador exported cacao, which was native to Mesoamerica and becoming popular in Europe, as well as cochineal, a red dye, and indigo.[10] *Indigofera suffruticosa*, also known as anil, wild indigo, or Guatemalan indigo, is a plant used to make blue textile dye.[11] During Spanish colonial rule in the late 1500s and early 1600s, driven by high demand for the dye in Europe, indigo, which was also widely cultivated in Guatemala, became El Salvador's largest export. The landed elite established large plantations, exploiting Indigenous people and sometimes enslaved people from Central Africa to cultivate the plants and produce the dye.[12] The work was labor-intensive and dangerous; continuous exposure to the toxins present in the plants, as well as to the swamp waters used to extract the dye from the plants, would both prove fatal over time.[13]

By 1871, indigo demand had waned and coffee became the major export of El Salvador.[14] Landowners continued to expand their plantations and intensified the exploitation of the indigenous people by cutting wages in half and seizing more land from the *campesinos*, the Indigenous peasantry who worked for meager wages. Soon, over 90 percent of the land in the country was owned by only fourteen families, known as *las catorce*. Over time, popular dissent began to brew. In 1932, Farabundo Marti formed the Central American Socialist Party and led popular demonstrations against the government where workers gathered in the thousands. Despite calls by party leaders not to commit violence, some followers killed several government officials. The oligarchical government retaliated on January 22, 1932, by killing over thirty thousand people—around 4 percent of the entire population at the time.[15] Suspected communist sympathizers and supporters were killed by firing squads and large massacres were carried out in rural villages.¹⁶ *La matanza* (the massacre) is regarded as an ethnocide, as most of the thirty thousand people who were massacred were Indigenous.¹⁷

The strained relationship between El Salvador's landed elite and the laborers continued. Over time, many of the country's poor migrated to Honduras to take advantage of free, vacant, and arable land. In the late 1960s, however, the Honduran government passed land reforms and ordered the Salvadorans to leave. In 1969, the border tensions intensified as the Honduran government expelled some Salvadorans forcefully, and the newly repatriated Salvadorans, now landless and unemployed, strained government services. Tensions further erupted during the World Cup qualifying soccer matches between the two countries. The "Football War" between El Salvador and Honduras began on July 14, 1969; only six days later, more than two thousand people from both sides had been killed.¹⁸ The 1970s marked a period of economic and political instability in El Salvador. Land and the coffee trade were controlled by less than 2 percent of the population.¹⁹ The Oil Crisis of 1973 further exacerbated tensions between the oligarchs and the impoverished as prices of goods rose across the nation but wages were kept low. In 1974, President Arturo Armando Molina made several attempts at land reform to appease the growing unrest among the masses, but his government often did not enforce these policies. In addition, political dissent and opposition were met with increasing force by the military and paramilitary "death squads," presumably bankrolled by the oligarchy, that specifically targeted Christian-based communities, which were perceived as posing a threat.²⁰

The Salvadoran civil war officially began on October 15, 1979, and lasted over twelve years, ending in January 1992. It began when the deepening economic disparities among the population and the state-sponsored violence to silence political dissidents led to a coup d'état in October 1979 by younger officers of the country's military. The group quickly deposed President Carlos Humberto Romero and tried to establish control of the country. In November of that year, the military junta established reformist measures, including limitations on land holdings, the nationalization of some industries, and an election in 1982. The poor viewed these reforms favorably, but they angered El Salvador's elite and the ruling class.²¹ The new government failed to curb the violence erupting throughout the state. Conservative military officials carried out violence against left-wing factions of the population, fueling the chaos. At the same time, the past failures of the Salvadoran government to address deepening economic imbalances between the ruling and wealthy classes and the general population led leftist guerrilla units to threaten wealthy businesspeople and government officials.

On the international front, the civil war between the Salvadoran government and the Farabundo Marti National Liberation Front (FMLN) became another arena of the Cold War. The United States sent monetary support, estimated at $1 million to $2 million per day, as well as military direction, support, and training to the Salvadoran government forces in an attempt to curb the supposed influence of the Soviet Union in third-world countries in the Western Hemisphere. In turn, the Soviet Union helped fund and support the FMLN by way of Cuba and Nicaragua.[22] For twelve years, the lives of Salvadorans were marred by violence, much of it at the hands of state agents, including the assassination of Archbishop Oscar Romero and the massacre of six Jesuit priests, as well as by the army, which killed over two hundred civilians in El Mozote, and the FMLN, which kidnapped and assassinated mayors and other elected officials. After over seventy-five thousand Salvadorans were killed and eight thousand went missing, the Chapultepec Peace Agreement was signed by the government of El Salvador and the FMLN on January 16, 1992, in Mexico City.[23]

During the civil war, those who did not die often fled their land and possessions, seeking refuge in other parts of the country as well as in Honduras, Mexico, or the United States. In 1980, the Salvadoran population in the United States was low, at only ninety-five thousand; through chain migration, social networks, and family reunification, that number would increase to nearly 1.17 million by 2015 and to 2.3 million in 2017.[24]

Before the war in El Salvador, many people could make a living through subsistence farming on their land.[25] Their lives were humble, not extravagant, but they and their extended family could do well enough for themselves. Many extended families still lived on larger plots of land (though nowhere near as large as the plantations owned by the fourteen families were) inherited from other family members. On these farms, there might be multiple small houses with basic rooms and kitchens and a main house with more amenities, such as a bath. Landowning was common, but when the war came many had to abandon their land and flee.[26] Areas were completely decimated, and it became hard to work the land. Polarization into opposing factions tore families apart, making it harder to survive based on common land tenure. Some people went to larger cities or surrounding countries, but the labor demand was in the United States. Of those who migrated north, few could apply for political asylum because it would have been seen as the U.S. government taking a stance against the Salvadoran government, which in fact the United States was supporting.[27] If they did apply for asylum and the request was denied, they were deported back to a country in the hands of the right-wing dictatorship that they had tried to escape and that many feared would retaliate against them for having left. So the Salvadoran migrants of the 1980s often had little choice but to come to the United States undocumented and stay below the radar. Later on, Congress created temporary protected status (TPS), a liminal category that temporarily protects from deportation immigrants from countries in distress, but it does not provide a quick path to citizenship.[28]

Research documents that the first Salvadoran immigrants settled in the regions surrounding Los Angeles, Long Island, and Houston.[29] Soon after, Washington, D.C., became a magnet location for Salvadorans.[30] Today D.C.'s largest single national immigrant group is Salvadorans: over twenty thousand Salvadoran immigrants live in the city and two hundred thousand live in the region.[31] Washington, D.C., is home to various sizable immigrant groups from all over the world, including Guatemalan and Honduran migrants.

It is undeniable that some immigrants arrive in the United States with more assets than others. Sarah Mahler and Patrick Scallen explain that many Salvadorans who owned land and were well-off in El Salvador also migrated to the United States.[32] However, many of them experienced not only symbolic but real downward social mobility after they moved into tightly packed living situations in the United States, worked long hours, and experienced negative stereotypes about Latinos and Central Americans.

## Honduras: Interventions, Imperial Dreams, and Suppressing Democracy

By the nineteenth century, the United States had a broad history of invasions, interventions, and intelligence gathering throughout Latin America. There were direct invasions by the U.S. military itself, the power exerted by U.S. companies (backed by the government), and the "private invasions" of U.S. citizens. One such private invader, William Walker, declared himself "President" of the states of Baja California and Sonora in Mexico, was forced back into California, invaded Nicaragua more than once, declared himself "President" of Costa Rica while simultaneously invading the country, was temporarily imprisoned by the U.S. government, and then invaded Honduras on his way to retaking Nicaragua in 1859. There he was tried and executed by a firing squad after being captured by the British.[33]

Honduras's twentieth-century history is similar to that of Guatemala and El Salvador: the U.S. government vehemently protected, with force, the interests of the fruit companies that owned most of the land and perpetuated exploitation and income inequality.[34] There were direct military interventions in 1907 and 1911, and the United States also began to control banking and mining in the country. From this time, the United States began to train and develop Honduras's military, which continued into the Reagan years. As Nicaragua's Sandinista government took power, the U.S. military was again stationed in Honduras, where they trained the Contra paramilitary, a U.S.-financed counterrevolutionary faction.[35] The Reagan years also had a substantial effect on the Honduran economy, including the deregulation of the coffee industry. Following constant decades of U.S. involvement and destabilization, Honduran migration to the United States picked up in the 1990s.

As it did in El Salvador, the U.S. government applied pressure in Honduras to stamp out left-leaning social movements with the National Security Doctrine (NSD).[36] In reaction to leftist revolutions in Nicaragua and El Salvador, the NSD expected the Honduran state to do anything it could (constitutionally or not) to stamp out any chance that a similar uprising would occur there. The resulting kidnappings, torture, disappearances, and death squads sent to murder leftist militants created a generalized state of fear and instability, and students, union leaders, workers, and activists started leaving the country in fear for their lives. Then, after Hurricane Mitch hit the country in 1998, the U.S. government granted TPS to many Hondurans in response. Between 2000 and 2017, the Honduran immigrant population in the United States went from around 180,000 to 579,000.[37] Finally, a military coup ousted a progressive and reformist democratically elected president in 2009.[38]

Constitutional rights were suspended, the media was censored, and military force was used to stop protests. Gerardo Rivera and his colleagues state that the suspension of rights and the use of military force show that the Honduran government was built through a violent process and that government officials do not fear using violence to stay in power.[39] As a result, Honduras has been left in a state of violence and instability. Like many Salvadorans, for Hondurans, at some point emigration no longer feels like a choice to leave but a necessity for survival.[40]

We do not write about the experiences of Nicaraguan immigrants in this book, but would briefly note here that neighboring Nicaragua provides another clear example of the extent of U.S. interventionism in the region. U.S.-backed forces ousted the liberal government of Nicaragua in 1909, and U.S. Marines occupied the country for the next twenty-four years. With active U.S. support, the dictator Anastasio Somoza García and his family remained in control of Nicaragua from 1933 until the Sandinista National Liberation Front came to power in 1979. The Soviet Union was not active in the region during this era of Cold War paranoia, but the Contras, backed by the United States, started attacking government agents. In the 1990s, the conservatives returned to power with Violeta Barrios de Chamorro.[41]

## Guatemala: United Fruit Yes, Democracy No!

In late 1944, Juan José Arévalo became Guatemala's first democratically elected president. Earlier that year, popular uprisings had toppled a military dictatorship.[42] Arévalo would institute democratizing reforms, enact a minimum wage, and grant near-universal suffrage. After taking office in 1951, Jacobo Arbenz Guzmán instituted land reforms and gave uncultivated land from large estates to the laborers so that they could have their own farms. These actions taken by Arbenz Guzmán and Arévalo reduced the profits of the United Fruit Company and were seen as akin to communism by the United States.[43] The secretary of state at the time, John Foster Dulles, had close ties to the United Fruit Company, and several members of Congress were extremely vocal about what they saw as the Guatemalan government's mistreatment of the company. Of course, the company did not do much for Guatemalans, and the newly elected leaders were making fundamental changes. In 1954, the CIA, directed by John Foster Dulles's brother, Allen Dulles, overthrew Arbenz Guzmán and installed a military dictatorship, ending the ten years of democratic rule in Guatemala known as the time of the Guatemalan Revolution.[44] Soon after the CIA's "Operation PBSuccess" toppled democratic rule, a civil war broke out that lasted from 1960 until 1996.[45]

During this thirty-six-year period of armed conflict, two hundred thousand Guatemalans were killed or disappeared. The civil war internally displaced over one million people, and two hundred thousand fled the country, of whom forty-six thousand lived in refugee camps in southern Mexico, according to the United Nations High Commissioner for Refugees (UNHCR).[46]

Even with the civil war officially ended, Cecilia Menjívar shows, structural violence still manifests in Guatemala and affects low-income women, even Ladinas (mixed Indigenous and Spanish heritage) in areas of Guatemala that saw less physical violence during the civil war but nevertheless suffered a "slow death" because of it.[47] In the 2000s, despite the formal end of civil war and democratization in the region, there are regions of Guatemala with some of the highest homicide rates in the world because everyday violence continues, fueled by nonpolitical gangs, cartels, and paramilitaries.[48]

## Transnational Connections between the United States and Central America

When Central Americans in Los Angeles experienced racism and exclusion and became the targets of violence in the 1980s, gangs emerged to provide self-defense for their communities. U.S. policing, along with U.S. drug and immigration policies, led to the export of drug- and gang-related social problems to Central America, which then produced more emigration.[49] As anthropologist Susan Terrio writes, summarizing many expert testimonies at the hearings of asylum court cases,

> Punitive U.S. immigration laws, harsh gang abatement policies, and the war on drugs have a corrosive effect on life in Central America and Mexico. Thousands of Mara Salvatrucha and 18th Street gang members in Los Angeles who are deported back to the "home country" reconstitute themselves in El Salvador and spread their operations

to Guatemala and Honduras. The exportation of U.S. zero-tolerance policing strategies to Central American alongside the deportations of gang youth fuels more undocumented immigration, this time as a result of the combined pressures from gang, cartel, and state violence. The insatiable demand for drugs in the U.S. market has spawned new criminal cartels, creating murderous competition over smuggling routes and distribution networks. Young people see firsthand the intensification of lawlessness, the political corruption, the extrajudicial killings, and the armed gangs and drug cartels that infect all spheres of social life. Migration is a calculated wager against the certainty of a social or a physical death if they remain at home. As an expendable, surplus workforce in their home communities, young people understand that selling their labor abroad is the only option.[50]

Central American economies have grown at modest rates, but not enough to create opportunities for many low-income rural and urban young people. For them, migration is not only a dream but also a reality, in that many already have family members and friends living abroad. Social networks and established path dependencies and migration corridors make future migrations easier than early ones, as Massey and his colleagues observe in their "cumulative causation of migration" theory.[51] The war on drugs and organized crime's overt control of certain areas of these countries further fuel immigration, as Terrio writes.[52] Structural family separation and family-propelled migration to reunify move this circuit even more toward closure.

## Outcomes of the Cold War

Central Americans have been victims of paranoiac, dangerous, counterproductive, and misguided U.S. policies designed to fight the supposed spread of communism and the influence of the Soviet Union in the Americas. As Marcelo Suárez-Orozco writes:

> The United States–Soviet Cold War and the proxy wars it engendered in Africa, the Americas, and Asia created massive displacements. . . . At the height of the Cold War, the best predictor of who would arrive as a refugee in the West was someone escaping a Communist regime: from 1975 until 1995 more than two million Southeast Asians fleeing Vietnam, Laos, and Cambodia were settled in the West. . . . Likewise,

more than a million Cubans fleeing the Castro regime in various waves were favored refugees in the United States. Least favored were the casualties of the proxy wars in Central America. Escaping barbaric but, alas, anticommunist regimes in Guatemala, Nicaragua, and El Salvador, millions of folks arrived in North America in search of refuge. Few became formal refugees.[53]

U.S. interventionism under the Monroe Doctrine, and then during the Cold War, created many casualties and much displacement in Central America. Suárez-Orozco continues:

> The sources of the forced movements of people in Central America have disparate and complex histories, finding their distal origins in the Cold War, inequality, and uncontrolled criminality. The Cold War drastically destabilized Latin America and the Caribbean, setting the stage for multiple cycles of mass forced migrations. Armed with the "doctrine of national security," state terrorism was installed throughout the region. From 1976 to 1996, the Cold War in Central America would leave more than 250,000 dead, more than one million internally displaced, and more than two million seeking shelter, the vast majority in the United States.[54]

Beyond the direct legacies of the Cold War, structural issues, such as categorical inequality and impunity around violent acts by organized crime, further compel some to emigrate. Suárez-Orozco explains:

> Honduras and Guatemala are also the countries with the highest levels of inequality in North, Central, and South America. In Honduras the Gini coefficient ratio was 55.7, making it the tenth most unequal country in the world. Honduras has a chilling rate of violence of 90.4 murder deaths per 100,000 inhabitants—the highest per capita in the world. By 2013, more than one thousand children and youth under the age of twenty-three had been murdered in that country.... The vast majority of Honduran children detained at the U.S. southern border originate in San Pedro Sula, first in the ranking of the fifty most violent cities in the world, with a rate of 159 murders per 100,000 inhabitants ("San Pedro Sula" 2014).[55]

Therefore, emigration from these areas should not be surprising, and the U.S. government should recognize its responsibility in creating many of the dynamics that have long caused the displacement of Central Americans.

Likewise, Abrego's seminal work on Salvadoran transnational families is grounded in an analysis of the political and economic drivers (the 1979 Salvadoran civil war and later neoliberal policies) that led to the migration of parents to the United States. She shows that structural forces determined both economic and emotional outcomes for these families and analyzes how U.S. immigration policies exacerbated threats to the economic and emotional well-being of children and their parents.

An analysis of youth migration from Central America imparts important lessons about migration and immigrant integration and sheds light on the effect of U.S. social and education policies and social services administration. To begin, Central American migration itself is not new. Many of the parents and grandparents of recent migrant minors came to the United States in the 1980s. Prior to the 1980s, unaccompanied minors from El Salvador and Guatemala were uncommon.[56] When they did arrive and were arrested by the Immigration and Naturalization Service (INS), they were usually released on bail to a responsible adult, often their attorney. However, when the number of children arriving grew in 1984 because of the civil war in El Salvador, the INS established a policy that no minors could be released to anyone but their parent or legal guardian.[57] This posed an issue for many Salvadorans and Guatemalans, who were being discouraged from asking for asylum by the Reagan administration, given the U.S. Cold War stance on the conflict in El Salvador and its support for the military regime in Guatemala.[58] Therefore, without papers, they were forced to go under the radar as they fled the violence and sought work and safety in the United States. As a consequence, many parents were unable to pick up their children from INS custody out of fear of the legal ramifications and of being deported back to the civil war they had fled in fear for their and their children's safety and well-being. In other cases, the parents were still in Central America and thus unable to collect their children, who were then held indefinitely in INS custody.

One such minor held indefinitely was named Alma Yanira Cruz-Aldama. She was twelve years old and had to leave El Salvador after her grandfather and uncle were killed, presumably leaving her with little family in El Salvador to take care of her. When she came to the United States, she was arrested and held. She and two others, Ana Maria Perez

Portillo and Jenny Lisette Flores, were held indefinitely in an INS facility in Pasadena, California, where conditions were inappropriate. They filed a class-action suit against the government, *Flores vs. Reno*, which detailed the conditions of their detention. They were given no educational instruction or materials and no medical examination, they received no outdoor recreation time, and they were not allowed familial visitation. The children were held alongside unrelated adults in the INS facility and were subject to strip and body cavity searches by the INS. The INS made no effort to identify other suitable adult relatives or family friends to whom to release these children. Instead, they held them indefinitely in hopes of interrogating their parents about their immigration status.

The class-action suit of the three Central American girls was later decided in what is known as the Flores Settlement Agreement, and it settled three major topics of contention. First, the government would release children without delay to their parents, legal guardians, adult relatives, or other individuals designated by their parents, guardians, or government officials as sponsors. Second, addressing the improper conditions in which Cruz, Portillo, and Flores were being held alongside adults, the government would place children in the "least restrictive" settings. Third, stronger standards for the treatment of immigrant children in detention by the government would be implemented.

The lawsuit, initially filed in 1985, did not reach a settlement agreement until 1997.[59] Since then, each presidential administration has added to the protections afforded to youth migrants until the Trump administration came into office in 2017 and disregarded many of these protections.[60]

## Gang Violence and Immigration Policy

An ever-present topic of discussion surrounding Central America is that of gang violence, which was a cogent factor in respondents' decisions to migrate (as discussed at length in the next chapter). With any instance of widespread societal violence, it is important to question the sociopolitical context in which that violence developed: What started the violence? What enables it to continue? What could stop it?

The transnational gang MS-13, or Mara Salvatrucha, is possibly the best-known organized crime group active in the region. However,

MS-13 did not develop in Central America. As previously mentioned, the Reagan administration's support for the right-wing government in the 1980s Salvadoran civil war had rendered Salvadorans largely ineligible for asylum, so many of them had to come without papers. Undocumented immigrants usually find only jobs with low pay and poor protections, and many Salvadorans relegated to these jobs were ending up in poor neighborhoods that already had a lot of gang activity. With many gangs targeting the recently arrived Central Americans as easy prey, some eventually turned to self-defense, forming MS-13.

In the 1990s, the Clinton administration ordered mass deportations of foreign-born people convicted of a wide range of crimes; as a result, an estimated twenty thousand people were deported to El Salvador, Honduras, and Guatemala. The United States gave little warning to these countries, which were not prepared for such an exodus. Many of the deported had spent very few years in the country they were sent to, and others had not been there for more than ten or fifteen years. As they struggled to find regular employment and to integrate back into the society, these people found that joining a gang or continuing their membership in a gang was one way to have a social support system. At a point when El Salvador was still recovering from the end of the civil war, the gangs capitalized on the instability to gain members and influence. In this way, harsh and hastily administered U.S. immigration policy preceded and fueled the virulent growth of MS-13 in Central America. As mentioned in the introduction, anti-immigrant rhetoric about Central Americans highlights MS-13, positing that people from Central America are criminals, yet this is a gross misrepresentation of the facts. Many of those attempting to migrate to the United States are fleeing situations caused by gang activity.[61]

## Understanding Family Separation, Reunification, and Remittances in a Sociohistorical Context

For political, economic, and social reasons, Central Americans, like previous immigrant groups, have established themselves in many cities in the United States as time passes and their social networks expand.[62] When all other options have been exhausted and the situation remains dire, people will take the long, expensive, and dangerous journey north. Many need to provide for their children, but to do so, they must leave the children at home, causing family separation. In a few years or more, they may send for their children, or the children themselves may make the decision to leave in an effort to "self-reunite."

The ABC Settlement Agreement of 1991 was a response to the legal case *American Baptist Churches v. Thornburgh* that gave Central American adults stays from deportation, prevented many detainments, and allowed certain applicants to have their asylum cases reevaluated if they had arrived before 1990.[63] Similarly, the Nicaraguan Adjustment and Central American Relief Act (NACARA) allowed some Salvadorans, Guatemalans, and Nicaraguans who had fled in the 1980s to file for asylum.[64] Since the 1980s, and with the beginning of detentions of minors, most of those detained have been from El Salvador, Guatemala, and Honduras. For example, over 58 percent of the unaccompanied minors who came to the border in 2018 were Guatemalans.[65]

U.S.-backed dictatorships and interventionism paved the way not only for the poverty, corruption, low state capacity, and gang violence seen in El Salvador, Guatemala, and Honduras but also the migration to the United States from each of these three countries as individuals fled violence and sought economic opportunity. Interestingly, besides highly educated professionals, the most recent immigration from Mexico mirrors that from Central America in that families are trying to escape from the organized crime and impunity fueled by the U.S.-sponsored war on drugs.

After exploring the sociohistorical processes of family separation and remittances in the remainder of this chapter, we discuss in the next chapter the personal events and individual decisions that make some emigrate, but to reiterate here: these decisions are impacted by the long history of global exploitation and underdevelopment that have made it so difficult for many people to make a living.

As discussed in the introduction and chapter 1, the forces that cumulatively cause migration are largely the same throughout the world in recent history: people migrate to find employment and resources, to flee violence, and to be with family or reunite with other important social networks. Two historical examples are migration from Algeria to France and migration from Mexico to the United States. Pressure to provide for one's family and the lack of alternatives to increase household income created a social context in which emigration to France has been periodically encouraged by a local culture of migration among the Kabyle people of Algeria.[66] Similarly, chain migration from the Mixtec Mountains of Guerrero, Puebla, and Oaxaca, Mexico, to the United States has made the migration of a few family members with the explicit purpose of increasing family income with remittances a common household strategy for social mobility.

"Remittances" refers to the money and resources that migrants send to their place of origin. An important by-product and cause of migration, remittances are more than money and material resources—remittances represent the sweat and tears of migrants who work long hours far from home to provide for their families, friends, and communities.[67] The system of global capitalism that creates and upholds the need for remittances goes hand in hand with the systems that create structural family separation and the contexts in which most family separations occur.

Remittances reinforce existing social ties and commitments between family members—not only between parents and children but between extended family members as well—and they maintain trust networks and emotional bonds across distances.[68] Remittances are "a product of love" and carry an emotional load, but they cannot produce emotional closeness between family members living far away from each other.[69]

Remittances are incredibly relevant within the region: as of 2019, annual remittances surpassed 20 percent of GDP in El Salvador and Honduras and nearly 15 percent in Guatemala.[70] Remittances can be essential lifelines during times of violence, turmoil, and social upheaval—as we saw during the COVID-19 pandemic—as well as in more peaceful times. Nonetheless, they also create economic inequalities between households that receive remittances and those that do not, to the point of exerting social and moral pressure on family members in nontransnational households to emigrate.[71] As Jason DeParle entitled his account of the Filipino migrant families he followed for decades, "A Good Provider Is One Who Leaves."[72] The social pressure to emigrate on people living in traditional emigrant-sending communities is enormous. For many, not migrating is seen as a parental failure to provide economically for one's children. Parents contemplating migration overlook the important psychological impact of their departure on the children left behind. For example, as Carola Suárez-Orozco and her colleagues show, the incidence of depressive symptoms increases in children enduring family separation.[73] There is tension between remitting parents' need to see themselves as providing economic resources for their family and the value that children put on living with their parents. Left-behind children can tend to dismiss the economic support, emotional pain, and sacrifices made by migrant parents for their benefit because another essential part of a parent's role is to provide emotional comfort. Clearly, however, the calculation changes when there is dispossession and violence.

Although the emotional costs to migrants and their children receive less attention than horse-race issues such as aggregate remittance flows to specific countries, the reality is that *a large inflow of remittances between countries implies many family separations*. Some analysts and some migrants themselves make a cost-benefit analysis between family unity and family economic improvement, but conclude a priori that income is more important. The existing evidence forces us to take a skeptical view of this conclusion and to argue that the choice should not have to be made.

Many research papers, policy reports, and newspaper articles make unrealistic predictions about the development potential of remittances at the macro level and downplay the social and economic costs of prolonged family separation and its psychological impact on the children who do not migrate with their parents.[74] It is important to consider the children's experiences and the long-term impact of early separation from their primary caregiver. While remittance aggregate figures may be impressive, they do not tell the full stories of those who send and receive them. Remittance-led migration can create traumatic separations between husbands and wives, and between children and parents. It can create economically united transnational households but socially separated and psychologically fragmented families. In transnational households, both departing parents and those left behind suffer. None of them are at fault—indeed, the money is necessary and often lifesaving. Instead, the blame lies with unequal economic systems that exploit the many to the benefit of the few and with immigration laws that treat immigrants not as family members but as vehicles of labor. Remittances are proof of an immigrant's sacrifices and serious commitment to the loved ones left behind, but they cannot fix global inequalities in wealth. Remittances at a macro level are a short-term solution to global social problems that separate families across oceans, border fences, and economic statuses. From the point of view of a child, parental separation is mainly experienced as parental abandonment, even if temporary and intended to provide financially.

Many studies have described the lives of the children left behind when their primary caregivers migrate for work.[75] With the tightening of border controls, these sojourns tend to last longer than expected, and children go years without seeing their parents. In her study of Mixtecs from Oaxaca settling in central New Jersey, Joanna Dreby looked closely at parenting and transnational families. She reports an average of 3.4 years of mother-child separation among her respondents and an average length of father-child separation of 9.2 years.[76] Rhacel Salazar Parreñas (2005) calculated that her respondents, migrant mothers from the Philippines who had permission from both the Philippines and foreign countries to work abroad, spent on average 23.9 weeks with their children during visits across 11.42 years, while migrant fathers spent 74 weeks with their children during an average period of 13.79 years.[77] Ironically, many mothers migrate to work as caretakers in wealthier areas where mothers work professional jobs. So, they take care of working mothers' children while somebody else takes care of their own children.[78]

Transnational household economies raise the issue of the division of labor across borders. In remittance economies, labor and social reproduction are divided geographically. Child-rearing and retirement occur in developing countries, while the productive working cycle is spent in developed countries.[79] What are the repercussions of separating the spheres of labor use and labor reproduction? The host nation reaps the benefits of a migrant workforce raised abroad, and the sending country takes in the remittances and cares for children and the elderly. This international division of labor could be analyzed with a Marxist lens as an extreme split between labor maintenance and labor reproduction.[80] Partial family migration externalizes the cost of labor reproduction to the communities of origin.[81] The subsequent distortion of demographics, with towns left predominantly populated by children and the elderly, increases the vulnerability of both groups. Behind remittances and the departures that enable them are separated families, empty community spaces, and diminished everyday lives for those left behind. Transnational families are also affected by changes in household economies and gender roles in the Global North.

With the rise of neoliberalism in the 1970s, real wages for traditionally male breadwinners decreased drastically, even in wealthy countries like the United States. In response, many married women who had not been working entered the labor force. The question arose of who would take care of the domestic labor that stay-at-home wives used to do. The labor of internal and international migrants provided a partial answer to this dilemma. Nonetheless, the wages that working-class and even middle-class dual-earner households could pay were relatively limited since they did not have much disposable income.[82] Michael Burawoy argues that countries in the Global North often prefer that so-called low-skilled workers immigrate alone because the meager wages they are paid would not allow them to sustain a family there. For home cleaners and care workers, who may be single mothers, the typical pay puts the possibility of sustaining a family even further out of reach.[83]

## Reproduction of Migration Patterns across Generations

Tensions in migrant families are common. Intergenerational conflicts often result when parents, feeling that they have made many sacrifices for their children, let them know that they have high expectations for them.[84] Years of separation due to staggered migration contribute to this tension. The idea that remittances could make the migration of the next generation unnecessary is sometimes unrealistic. The migration of a family member changes family dynamics and may exact a high emotional toll on both parents and children. Yet once migration and remittances create a transnational household economy, it is hard to stop sending and receiving remittances. When the pioneer family migrant must return because of deportation, sickness, or retirement, a new family member often must take their place. Sarah Mahler explains:

> Increasingly visible are older returning migrants, generally men in their forties to sixties who fled El Salvador during the war, leaving behind their spouses and young children. With limited education and skills for advancing economically on Long Island, many of these men desired to return home—indeed their families begged them to return—but the families had also grown too dependent upon remittance income to forsake migration altogether. So, before returning, migrants first sponsor the migration of at least one child, grooming

him or her in the basics of migrant life—housing and job. The children ensure that remittances will continue to flow homeward, cash that even highly self-sufficient farmers need to purchase fertilizers and pay for clothing, medical care, and so on.[85]

Once the household economy becomes transnational, it is hard to go back in time despite all the emotional costs, risks, and drawbacks of the new status quo. Moreover, migrant-sending towns, contending with the long-term absences of working-age people, need to attract internal migrants to build houses and work the land. Meanwhile, employers in industrialized nations paying foreign-born workers under the table quickly get used to using labor from abroad for which they do not need to provide a social safety net, education, paid vacation, sick leave, workman's compensation, or any other benefits.

## Economic Development?

While some researchers look at the emotional consequences of family separation without considering their implications for immigrant integration into the receiving society or the economic development of the place of origin, other researchers concentrate on the economic aspects and disregard the economic consequences of the subjective perspective and the meaning-making aspects of the migration experience. Viviana Zelizer is one of the few scholars who has successfully analyzed the interplay between the emotional experience of migration and socioeconomic factors.[86] Emotions affect economic decisions, and economic decisions affect emotional states. In the case of transnational household economies, not only are emotions embedded in remittances, but there is a dialectical relationship between the economic logic of migrating to provide for the family and the emotional logic of doing so as a moral duty and an act of love. Ironically, this relationship overlooks the economic and emotional costs of the decision to migrate. Thus, we argue that the suffering of the children left behind is an intrinsic part of the logic of remittance economies. Given the low wages paid to many migrants, covering their children's expenses in the host country would be close to financially impossible. To put it dramatically, an immigrant sending remittances cannot avoid the psychological trauma caused by migration and family separation.[87]

Our current migration and economic systems leave children vulnerable, parentless, and lacking physical, psychological, and emotional protection in order to provide possibly greater financial protection through remittances. Some commentators believe that money can compensate for the hardships imposed by family separation.[88] Although a household's economic resources may increase with remittances, the debate on development has rarely concentrated on the family's overall well-being, *especially concerning the social and psychological needs of those left behind.*

Transnational families suspend many facets of their social life as they wait for reunification on one side of the border or the other. They face a spatial and temporal split that creates uncertain and novel relations between family members in the home country and family members abroad. Members of these families put their hopes abroad but stay attached to local institutions and identities. They continue to make emotional investments that are as powerful and influential as economic investments and that migrants take into consideration when making decisions. Social mobility for members of the family of origin often comes at the expense of marginality and exploitation in the place of work.

### Migration by Unaccompanied Minors

As Sonia Nazario recounts, friends of a Guatemalan child told him, "You have it all. Good clothes. Good tennis shoes." The child answered, "I'd trade it all for my mother.... You can never get the love of a mother from someone else."[89] This sentiment was constantly repeated by the interviewees we spoke to, whose main motive for migrating as a minor had been to reunite with their parents. The 2020 movie *Half Brothers* similarly depicts some of the dramas caused by family separation due to migration—father absence, racism, closed borders, and the formation of new families. So, for this Guatemalan child, family unity was more important, even if it would have meant greater poverty for the family.

Like Nazario, Cecilia Menjívar also shows how challenging the experiences of Central American children can be when they try to get to the United States: they must first cross Mexico, without papers and with few resources, and they face many risks in doing so (see chapter 4).[90] Nazario tells the story of a Honduran boy, Enrique, who risked his life by riding on top of freight trains from Honduras to the United States, facing perils such as gangs, criminals, police abuse, immigration agents, and hunger as he crossed Guatemala and Mexico. As the Mexican movie *Al otro lado* (2005) and the Mexican-American movie *La misma luna* (2007, *Under the same moon*) illustrate, sometimes children's longing for their parents is so strong that they will risk their lives in order to try to reunite with their parents abroad, even if it means running away and traveling alone along unknown routes.

## Indigeneity and Migration Today

Many Central American immigrants speak Spanish, but for many others an Indigenous language is their mother tongue. El Salvador still has Nahuatl speakers, the *pipiles*, and historically most of southern Mexico and Central America were Mayan areas. Contemporary Mayans identify with their local group and may speak local languages. For an excellent discussion of K'iche' Mayan people living in Providence, Rhode Island, and the implications of political violence in the diaspora, see the work of Patricia Foxen.[91]

Not being a native Spanish speaker is a particularly common experience for those born in Guatemala. Indigenous Guatemalan migrants are doubly excluded and stigmatized in the United States, as they were in their home country. Juan Gabriel, a seventeen-year-old, told anthropologist Lauren Heidbrink:

> The Guatemalan government treats us like we don't belong—even on the land of our ancestors—and blocks us at every turn. Bad schools, no work, no medical care. They treat us like *inidios sucios* while they rob gold from our lands. Believe me, I never wanted to migrate. I'd heard the stories from my cousin—about the dangers of the journey, living in a cramped apartment, working twenty hours a day and never saving—but I had no choice. My mother and sister got sick; the mine contaminated our water and spoiled the crops. They call it *desarrollo*, but it is not developing our communities; it is devastating them. They are killing us slowly.[92]

Indeed, the Guatemalan government has been engaged in genocide for centuries. Juan Gabriel migrated with his twenty-eight-year-old cousin. Traveling with an extended family member is common, and thus the term "unaccompanied" is partly a misnomer. As Heibrink writes, "Many children classified as unaccompanied minors may not be unaccompanied at all. Of the children whom I have encountered, the vast majority were *accompanied*"—by extended family or close family friends. Others were *entrusted* to brokers, facilitators, community members, or known coyotes. "Unaccompanied children are rarely 'on their own,' 'unattached,' or 'abandoned' by 'bad parents.' They are children, siblings, cousins, partners, friends, and community members."[93]

It takes a lot of financial resources, family ties, and know-how to migrate successfully to the United States without a visa. Most youth in similar conditions never make the journey or are deported. Indigenous Guatemalan youth are the most likely young Central Americans to migrate, and the most likely to be deported after they arrive. Heidbrink studied deported youth and described conditions that made them migrate that are comparable to what we describe in chapter 3. Although some made it to the United States, some never did despite multiple attempts.

Similarly, anthropologist Amelia Frank-Vitale documents the lives of youth who were never allowed to settle in the United States and were deported back to Honduras. She describes the violence that threatens them there, as well as the political instability and lack of economic opportunities for peasants and the working class. Frank Vitale shows how commonplace undocumented migration and deportation have become in some marginalized neighborhoods and towns in Honduras. The takeaway from the important counterfactual evidence presented by Frank-Vitale and Heidbrink is that the people who make it to the United States and manage to stay are lucky in having defeated the odds, but not extraordinary in their suffering, need, and humanity.[94]

CHAPTER THREE

# REASONS TO EMIGRATE

> I came because my dad lives here. I only wanted to see my dad.
> —DANIELA, eighteen, El Salvador

> Life is better here. I have many more opportunities than in El Salvador, and it's much better without the Maras.
> —ALBERTO, sixteen

Immigration is most often not an individual decision but a family calculation and shared decision. Age profiles, local parenting expectations, gender dynamics, and established social networks largely determine who migrates, when they go, and how they migrate.[1]

Three common experiences uncovered by our data illustrate the more prominent reasons that led Central American minors and their families to migrate: gang violence, lack of educational and economic opportunity, and a longing for family reunification. These three experiences were interconnected: gang violence, recruitment, and harassment often compromised educational opportunities, with negative impacts on economic opportunities, and the lack of economic opportunities motivated young people's parents to leave their home countries in search of ways to provide for their children. Sara, who was eighteen when she was interviewed, described several reasons why she came to the United States from Guatemala:

> One reason is that I hadn't seen my father in fifteen, fourteen years. He left when I was two years old. Another is because, when you're a kid, you have a lot of goals, so I wanted to come to learn English, work,

fix my house in Guatemala, and do everything I need to do in order to go back, you know? And if not, then I want to bring my mom here.

Although she wanted to go back, Sara acknowledged that she did not know if it would be entirely possible; in that event, she wanted to provide for her mother and eventually bring her to the United States. She felt that leaving would ensure her future well-being and did not see remaining in Guatemala as a feasible option. She saw her departure as motivated by a desire to see her father combined with a wish to improve her future.

The main motives to leave vary between families. A family's economic starting point can greatly affect the urgency they feel about the need to migrate: if they are in less active danger and have more resources, they have time to better plan the trip. Some families in our study who were documented had been planning reunification for a long time, filing paperwork with the aim of legally migrating through family reunification as allowed by U.S. immigration policy. Others were in much more dire situations. For instance, gang conflicts had made some unable to attend school because of threats to their physical safety. In these circumstances, youth and their parents felt that they needed to leave as soon as possible.

## Premigration Family Dynamics

The premigration home lives of those surveyed ranged widely, depending on their family's economic situation and whether they lived in an urban or rural area. Some said that they had enough to eat and that the remittances sent by their parents were enough to survive on; some even said they had been thriving. Others did not have enough to eat, shared rooms in cramped quarters, lived with extended family, and sometimes were being raised by people outside of their nuclear family. Their premigration daily household interactions also had a great impact on their adjustment to a new household in the United States and its emotional toll.

Young Central American migrants in our study had a range of experiences with parental separation. Many came from transnational families in which parents and children were already separated, or continued to be separated to some extent. Long-term family separation had notable effects on youth in school, on their behavior, and ultimately on their emotional well-being.[2] Family separation ultimately and fundamentally changes the nature of parenting: "Since the mother, father, or both are not physically present in the everyday lives of their children, they have to show affection, receive reports, and provide instructions and advice via the telephone, letters, and the Internet and through caregivers."[3] When it is an economic necessity for parents to migrate to ensure their children's health, education, and well-being, families should be allowed to be together, especially when the physical safety of youth and families is threatened in their community of origin. Not only is the experience of family separation potentially traumatic for parents and their children because ultimately they hardly know each other, but youth who reunite with their parents also suffer the trauma of leaving behind caregivers whom they have grown to see as their "real" parents.

The lives of those in separated families are in many ways lives of uncertainty. Parents and children not knowing when they will see each other again is an experience that can be a barrier to integration when families are reunited.[4] For years separated families have not been worrying about integration but about successfully using remittances to support two households.[5] Family separation affects the behavior of children and youths in their schools, within their families, and in their lives overall in their home country. Parents living in the United States, seeing no path to legal reunification, concentrate all their resources on earning and sending remittances to their families abroad to ensure that their children have proper food and schooling. However, their focus on working long hours and sending home as much money as possible may leave these parents with relatively few connections, meager savings, and little sense of belonging in their community, with possibly negative effects on their children when they do join them abroad. This structural and cultural isolation can prevent families from engaging with their communities in meaningful ways to become more integrated in them and develop extensive social networks. For example, their children may be less likely to engage in recreational sports leagues than U.S.-born White children.

Another experience of family separation is living apart from siblings. Juan, who was eighteen when he migrated, told us: "My brothers lived with me, but they had to travel to Ecuador because of the violence in El Salvador, so we stayed by ourselves." In El Salvador, Juan's family had a plot of land, where many of them lived. Even though his brothers and his mother were gone, other family members lived there, including his elderly aunt and cousins.

> So all of my cousins live there. We went into the main house, for example, for personal needs, such as to bathe, change clothes, and all of that, but the majority of the time we were at my aunt's house because she lives alone, and when my grandma couldn't take care of us, my aunt would bathe us when we were little, my brothers would iron our clothes, things like that. So she's like our other grandma.

Juan's mother had already gone to the United States and was able to help him move there too. "My mom alone had to pay for our school, food, and bills here. On top of that, she had to send money for my brothers in Ecuador, and my mom's budget here [in the United States] was very tight." For Juan and his family, schooling was a priority: "Even though there were times when the money didn't last us, for example, to pay bills, because we had to pay our school fees. Then there would be times we did have enough food, God bless, but there were other things we could not have." Migrating to the United States, however, had interrupted the schooling that he and his family were working so hard for: "I finished high school, and I only had two or three months left to become a technician, but the documents to come to [the United States] arrived specifying a time when you can enter . . . so I never finished the technical program."

Jorge, a sixteen-year-old from Honduras, explained that he was only able to complete fourth grade before he had to stop attending school because of threats from local gangs. His brothers also left school. Jorge had a lung condition and epilepsy; his mom had told him that he was not supposed to live past six years old. But because he did, he tried hard in school, though the schools were not well suited to deal with his health issues. In spite of his efforts, he had trouble: "More than anyone, I wanted to pay attention in school, but I couldn't, nothing stuck at all." Two years later, Jorge immigrated to the United States, "and now, still not much sticks, but I try really hard still."

Thirteen-year-old Beatriz left for the United States on what would have been her first day of seventh grade: "The day I was supposed to start seventh grade was the day that I left to come here. I finished sixth grade, but when I came here, they made me repeat sixth grade."

Beatriz's mother lived in the United States, so her grandmother, she felt, was raising her alone up until she and her mother were reunited: "My grandma raised me until I was eleven years old. My mom was consistently sending money to my grandma. She was my *mama de dinero* [money mom], but my grandma *me dio la crianza* [was the one who raised me]."

Beatriz's experience was a common one, and it exemplified the challenges faced by many immigrant minors in school and in their home lives. Diana, a thirteen-year-old from El Salvador, explained why she wanted to leave that country: "I came from El Salvador because I wanted to study more. I want to be a doctor. The school was not very good where I was." Her father helped the family, but because of where they lived, she had to travel far to find better educational options or indeed anything more than necessities: "My dad would help us a lot. . . . Where I lived, there were not many stores . . . there wasn't much to buy. I had to go very far in order to buy food like meat and things like that."

Having enough money to survive was related to their experiences in school. Diana did not always have enough to get by in school: "I would sometimes bring money to school, but sometimes I didn't. There was a store in my school, and sometimes I wanted to buy something, but I couldn't because I didn't always have money." Luis, who migrated at age seventeen, described his home life in El Salvador when he was little:

> One time my mom didn't have any money, and I came home from playing, and I told my mom, "I'm hungry," and she told me, "No, I don't have money," and I told my mom, "I don't like this." But because she's a mom, she knows what to do. So that we wouldn't be hungry, I think that she went to borrow money, and she went to buy groceries. But that time, I felt so bad because she told me, "No, son, I don't have money."

Things got better, however, once Luis's dad was able to send him money:

> Yeah, and she liked that I would go out and play. And when I would go out, she would tell me, "I don't have money to give you," and I would tell her, "Okay, Mom." And when I got older, my dad started to send money to me, and I would tell her, "Mom, don't worry," and I would give her money.

Remittances help families' situation, but they do not fully ease the stresses of family separation and of daily household interactions.

## The Reproduction of Parental Migration

Many U.S. citizens conflate Central America and Mexico in discussions surrounding immigration, in that all adults from both regions are assumed to migrate for work. But they are seen as dissimilar when it comes to the new visibility of immigrant Central American children and the discussion of family separation. What many fail to realize, because it is rarely included in the public discourse, is that child migration and family separation also happened in Mexican families.[6]

The choice to migrate is not an easy one. Sometimes it is planned years in advance, but in other instances it is a last-minute decision. When parents must decide to leave to provide for their children, the children often stay back. But as the children get older, those left in charge of them may die or be otherwise unable or unwilling to continue taking care of them. Years after their parents left, teenagers often find themselves targeted by local gangs for recruitment and fear for their lives if they do not succumb to the harassment. They may be unable to go to school because it is too far away or because of gang harassment. Some decide to go north to stay with other relatives or family friends rather than their parents. Either way, those we interviewed did not see internal relocation as an option, though it may be for some Central Americans. Our sample represents those who chose to come to the United States for various reasons, the primary one being reconnection with family.

## Under Threat from the Maras

Gang (*mara*) recruitment and activity are persistent drivers of out-migration for youth. For many, gang threats on their lives or the lives of their family members add significant urgency to their decision to leave. Fifteen-year-old Carlos briefly described the impact of gangs on his life in El Salvador: "They wanted to force me to join the Maras. And that is why you can't study: because I was scared to leave the house, to go to school, and then to come back home." Those who did not want to join the gangs often received death threats. Carlos continued: "They only followed me once, but they didn't get me. I headed home. If someone doesn't join the Maras, they kill you, young. There are no options. If you don't join the Maras, they kill you. I felt a lot of pressure."

Carlos felt as though coming to the United States was his only option besides death or joining the gang. It was his idea to come and join his father. After Carlos spoke with his family, his father arranged and paid for him to travel north. This type of situation was all too common within our cohort of participants. Sofia, age sixteen, spoke about local gangs recruiting her and her brother and the gang turf war that kept them from going to school and was the reason they left El Salvador:

> My brother was going to a soccer academy. That day we stopped by, and there were a lot of people there. They told me when I was with my mom and brother, they [the gang] told me that one day I would be theirs and I don't know what else, and that if I didn't obey them, they were going to hurt my brother, and they were going to kill him. They also wanted to force him to join the Maras. That's why we decided to come. The neighborhood was divided between different gangs, so we couldn't even go to school.

Others reported similar problems, as well as the rumors that circulated about who was a member of what gang and where their territory was. Seventeen-year-old Jose said of his home in El Salvador: "Because there, I couldn't go out anywhere. They would always ask me where I was from. If I said I am from X place and a rival gang was in control there, they would kill me."

Luis, who was nineteen, elaborated on what it was like to be stuck in the middle of territorial disputes and rumored to be a member of the "wrong" gang—in his case, the 18th Street gang, or Dieciocho—in MS-13 territory:

> One time, we were in church, and my sister's boyfriend told some Mara members that he lived in a different zone, and the zone I lived in was MS territory, and the zone my sister lived in was Dieciocho territory. My sister's boyfriend told Dieciocho that I was a MS gang member and that that was the problem because of where I lived, they thought I was MS. So then my best friend from El Salvador told me that they're saying this and that. So I asked my sister's boyfriend why he's going around saying that, and I left the church, and I told my mom

what was happening. And she told me, "I don't want you to be here anymore.... I don't want you to go to school either, because I'm scared that members from Dieciocho go there looking for you."

As this narrative clearly shows, it does not matter in the end if young people are members of any gang or not if the other gangs think that they are. For Luis and his sisters, their mother was all that they had. Their mother did not have a job, their father worked in the United States, and the family depended economically on the remittances he sent from the D.C. area. Luis explained the burdens his mother carried every day and why she wanted them to leave El Salvador: "Poverty. If my sisters and I wanted something, only my mom was around. She was a mom, a dad, she's everything to us, and she taught me so many things too."

Like many others, Luis and his family decided to migrate to ensure their immediate and long-term well-being. They were searching for a better future without persecution by gangs and the struggles of poverty. His mother ended up staying in El Salvador, but she was aware of the risks her children faced and encouraged them to migrate as unaccompanied minors despite the many risks along the way. Their lives were already under threat, and if they arrived in the United States safely, their lives could improve because they would be at much lower risk of being killed by gang members.

## Inhibited Opportunity

Many people in Central America attend school daily without a problem, but the young people in our study often reported that they could not attend school five days a week. Sometimes it was frequent gang violence in the streets on the way to and from school that kept them away. Others lived in rural areas, and the schools were too far away to attend every day. Many said that they had no problem attending school but the schools were not very good; these youth could not see themselves attaining a higher education if they stayed in their home country. Sixteen-year-old Diana explained:

> I came from El Salvador because I wanted to study more. I want to be a doctor. Where I was living then, the schools aren't great. Well, they don't teach a lot of things, like math, or things like that. They only

taught us math twice a week, for thirty minutes. Same with science. So my parents wanted me to come here to study, and I also wanted to study, but where I lived, I couldn't study what I wanted to study.

Diana felt better able to attain her goals in the United States than in El Salvador. She continued:

> Here I think, when I'm twenty-two, or when I'm no longer a minor, I'll be going to university. I want to study. And where I used to live was very dangerous, and there were no opportunities to pursue higher education. Most people in my country only study up to high school and stop there. It is very rare that someone makes it to university.

Jorge, age sixteen, explained why he came from Honduras to the D.C. area: "I wanted to see my mom because it had already been ten, nine years of not seeing her, and it was also for my future. My future that's mine, where I can study here and become someone in life." Jorge also explained that he experienced occasional gang persecution by what he called *guirros*, Honduran slang for "boys" or "a gang of boys." They may not have been wholly affiliated with an actual gang, so for Jorge, who felt only lightly harassed by the *guirros*, the move was less about his immediate safety and more about being reunified with his mother and fulfilling his long-term educational aspirations.

Families leave seeking opportunities, whether they are economic, educational, or otherwise. Some Central American communities are connected to D.C. through social networks and long-standing community ties that can help new immigrants get settled, find work and housing, and stay in the area. Many respondents reported that a parent, or both parents, had left before they did, often many years before, seeking opportunity. Then, as the gang violence connected to the war on drugs and low state capacity got progressively worse, the parents felt it was time for the children to leave too. Civil war violence and persecution, the drivers of migration in the 1980s, have been replaced by networks, gang violence, dedemocratization, and climate change. Some of these factors may change in the future. As we see in El Salvador in 2023, gang violence has decreased.

Gang violence is not always the primary driver in a decision to leave. As parents see their children getting older, they recognize the need for them to have a better education. Higher earning opportunity abroad is paired with other educational and employment opportunities. If, in El Salvador, a child is afraid to go to school and attends only two times a week, the family may feel that the only option is for them to emigrate to the United States, especially if a parent or other friend or family member is already there to support them and finance the trip. Migrants rarely have only one reason for leaving; that is why migration, especially that of unaccompanied youths, is such a complex story. Every migrant had their own set of circumstances that brought them to where they were now.

## Family Reunification

Enduring family separation is a substantial sacrifice. Parents often initiate separation in their family to ensure that their children have money for food, clothing, and other essentials, as well as access to education. However, distinctive challenges arise with family separation, such as many children never having a chance to truly know their parents. Reunification also has its trials, as we discuss in greater depth in chapter 5.

It was very common for youth to report that when they came to the United States, they were meeting one or both of their parents for the first time since they were small children. Juan, who was eighteen when he was interviewed, said: "I came [from El Salvador] because it had been fourteen years since I had seen my mother, so it was like she needed to see us again already." Juan was four years old the last time he had seen his mother. Most people have very few, if any, memories from that age. Although Juan and his mother had stayed in touch and spoken on the phone, his story illustrates how compelling family reunification is for many as a reason for migration. Juan wanted his entire family to be together: "I wanted to be able to help to bring my brothers, so I decided to come more than anything for that reason. So that my brothers could be here and to help her."

The youth in our study had various living arrangements before and after migration. Some were leaving family members in their home country and going to other family members living in the United States. Some were leaving family and joining friends abroad or moving from an extended family to a nuclear family abroad. Sometimes the parent had gone first, the child grew up, and the primary caretaker could not handle them anymore, or had passed away. Beatriz, age thirteen, told us what happened in her family:

> Shortly after I was born, my dad was killed, and then my mom came to the U.S. and left me with my grandma, until she died in 2015. Then she entrusted me to my aunt. It wasn't the same as with my grandma because she raised me since I was little, and I loved her like a mother, and I wanted to go with my mom. It had been ten years since I've seen her, and for those reasons [I wanted to emigrate].

Beatriz wanted to be reunited with her mother, whom she had not seen since she was three years old. When her grandmother died, she was left with someone who was still family but not as well known to her. With her grandmother gone, Beatriz felt it was time to leave El Salvador to be with her mother in the United States.

## The Decision to Leave

Although the migration of minors is a shared decision within a family, some members may have more sway than others; either the parents or the children may feel more strongly about leaving. Many young people did not want to leave, but in other families it was the children's idea to emigrate. The decision can look different depending on whether legal immigration is even possible. Some youth have access to green cards and paperwork. They go to mandatory doctor's appointments before leaving and have time to process that they are moving. Others have little notice and travel with coyotes.

Sebastián, eighteen, explained how he and his parents, along with his uncle, came to the decision that he would leave El Salvador. A great analyst of his own experience, Sebastián alluded to the risks that he would face:

> INTERVIEWER: How did you decide to come?
>
> SEBASTIÁN: I see it as a type of recruiting on my uncle's part because I remember when he came to El Salvador. He started to get involved in seeing how everything was, how we did in school, and all that. He saw that I was hardworking and that I had good grades, so when he came back here, he offered me an opportunity.

He said that he would support me so that I could come [to the United States].

INTERVIEWER: And what did your parents think about this?

SEBASTIÁN: I think that my parents trusted me because I was a very good kid. I'm well mannered, educated, so they felt confident that nothing was going to happen to me.

INTERVIEWER: They wanted a better life for you, right?

SEBASTIÁN: Probably.

INTERVIEWER: Did you talk to them before about your decision to come?

SEBASTIÁN: No, it wasn't planned. It happened spontaneously. My parents didn't even understand why I made this choice, and I would say at that moment, I myself didn't even know what I was getting myself into. It was like exploring a new world; I wanted to experiment, I wanted to see [more], I wanted to explore the world.

INTERVIEWER: You can't know the risks.

SEBASTIÁN: Yes, that, exactly.

INTERVIEWER: You don't think that you're going to die on the way.

SEBASTIÁN: Exactly. We see many thirteen-year-olds along the way. It is better that we don't know all the risks. I think if I knew everything that was going to happen to me, I would've never done it, but to face it head on, I had no other choice than to do it. I came out victorious, I made it by the skin of my teeth, but I made it.

Sebastián was open about his imperfect information and irrational optimism. Nonetheless, the fact that his family members had left before was enough to convince him that he could do it too.

Thirteen-year-old Miguel also talked about the emotional difficulty of leaving for good:

MIGUEL: When we left home, we said our goodbyes. We went to my grandparents, we said goodbye to my cousin, the neighbors, some other neighbors, and from there, we went to Tejutepeque. The coyote would meet us there at 5:00 AM. We left from there, and I didn't eat because I was sad that my grandma, my grandpa, my family were staying. I told my mom, "I don't want to go, let's go back," and she told me, "We already came. We have to keep going." I didn't eat, I felt betrayed, and I cried.

INTERVIEWER: Were there other moments, like when you were both deported from Mexico, that you didn't want to keep going?

MIGUEL: I couldn't take it anymore.

INTERVIEWER: What would your mom say in those moments?

MIGUEL: She would cry from disappointment that we might go back to El Salvador, that we wouldn't be going home, and that we were going to be going on our own.

INTERVIEWER: Then, it was your mother who encouraged you to keep going?

MIGUEL: Yes.

For Miguel, the presence of his mother and her high motivation to migrate were essential in keeping him hopeful about their eventual success in reaching their family in the United States. As his story and those of others here make clear, family reunification is the main factor in migration decisions, which are accelerated by violence and the lack of economic and educational opportunities in Central America.

## Unaccompanied Minors

The U.S. government uses the term "unaccompanied alien child(ren)" (UAC), "unaccompanied child(ren)" (UC), or "unaccompanied alien minor" (UAM) to describe minors who arrive in the United States unaccompanied by an adult family member. This designation does not necessarily indicate that they crossed Central America and Mexico alone. Beatriz described what accompaniment looked like on her journey:

> "It was two days before I left that my mother arranged the trip. It was very last-minute, and it basically only left me a day till they said, "You

have to go," and I was okay with it because I had already decided to come, but they asked me first if I wanted to come, and I didn't want to go at first because I was scared of going alone, but then I found out that a young woman from my area was coming too, [and] it amped me up to come because I knew I wouldn't be doing it on my own.

Parents often pay coyotes to transport and protect their children to a certain extent. For instance, Carlos said that it was his idea to migrate to flee the Maras. His father then paid a coyote to facilitate the trip.

Parents are usually aware that their children are embarking on the trip to El Norte, but sometimes youth not only decide on their own to leave but completely organize their trip without alerting parents or family members. Traveling unaccompanied and without family sponsorship puts migrant youth in the most vulnerable position. These youth often board freight trains (such as La Bestia) to move cheaply through the territory, but such travel is not without risk.[7] In recent years, as Mexican authorities have cracked down on immigrants from Central America, patrolling highways and checking buses full of migrants, many more traveling youth have turned to La Bestia. The train helps migrants get from southern to northern Mexico quickly and without having to buy bus tickets or pay smugglers, but it is incredibly dangerous. It is notorious for physical violence on and around it, with people falling off, losing limbs, and dying in the desert. Those who ride the trains also risk sexual assault and harassment. Freight train companies and U.S. and Mexican authorities have made important changes to routes and routines to make taking the train to cross all of Mexico much harder. Among these changes are radical increases in the speeds at which it moves at certain times and halts in service for long periods. According to the Migration Policy Institute, "The response changed in July 2014 when the Mexican government announced measures to prevent migrants from climbing aboard the trains—including increased border patrols and road checkpoints—and the railroads ordered an increase in the speed of the trains."[8]

Given the increase in Mexico's internal policing and changes in freight train movements, more people have been pushed to hire coyotes and smugglers. The subsequent increases in the prices and profitability of this business, in turn, have made it increasingly attractive to organized crime and drug cartels. Paying a coyote to traverse the land is safer than riding La Bestia and more likely to lead to a successful crossing into the United States undetected. None of the youth interviewed reported riding atop freight trains. Those who ride the trains are less likely to have family connections in the United States or make it over the border.

Some interviewees, like nineteen-year-old Gloria and her brother, become unaccompanied migrants with the consent and knowledge of one parent but not the other:

> My mom had paid for the trip and everything, but my dad [in the United States] didn't know that we were coming. He didn't know our situation in El Salvador, so as not to burden him. He did not know until the day immigration [Border Patrol] detained me. . . . I asked for my brother all the time, but, um, after they took me to an office where they were going to decide whether to send me to a children's center or to see if my dad could get me or something. I was in some cells. They call them the hieleras [freezers]. From there, they moved me to a different center where they gave me clothes, food. I showered, and I talked to my mom and dad once or twice a week. There I'd ask for my brother because it had been a week since I had heard anything about him. From there, I came with my dad until I found out that my brother had been kidnapped, and they asked for money to turn him in to immigration. He suffered the most on the journey. It was very hard. Hard . . . to come by yourself, without a parent, without anything, because we were separated from each other. When I saw him again—I was released to my dad on August 14, 2014, and he on the fifteenth—I saw him skinnier; I saw tick bites on him. His guide didn't give him any food. He spent many days without eating.

Even when migrants turn themselves in to immigration authorities and legally apply for asylum, the trip north leaves many physical and emotional scars, and getting asylum depends on having a clear and simple case that is easy to make by a legal counsel—when there is one available.[9]

## Legal Reunification

Other child migrants were lucky in that they had family members with legal immigration status in the United States and so could petition for family reunification. Luciana, age seventeen, explained that her mother had submitted a petition for her immigration years before, but without telling her; she had wanted to wait until the petition was approved. Luciana described the paperwork and doctor's appointments associated with coming, as well as the emotional toll of leaving El Salvador.

> Suddenly, she told me that she had it all planned, and God willing, we would join her.... I thought it would not happen. Then when the documents started to arrive in the mail and all that, they said that we had to get bloodwork done. I was like, is this really going to happen? Sometimes I wouldn't want to go, and I'd cry.

Luciana saw it as almost a miracle that she was able to migrate legally. Nineteen-year-old Gabriela had a similar experience:

> Because it started to become really dangerous and because I think that there's a better future [for me] here than over there. My dad had already submitted the paperwork and said that we would all be together, and that this way he wouldn't have to keep going to [El Salvador]. He told us that we'd be better off here, and we would have everything we needed, including residency [green cards].

Alexander, age twenty and also from El Salvador, shared a similar story:

> My mom arranged for our paperwork to go through. She was who brought us. My stepdad requested us. We came with visas, while waiting for the green card here. My mom said that she was going to arrange for us to come one day and that the paperwork was in process, that we should stay out of trouble, and that we'd be able to be here with her. We came when all the paperwork went through.

Access to legal migration through family reunification processes allowed Juliana, Gabriela, and Alexander to immigrate to D.C. and join their families without having to face the risks of crossing jungles and deserts and other dangers on the road while spending thousands of dollars on an uncertain trip. These three examples show that the process of migrating legally is more orderly and humane and that the motivations of those seeking legal immigration status are not very different from those of migrants who have no documents or are asking for asylum since many also faced violence and persecution. Increasing avenues for legalization and legal family reunification would sharply reduce human suffering.

Why would someone migrate "unaccompanied"? The reasons why minors and adolescents come to the United States vary, as do their willingness and desire to migrate. Many are on board because it means that they can escape gang violence, pursue educational and work opportunities, and, for so many, reunite with family members in the States. We argue that the main motivation to leave is a desire to reunite with family members who are already abroad. Nevertheless, the decision to leave can also be very painful. They are leaving behind their homes and family members and entering a new country with different customs and languages. The journey is well planned for some, while others must leave suddenly because a parent felt it was important to do so. The autonomy of leaving, or the lack thereof, is crucial in their experience. Some youth feel reluctant to abandon their connections in their home country. Family members such as their grandparents may feel more like their mothers and fathers than their actual ones in the United States. Leaving means saying goodbye to their friends, their culture, and their country. Many youths interviewed expressed a desire to return to their country after they had moved up socioeconomically in the United States. It is also important to state that most Central Americans cannot or do not want to leave.

All in all, these decisions are made out of necessity. Whether motivated by a search for immediate safety or aspirations to become a doctor or a lawyer, leaving is never easy. Whether leaving was decided for them or they decided on it themselves, the future of these young people is in the United States.

### Bittersweet Departures

INTERVIEWER: Could you describe to me a little about how you felt when you left your family in Central America? (*Jose chuckles*) It's still a recent experience, right?

JOSE (age seventeen at migration, from El Salvador): Yes, I felt bad, terrible, but at the same time it gave me strength knowing that I was going to see family here.

INTERVIEWER: How did it feel to leave?

BEATRIZ (twelve at migration, from El Salvador): Well (*chuckles softly*), I felt very sad, to be honest, because all of my family is over there and, well, just very sad more than anything else. Two days before [I left], well, my mother arranged the trip quickly, and I basically only had a day left [at home] to say my goodbyes. They told me, "You're leaving this day," and I said "Okay," because I had already decided to come, but they asked me first if I wanted to go. [At first], I didn't want to go by myself, but then a woman from my neighborhood came to guide me, which gave me the strength to come because I knew I wouldn't be going alone.

Youth expressed great sadness at leaving their home countries. For most respondents, this sadness was rooted in leaving the family who had raised them—whether parents or other family members—their friends, and other people they knew well. Their sadness stemmed from leaving the place that they had known and called home, along with everything related to country, place, and home—the customs, traditions, mores, and interpersonal understandings that colored everyday interactions and shaped their habitus. However, most intuited that the move would be good for them, even with the dangers of the journey northward, the difficulty of navigating the U.S. immigration system, and all the new things they would have to learn once they were in a new country. Some of them did not even know their parents who were already in the United States and would meet their parents for the first time. Others left knowing that they could be with their parents again after extended periods of separation sprinkled with long visits.

Leaving home is an intensely emotional experience, no matter the age, and being aware of opportunities and being told they would enjoy a "better life" does not make it easier. Some youth did not even have a chance to say goodbye to those who had been taking care of them. Others were fixated on times when they fought with their families in their last days before leaving. Many also knew of the physically demanding journey ahead of them. Stories of violence and danger on the trip to the United States are widely known and circulated in Central America. Finally, while some seemed to care most about the people they had to leave, others made it clear that they would miss more than the people they lived with. They would miss neighbors, street vendors, old teachers, priests—each of whom may have been very significant and who together had made the place what it was.

When asked how he felt when leaving El Salvador, sixteen-year-old Antonio responded: "Very bad, very sad, because my entire life has been there... my childhood. I had to leave my grandmother too, my cousin... but above all my home country." Elizabeth from Guatemala, also sixteen, reported feeling "at the same time scared and... happy. I felt scared because I didn't know what would happen to me, if it would go well. If I would be able to get there, I didn't know. And I felt happy because, for the first time, I was going to meet the person who says she is my mother."

Many youth wished to stay but felt that they had no choice, not because their parents said so, but because many found themselves in dire situations. Alexander described the emotional processes associated with leaving and the reasoning behind it:

> Sad, you know? Because there [in El Salvador], for the most part, you're just living your life there, and when you realize that you're going to come here, you start to think so much about so many things that you will not experience there but in a different country where you don't know anyone, and you're starting from square one. For me, it hurts. It hurts to be so far from home, away from all my cousins and everything, do you understand? But what can we do? This is a country of opportunity, and you have to get ahead. However it may be.

This sentiment was echoed by Avery, who migrated from El Salvador at age seventeen. They said:

> Well, I only focused on the positive. Let's say, many would say that I am being heartless, but it's not like that. It's just leaving your emotions behind. Why cry if you know you're going to return one day. I didn't cry at all; I didn't even think about missing my family. I only said to myself, I want to come to America, and to America I will go. Because if I don't get there, I won't accomplish my dreams.

Of course, there were also bonds between migrating youth and friends and other community members. Juan, who was eighteen when he left El Salvador, highlighted the role of the entire community in his life before he left.

> My friends became my family too. For example, they would stay at my house for three days at a time, and well, I've always gone to church, so it was my turn to serve in the ministry. There were older people, they were sisters who were more than fifty years old, forty-five, thirty-eight. So, it was like having four moms who always took care of me.

They would come to cook at the house, and they would be there washing dishes with us, and they practically became part of my family. It was a strong bond. It was tough when they heard I was leaving. They cried a lot, so I became very attached to all of that, so I knew to come here would be a big change, to get to know new people, and all of that.

Additionally, the sometimes strained parent-child relationships that are normal during adolescence were sometimes cut off abruptly. Luis described his last day at home, when he had an outburst at his mother and then was unable to apologize before leaving for what might be a very long time:

LUIS: It was the day after my seventeenth birthday that day. I left without saying goodbye to her.

INTERVIEWER: Did she know that you were about to leave?

LUIS: Yes. But that's not what hurts me. What hurts me is the day before I fought with her. . . . We were together shopping, and I didn't buy anything for myself, only for my sisters, and we got back very late. While we were out, I told her, "Mom, I'm hungry," and she told me, "Wait till we get home." At the time, I didn't remember that Real Madrid and Barcelona were going to play each other. Later I told her, "Mom, I'm hungry, but when we got home, I was going to see Real Madrid and Barcelona play each other with a friend." And she said, "Wait till we get home and I'll make you something to eat," and I started to yell that I was hungry and that we never had food. She got very mad at me because I yelled at her very rudely. Despite being poor, she always had something for me, and I never even realized it. That day she told me, "Look what I have in the drawer," and she had clothes and shoes for me, and I never saw her buy them. I felt so awful, and that I couldn't tell her to her face to forgive me for everything I had said that day.

Common family disagreements were sometimes the last in-person memory of those who are departing. These moments filled them with guilt and anguish, and they could ruminate on these sad memories for a long time.

Parents are often the ones who arrange these migrations, sometimes with very little turnaround time. "We came because my mom ordered us to come," said thirteen-year-old Fernanda, who migrated from El Salvador. She added, with a laugh, "I didn't want to come here."

## The Journey

Beyond the emotional toll of leaving friends and family members, there is also the physical toll of the journey itself. Gloria, age sixteen, described the conditions of her journey north from El Salvador:

> I would've been stuck, thrown away in the middle of nowhere. I needed water, and ants had bitten my whole left hand and had given me some big welts. Where I would've been stuck was in the mountains, so obviously, snakes would come. One slithered by my feet; I felt it because one foot didn't have a shoe.

Gloria's group spent hours walking without stopping, sometimes leaving her behind because she struggled to keep up. She also described the terror of crossing a river in an inflatable raft because she did not know how to swim. The exhaustion and dehydration made her feel relieved when the trip finally ended, even though she was then taken in by migration authorities.

Despite being open about other topics, many youth did not want to discuss the trip or how the coyote treated them. Immigrants who employ the services of coyotes are often still indebted to them, and failure to pay this debt is sometimes met with a threat of violence. Thus, it is a sensitive topic that immigrants may not want to discuss with researchers or anyone else. Additionally, the trip was often traumatic and not something many wanted to discuss, as ten-year-old Angel, a migrant from El Salvador, made very clear:

> INTERVIEWER: And overall, how was the trip? Did you have enough food? How did you feel?
>
> ANGEL: I felt bad because I had left my aunt, but at the same time happy because I was going to meet my parents.
>
> INTERVIEWER: But, for example, regarding food, did you get enough food?

ANGEL:  Yes.

INTERVIEWER:  And the man, the coyote, who brought you, how did he treat you?

ANGEL: More or less. I don't want to talk about it.

Walter, who was nineteen when he came to the United States from El Salvador, described the end of the journey. After the coyote led them to CBP, they experienced state-sponsored trauma at the hands of the U.S. government and its agents:

> Immigration got us because the coyote basically handed us over to them. The coyote told us to cross the river on foot and continue walking and that, behind a wall, there would be a car waiting, which there was, but it belonged to Immigration [the Border Patrol]. They took us to the hielera, and that is super-complicated. When they questioned me about why I was there, I told them everything that I just told you now. He started laughing. He didn't believe me at all. He thought that we were stupid. He said that everyone that comes says the same thing, and I began to cry. He called the other agents to laugh at me, they told me they were going to deport me, and I said if they sent me back, I would be killed, and they told me that my life didn't matter. Finally, they took me to a jail to see if they would let me go through or not. It was like a cell in jail, and it was filled with all the beds in the same cell. One of the guards befriended me because he saw me not eating, and barely sleeping. He knew I'd never been in jail before, and he would tell me stories of other people who were able to get out of there. I was there for four months. Afterward, they transported me to another jail in New Jersey, where ten people would sleep in one room, and they'd lend us games. It was better. The other people there didn't have documents either. I had my interview there. We'd ask each other for advice between the ten of us who were there about what to say in our interviews. There were also gang members there that asked us what to say so they wouldn't get deported. During my interview, the man who interviewed me basically wrote down what I said with the help of a translator. Afterward, they sent me outside to wait. Then a woman came out to say they accepted my case, and I'd have to wait for the court to process my bail. I was there for ten more days until they transferred me to a different, real jail, called Elizabeth, where inmates

were distinguished by colors, and those wearing orange were the most dangerous criminals. I was there for four days. I went before a judge in Elizabeth, who told me how much my bail was. I called my godfather to tell him how much the bail was, and he paid it the next day. I was happy to find out my bail got paid. That's what made me happy. My godfather paid my bail of $5,000. The day after he paid my bail, they opened these big gates at 8:00 PM and told me, "Good luck." I left and had no idea which way to go. There was nothing there. But after five minutes, my godfather showed up. Twenty-three days. So the trip took basically a month and a half through a coyote."

When asked who paid for his trip, Walter said, "My godfather paid for everything; it was around $3,500. It was going to be $7,500 had they brought me to where he was, but they only got through the border, so he didn't pay the rest."

Walter was lucky because he had resources in the United States, including a godfather who was able to fund the trip, post bail, and advocate for him outside of the prison system. His godfather could not change the fact that he had to enter the country without papers, face verbal abuse by CBP officers, and spend months in jail awaiting an immigration court date. This is what many asylum seekers and immigrants go through, and these experiences inform what they need to feel safe, at home, and integrated when they finally make it into homes with their sponsors. The first experience of the United States for many is the violent immigration system, which often leaves a negative first impression that produces an emblematic mix of feelings in many new arrivals about the United States. They find that many people will put them down, while some may support them. They may want to come to the United States to be with their parents, or to seek opportunities and education, but they do not want to leave what they know, where they were raised, and the people who raised them. Then they come to the United States, which they have been told is a good place, but immediately face arcane immigration laws that produce what Cecilia Menjívar and Lesley Abrego call legal violence.[10] Immigrants experience immigration policies as a series of bureaucratic attacks and the opposite of a welcome.

Antonio's comment that he would very much miss his home country rang with the kind of pride that almost anyone would feel for where they are from. Such pride does not represent blind support for one's country so much as a great sense of belonging and joy in one's own traditions, cultures, mores, and understandings, which even two strangers can share if they are from the same place. For Antonio, the hardest part of departure was leaving all that was familiar at home and journeying toward the unknown. He would have to pick up a new language and understand a brand-new place with different cultural practices and symbolic rankings.[11]

Undeniably, our interviewees saw the United States as a land of opportunity, not only because of idealized views of the land, culture, and people but also because they knew there was work to be had here. Nonetheless, most interviewees wished to return eventually to Central America. It is a common experience for immigrants to come to the United States, work for some years, and eventually return to where they came from, sometimes when they retire and sometimes earlier. Others end up settling in the United States for good. Of course, those who are undocumented or whose legal status is precarious are unable to travel abroad and face drastically increased costs and risks returning to the United States, because legal ports of entry would not be an option for them.

This chapter has illustrated the ways in which young migrants from Central America depart from their natal countries. Their reasons for leaving are similar to those of other migrants around the world: a wish to reunify with parents or other important caregivers, a desire to flee violence, and hopes of improving their chances in life by gaining education and work opportunities. Importantly, these factors are often inextricably interwoven, as our data show. Steps toward family reunification may start being taken when primary caregivers die or when violence and gang recruitment rises.

Motives for migration also are inextricable from the experience of the journey and the context of reception. A young person who feels more comfortable with leaving and who has a feeling of belonging and being at home after arriving is likely to integrate quickly and easily. On the other hand, traumatic experiences in the sending country and on the journey make for more challenges upon arrival. There is no one way to define integration, and it is possible to have experiences and feelings of both exclusion and inclusion at once. How immigration policies and asylum rules are crafted, how funding is disbursed to schools and community organizations to aid and house newcomers, how teachers, counselors, and families interact with, talk to, and speak about youth migrants—all of this makes a big difference in the lives of recent arrivals in both the short and long terms.

The next chapter discusses the journeys of youth migrants through Central America and Mexico, their encounters with the U.S. immigration system, and finally, their journey's end when they arrived at homes in the Washington, D.C., metropolitan region.

CHAPTER FOUR

# CENTRAL AMERICANS AND THEIR PASSAGE THROUGH MEXICO TO THE UNITED STATES

This chapter focuses on Central American children and young adults born in northern Central America who were part of the migration that began in 2014 and, to a certain degree, continues today.[1] We present individual cases that illustrate the journey through Mexico and arrival in the United States.[2]

Substantial work has cataloged the reasons why migrants leave their home countries, including violence in their region, whether gang-related, institutional, or both; it has also delved into family-related issues in migration, such as separation and reunification, which we discuss in chapter 5.[3] Furthermore, research has been done on the traumas that migrants may experience during the trip between their sending community and their destination, which we discuss (using validated psychological scales) in chapter 6. Many are fleeing gang persecution and recruitment and fear for their physical safety on the journey to the U.S. border; then they undergo state-sponsored trauma in Customs and Border Protection (CBP) custody once they reach the border.[4]

Many of the youth we interviewed did not construct their lives around the idea of migrating to the United States. On the contrary, many expressed profound sadness about needing to leave their country. Some left their parents in Central America. Many more were meeting their parents in the United States, maybe for the first time, and had to leave behind those who had raised them. It is a challenging and emotional task—especially for youth—to leave one's family, as well as one's friends, culture, and familiar surroundings.

Although travel problems were common among these young interviewees, they often kept them to themselves. Many of them understood

https://doi.org/10.7758/dvxg2393.1162

that their reasons for migrating and their interactions with coyotes, authorities, and organized crime along the way were considered private information that, for security reasons and to avoid worrying their family members, they should not share with friends, neighbors, or sometimes even family.

There is a silence implicit in "illegality"[5] that leads many immigrants to avoid talking about their journey and status with strangers. Most Central Americans travel "illegally" through Mexico, and many will enter the United States outside of ports of entry. Recently, Mexico has offered transit visas and permits to some Central Americans on their way north, but this visa does not make migrants somehow "legal" when confronted by authorities.[6] In addition, Central American migrants may encounter the genuinely illegal actions of smugglers, more and more of whom are what Charles Tilly calls "violent entrepreneurs and violence specialists" working in cartels as well as in government police and military forces.[7] When they arrive in the United States and experience the widespread stigma against immigrants there, even those who immigrated legally and have been granted asylum or temporary protective status are often framed as "socially illegal."[8] No wonder then that most immigrants avoid talking about their journey and their status with strangers, knowing that many people assume their illegality rather than ask about it, and that revealing their immigration status might lead to their deportation.[9]

The following two observations are based on the experiences of several immigrants and challenge the xenophobic sentiments that have come to dominate the discussion surrounding Central American immigrants in the United States. First, migrants do not wish to come to the United States strictly for economic reasons; they would generally prefer to make a living in their home countries, but global economic structures, violence, or both, may have made that impossible. The young people who leave Central America and arrive at the southern border of the United States are essentially following the path taken by their parents, who either are migrating with them or have already migrated years or even decades before. Leaving their home countries is a very sad and painful event for them. Second, those who oppose immigration to the United States tend to assume that the governments in Central America and Mexico make no effort to prevent migrants from crossing their borders. Some U.S. politicians also insist that Central American governments fail to do enough to maintain their citizens within their borders. Contrary to these misconceptions, Mexico and other countries in the region restrict migration to such an extent that they have created great obstacles and a dangerous environment for those who decide to migrate.[10] Many countries' immigration enforcement agencies detain and harass a great majority of the immigrants who try to cross their territory.[11] Accounts of officer bribery, deportation threats, and sexual abuse are common.

Mexican cartels also take advantage of the vulnerability of migrants. Since those in transit cannot get help from local authorities out of fear of deportation, migrants become targets for extortion—so much so that organized crime has become the principal authority encountered by migrants trying to pass through certain parts of Mexico. It has been reported that cartels keep some migrants as hostages until they receive payment of the "border tariff," and our data confirm that this happens.[12]

Although the migrants mentioned their concerns about these risks, several insisted that they feared the police more than gangs or organized crime. Given that the police act as representatives of the state and play a role in the judicial system, they can in fact present a greater threat to migrants. The police do not have to keep their presence secret, as criminal groups do, but can operate day and night openly without their presence being questioned. Immigrants' fear of state authorities is one example of the failure of immigration systems at the international level. Politics and the prevailing discourse assume that the principal dangers faced on a migratory trip are petty criminals, but beyond organized crime, the greatest threats to migrants are the police and other state agents.

One example of such systemic dysfunction has been revealed by several reports regarding interactions between migrants and immigration officials at the U.S.-Mexico border. Some migrants are greeted at the border with the statement "Welcome to the United States," while others are not even informed about their right to plead for asylum in the United States. Apparently, the way Border Patrol agents interact with them is one of the most important factors in many migrants' experience and early opinion about the United States.

The image of the undocumented migrant who has to board a freight train to cross through Mexico to reach the U.S.-Mexico border, fleeing violence and gangs, is just one of the common accounts. It accurately describes the journey of many Central American migrants, but not all of them.[13] Specifically, the Mexican government has changed the routes of La Bestia by canceling trains or running them much faster with the explicit intent of discouraging migrants from using them as a method of transportation. That sometimes works, but many migrants continue to lose their hands, arms, legs, or lives to the dangerous conditions set by the state.

The stories presented in this chapter demonstrate how the interplay of personal connections and environmental factors and history promote migration. These interviews reveal that, because of the antimigratory context and militarization of the border, engaging the expensive services of coyotes is the principal method of getting to the border. Joining a caravan is a solution to both the dangers of the trip and the cost. Traveling with a caravan is both much cheaper than paying coyotes and funding organized crime and safer because of the strength in numbers. Small criminal gangs are less likely to attack a large caravan and extort its members for payment. The likelihood of cameras and local and international media coverage also increases protection in the short term. When caravans arrive at a location along the way, local nonprofits, churches, and governments may offer places to spend the night, food, clothes, and even transportation to keep moving north.

Unfortunately, caravans garner more public and media attention and present a visual image of an "invasion," leading some to call for officials to do something about them, as we saw during the 2018 U.S. midterm election season.[14] Our respondents arrived before caravans became a more common mode of travel, before the implementation of the Trump administration's "Remain in Mexico" program, and before Title 42 was used to close the border to many owing to public health concerns at the onset of the COVID-19 pandemic. (These policies are discussed at further length in chapter 8.) The migrant experiences detailed here were hard enough, but soon after, they got even tougher as Mexican and Central American authorities became more aggressive in blocking and disbanding caravans.

## The Migration Journey

A slight majority of interviewees lacked visas when they undertook the journey to the United States. Most of them arrived at the border, turned themselves over to CBP, and formally requested asylum. The length of the journey varied widely among them: some traveled only a week or two before reaching the border, while for others the trip took much longer. For some, it took more than three months to arrive in Washington, D.C. One of these migrants was fifteen-year-old Carlos:

> From El Salvador, I went to Guatemala, from Guatemala I took a bus, I got off, took another bus, got off, at night the buses ran.... I must've taken around twenty buses from Guatemala to Mexico. From Mexico to the United States, I went by bus and by taxi. I crossed the border and was walking when they detained me, they took me to Immigration, they interviewed me, I explained my case, why I came.... I was at the center for minors for about half a month. I played there, they had classes, and from there I went with my dad. The trip took around three months.

For many, traveling through Mexico was a long and uneasy step of the journey that sometimes took months before they interfaced with the U.S. immigration system and could be reunited with their families. Many experienced difficulties getting into Mexico in the first place, owing to gang activity and the Mexican government's efforts to curb the unauthorized migration of Central Americans through the country. Some of the respondents from El Salvador mentioned that Guatemala felt less foreign and safer than Mexico. Salvadorans experienced almost no issues in Guatemala, but they felt more uneasy in Mexico. Seventeen-year-old Jose, for instance, said that he felt safe in Guatemala but not in Mexico: "Guatemala, yes, of course, because they're practically brothers with El Salvador, but Mexico, no."

Jose mentioned feeling out of place and scared in Mexico. Anti-immigrant attitudes are strong in Mexico, as revealed, for example, in the 2018 demonstrations in Tijuana, when hundreds of people protested against the immigrant caravans coming from Central America. Central American immigrants are discriminated against and associated with both crime and a bad economy, in much the same way Mexican immigrants have been scapegoated in the United States.[15] These sentiments are profoundly rooted in anti-Black and anti-Indigenous racism that infiltrates everyday life, creating a hostile and dangerous environment for immigrants making their journey north.[16] Following a colonial logic, Mexicans assume that people on the move who look Indigenous and speak differently are poor and therefore unwelcome.[17] Luis explained why he felt unsafe in Mexico and how getting into Mexico has become more difficult: "They had me in Guatemala for two days because to get into Mexico was—it wasn't possible because there were too many immigration officers there. The coyote had a house in Guatemala, and we waited there to pass."

In addition to Mexican immigration and other federal officers, many were worried about gang activity, such as kidnapping and extortion, in Mexico and along its border with Guatemala. Gangs would often slow down the already long and arduous journey. Dominic, who migrated from El Salvador at the age of twelve, described this ordeal: "The coyotes have to ask them [gangs] for permission to pass through, and they have to pay them to go through. Otherwise, they would kidnap us, or something like that, and ask us for money." Samantha, a fifteen-year-old from Honduras, experienced a similar threat. Her group was held up near the Guatemala-Mexico border, she said, by gangs wielding firearms and threatening to light their buses on fire, with everyone inside, unless they all paid a fee. She had to sleep in a field for four nights while the coyotes made an arrangement with the gang to let them pass:

SAMANTHA: And they went around in cars too, with firearms and all that. They would go in front of cars and wouldn't let them pass. Supposedly, that post is controlled by them.

INTERVIEWER: In which country was this?

SAMANTHA: Guatemala, and I think it was on the border with Mexico. And if you didn't pay them a certain quantity of money, they wouldn't let you through. Supposedly, they were going to set the buses on fire because they were locked from the outside. I mean, no one from the inside could open the doors or anything. The others couldn't open them or anything.

INTERVIEWER: How was this problem resolved?

SAMANTHA: I don't know how they resolved it. They, I think they went back to where they came from. We were left at that sports field that I told you about. We slept and spent around four days there.

INTERVIEWER: In the field?

SAMANTHA: Uh-huh, sleeping in the cold and everything.

INTERVIEWER: So then you were on your way?

SAMANTHA: Uh-huh.

INTERVIEWER: You were stopped.

SAMANTHA: Uh-huh.

INTERVIEWER: Those people are saying you need to pay and if you don't . . . they'll kill everyone?

SAMANTHA: Yes.

INTERVIEWER: Including the bus driver.

SAMANTHA: They made an agreement with them. And they gave them, the people that had to give them money, I believe a week. And if not, well, that they'd do away with us. Uh-huh, and I think they were able to get it, and afterwards we were let free. And we left.

Samantha said that she was given food to eat only once a day during the trip; otherwise, she just drank water. Compounding these intense physical demands was the precariousness of traveling through Mexico. Alberto, who was fourteen when he migrated from El Salvador, explained that, "in Mexico, the traffic at first was really slow, [because] around . . . the border there are Mexican immigration officers, as well as federal officers. Going through Mexico wasn't too difficult, but we did have to proceed carefully because the locals quickly realized that we were immigrants."

Many were apprehensive of Mexican immigration authorities out of fear of deportation, which would both lengthen their journey and raise the cost, given that they would have to try again later. Fourteen-year-old Ana Cristina spoke about the experience she and her brother had in Mexico when they were migrating from Honduras: "In Mexico, we had a cell phone, and we could call our mom. We had a bit of money, but then it ran out, and we had to bear the hunger for a couple of days. We were scared, and my brother would cry and want to go back, but I told him we had to keep going."

Besides some private citizens, networks of immigrant shelters, churches, and organized groups, such as Las Patronas, provide food and shelter to migrants traveling through Mexico, but not all immigrants happen to interface with them. There are shelters along the way, which are most often used by single men or family units, but most of the immigrants we interviewed for this study, because they arrived legally or traveled with coyotes, did not use them.[18]

## Arrival at the U.S. Border and U.S. Authorities

When Customs and Border Protection apprehends unaccompanied minors at the border, the minors must prove that they have a legitimate fear of returning or are victims of trafficking.[19] The William Wilberforce Trafficking Victims Protection Reauthorization Act (TVPRA) of 2008 grants youth—other than those from Canada or Mexico—eligibility for protection if they are victims of trafficking or exploitation. In this case, CBP must send the youth to the Office of Refugee Resettlement (ORR) within seventy-two hours.[20] The ORR then places the minor with an adult sponsor while they wait for their immigration case to be heard. If the ORR cannot locate an adult sponsor, the minor is placed in foster care or a group home.[21] After they turn eighteen, they can be placed in "post-eighteen" programs like those available through the Latin American Youth Center (LAYC) or the federally administered Unaccompanied Refugee Minors (URM) program. According to Jodi Berger Cardoso and her colleagues, between 2013 and 2016, "approximately 90% [of the 123,000 placed unaccompanied minors] were released to a parent or other family member."[22] Once youth are placed with a sponsor, the government is minimally involved in their lives outside of the courts and schools. There have been multiple troubling reports that during the Trump administration CBP and the ORR lost track of thousands of youth entirely and are unable to check in to learn whether they are continued victims of trafficking.[23]

As they approached the border toward the end of their migration journey, youth reports on crossing the river and being picked up by CBP differed. Alberto discussed his experience:

> ALBERTO: U.S. immigration officers detained us. We went through the detention center and contacted my father. He is my official sponsor.
>
> INTERVIEWER: Was that the plan? Did you know that they would let you live with your father?

ALBERTO: Yes. Well, we were out of supplies and the coyotes only left us and told us to cross the river and "walk straight ahead," but we couldn't find the road. The best thing was that ICE [U.S. Immigration and Customs Enforcement] would detain us because it would be the easiest option.

Diana, age sixteen, also spoke about her experience crossing the border and being kept in CBP custody:

> We were in a house, and then a man told us that he was going to leave us in a forest. There was a forest, and you could hear a river. And we were on a rock with some other men, who were also with the man who brought us. And you could hear animal noises, and they were very scary. We were scared. It was around five in the morning, and we were there for around two hours, and the man who was supposed to guide us across the river never came, but then he arrived. We passed the river once, but that was what we were going to walk along in the desert. Then we came back and did another loop because the man was mistaken, and he said that we were going to pass through there to Mexico. So, then we came back to go through the United States, and the man was mistaken again. So then we came back to Mexico, and then the next time we crossed it was where cotton was being grown, and then we walked a lot, a lot, to get to a big black gate where there was an immigration car waiting, and they detained us. They asked us our names, and they loaded us in their car and took us to a little house where there were only around fifteen girls there. They gave me a blanket around, well, it must've already been nighttime by then. They took us to shower, because our clothes were all [dirty], and they gave us [new] clothes. The next day they took us to the detention center.

Like Diana, sixteen-year-old Valentina was from El Salvador. She described a similar experience, as well as what is known as the hielera.

VALENTINA: When we crossed, immigration was practically already there waiting for us. They told us to take off everything that we brought with us that was pointy or sharp, like rings, bracelets, earrings, and they took us to the hielera.

INTERVIEWER: What is the hielera?

VALENTINA: It's a type of room, but super-cold.

INTERVIEWER: And you were there with your mom and brother?

VALENTINA: No, just my mom. They separated my brother in a different room, because he was ten years old, and in that room there were only women with small children because the bathrooms were right there in front of everyone. That's why they took him and sent him where the other boys were.

Alison discussed getting sick because of the crossing and then the time she spent in the hielera. The fourteen-year-old Salvadoran explained that if she wanted to go to the bathroom while she was being held, she had to use a single toilet shared by everyone, completely visible to all eyes.

ALISON: We crossed the river in a group, in a raft. Afterwards, we walked for three hours at night. I was wet because I was in the river, and I couldn't bear to walk anymore, and I sat down for a little while, and more time passed, and after four hours was when they detained me and a woman who came with me. Then they took us to a very cold place and didn't give us blankets. A cell, but because I was wet, it was even colder.

INTERVIEWER: Did you get sick afterwards?

ALISON: Yes.

INTERVIEWER: So, immigration got you. When they detained you, what happened?

ALISON: They told us that we should take off our shoes, and they took us to the cell. Around twenty-four hours later, they interviewed me, asking why I came, and they called my mother to let her know I was there.

INTERVIEWER: What happened after that?

ALISON: They took me to the shelter, and I was there for thirteen days.

INTERVIEWER: And how was it in the shelter?

ALISON: It's good.

INTERVIEWER: What did they give you there?

ALISON: When I got there, it was dawn. They gave me food, clothes, and shoes there.

INTERVIEWER: And did you have the flu at that time?

ALISON: No, afterwards.

INTERVIEWER: In the twenty-four hours that you were in that cold space, did they give you food, water, and access to a restroom?

ALISON: Restroom, but everyone always needed to use it and there were plenty of people, and everyone could see when I went.

INTERVIEWER: Did they give you something to eat, water, anything else?

ALISON: Only a sandwich. Just that.

INTERVIEWER: And during those thirteen days at the shelter, what did you do?

ALISON: I went to school, because they had a school there, and just that. They also had games. It was all girls and boys my age.

INTERVIEWER: How did you feel at the shelter?

ALISON: Good, it was fun.

The way these respondents described it, the ORR shelters seemed to be a much better place for young people. While still imperfect, the ORR is run by the U.S. Department of Health and Human Services (HHS), which, as implied by its name, is concerned with human services and well-being; by contrast, CBP is run by the U.S. Department of Homeland Security (DHS), a law enforcement agency. Immigrant detention is often subcontracted to for-profit services that have bad track records in protecting the people under their care.[24] During their time in the ORR shelter, these youth often felt better and unburdened by the events of the past several months. Even after experiencing the hielera, Alison was able to describe the ORR shelter as "fun." Their accounts during interviews may have been colored by the stark differences between their journey northward and their stay in the ORR shelter, and also by the instructional and recreational activities organized by the shelter. However, it is also possible that their answers were informed by a fear of the government or by legal concerns. The study was methodologically crafted to minimize this possibility, and honest answers about CBP conditions suggest that they are accurate accounts, but the other explanations cannot be ruled out.

Fourteen-year-old Ana Cristina's account of her crossing and the time she subsequently spent in an ORR youth shelter was typical:

> We were able to cross the bridge, and the immigration officials [who] were there didn't say anything to us. When we turned ourselves in, they called my mom, and I don't know what they asked her. At Immigration, they asked us if we wanted to return to Honduras. We said no, and they sent us to the shelter, and we were there for two weeks and [some] days. We enjoyed it there, we had a room for just my brother and me, and they treated us well. There were kids from different countries, and they gave us food and clothes. There was a counselor, and we were able to go to school if we wanted.

Youth would stay in the shelter for a few weeks before the details were worked out for their sponsorship, placement, and departure. Sometimes they went to parents who had taken the journey north together and been separated at the border, then were later reunited, while others were meeting one of their parents for the first time in many years.

## Migration via Mexico

Five findings that stand out from our interviews with minors regarding the trip contrast with many of the points made in journalistic accounts and in policy discussions, which focus on immigrant encounters at the border, overcount people, cannot go in-depth, and may paint a distorted picture of the dynamics at play.[25] Our five findings derive from interviews with those who made it to D.C. and who have some ties and connections in the area.

*1. The incidence of violence is not as high as reported.* Respondents reported various instances of violence along their journey through Guatemala and Mexico. In one incident, a young respondent was kidnapped for ransom, while another youth was the victim of both excessive use of force by Mexican immigration officials and threats made at gunpoint by a criminal actor. In one violent incident that seemed to involve the entire migrant party, the girl we interviewed may have been protected from harm by the party's guide and by fellow migrants.

There may not be as many violent incidents as we would expect, given journalistic reporting. Although youth are highly likely to experience less violence during the journey through Mexico, that is not everyone's experience. That the interviewees for this study were not generally victims of violence or of organized crime may be attributable to the additional protections coyotes afford youth migrants. This hypothesis is supported by the fact that both the routes and modes of transportation typically used to convey youth migrants northward are generally safer than those used by adults. For example, younger migrants are more likely to travel by bus and car than they are to get on board La Bestia or to go on foot. This is not to say that the experiences of young people traversing Mexico are anything less than harrowing. Ruben, who was sixteen when he left Honduras for the United States, spent a month and a half trying to reach the border. Things were very difficult for him in Mexico. On two separate occasions, he had to flee from Mexican authorities.

If coyotes were indeed making a concerted effort to shield youth from both genuine and probable harm, their actions were less likely altruistic than reflective of the outcome-based business model of the human smuggling enterprise. To have migrant youths repeatedly dying on their watch could prove devastating to future business prospects. In one extreme case of "coyote care," a female respondent reported that she flew to the United States using the documents of the coyote's daughter after the coyote's wife took a liking to her.

2. *The heightened immigration enforcement activities of Mexican authorities have had mixed impacts.* Under increasing pressure from the United States following the increased arrival of child and family migrants at the U.S.-Mexico border in 2014, Mexican federal and state governments have tightened security measures along their southern borders with Guatemala and Belize and throughout the country's interior. Consequently, detentions of child migrants by Mexican authorities increased from 9,630 in 2013 to 40,114 in 2016. Deportations of child migrants from Mexico have followed a similar trajectory, jumping from 8,477 in 2013 to 38,555 in 2016. Between 2015 and 2019, Mexico

deported at least 635,761 Central Americans in total.[26] Lately, Mexico has deported more Central Americans than the United States has. Thus, it may be surprising that, in the context of this clampdown, only two of the fifty-eight youth we interviewed had been formally detained by immigration agents in Mexico. Carmen, who was thirteen years old and coming from El Salvador, and Miguel, who was twelve and also from El Salvador, each made three separate trips trying to reach the United States.

Increased enforcement activities in Mexico have undoubtedly impacted the human smuggling enterprise as a whole by both redrawing smuggling routes and forcing coyotes to make provision for the possibility of making up to three trips before successfully reaching the U.S. border, as is frequently reflected in some of their higher-end fees. It is likely that we have not included in this study migrants who were detained or deported in Mexico and were thus unable to finish the journey. It is also likely that those respondents who made multiple attempts would report having been detained in Mexico. In 2024, the chances were higher that immigrants passing through Mexico would be stopped, detained, and possibly deported.

3. *Repeat migration is one factor behind the ballooning number of detentions and deportations in Mexico.* Despite an upward trend in immigration enforcement activities in Mexico, those efforts may prove ineffective in preventing child migrants from reaching the U.S.-Mexico border and presenting themselves to Border Patrol agents. Paradoxically, increased detentions in Mexico coincided with increased apprehensions at the U.S.-Mexico border in 2016. It is not altogether implausible that greater numbers of youth may indeed be leaving the Northern Triangle and thus accounting for larger numbers of apprehensions on both sides of the border, but another possible explanation is suggested by the experience of the study's two youth migrants detained in Mexico. Carmen and Miguel had been detained and deported by Mexican authorities twice before making it to the United States on their third attempt. On the first occasion, Carmen was detained and deported along with her younger sister. The younger sister managed to reach the U.S.-Mexico border undetected on her second attempt. The fact that these two girls accounted for five apprehensions by U.S. and Mexican authorities frustrates researchers' use of detentions, apprehensions, or, even worse, "encounters" as a proxy for the number of individuals

intending to immigrate into the United States.[27] Their experience also underscores the relative futility of Mexico's immigration enforcement activities when migrants clearly intend to migrate and are willing to make the attempt multiple times—as was the case for decades for undocumented Mexican migrants.[28]

4. *Family separation has been shown to be the single most important factor affecting multiple attempts to migrate.*[29] One mother's account of her daughter's deportations from Mexico seems to extend this finding to at least a subset of youth migrants. When asked whether her daughter had been offered asylum in Mexico, the mother responded affirmatively; however, she added, the family had no interest in asylum in Mexico since the purpose of the journey had always been to have her daughter with her in the United States. Unlike the United States, Mexico has yet to impose harsh sanctions on repeat unlawful entry. So, "revolving door" migration is likely to continue to be the norm among migrants who are fleeing adverse conditions in their countries of origin and are determined to reunite with family in the United States.

5. *Human smuggling networks are increasingly sophisticated.* At the time of this study, around 2016, rather than remaining with a single coyote for the duration of the journey, youth routinely reported being transferred to different coyotes during the various legs of their trek— a finding that points to the growing complexity of smuggling networks. As migrants pass from one cartel-controlled sector to another, they are handed off to a different coyote who is "authorized" to transport goods and people through that criminal group's territory. Presumably, this increasing sophistication has also allowed coyotes, who are now limited to managing just a subsection of the journey, to become more effective at either evading local law enforcement officials within their bounded territories or paying them off.

## The Implications of a Torturous Journey

This chapter has described the myriad obstacles that both minor and adult immigrants face on their journey through Mexico and when they arrive at the U.S.-Mexico border. As discussed in the following chapters, migration trajectory and integration are interconnected processes: the easier the migration journey is, the easier integration ought to be. Traumatic experiences can add barriers to integration, and the U.S.

externalization or remote control of immigration forces children and families to take potentially traumatic ground routes north. Those who can fly to the United States with legal authorization presumably suffer a great deal less than those who travel through Mexico with coyotes or on La Bestia. By examining the experiences of unaccompanied youth coming to the United States, we can better understand how others of any age and background experience immigration through Mexico and how it affects them.

CHAPTER FIVE

# LEGAL UNCERTAINTY, FAMILY REUNIFICATION, AND LEARNING A NEW LIFE

In this chapter, we describe some of the anti-immigrant policies and tensions that both accompanied and unaccompanied immigrant children and youth face when they reunite with family members after years of living separated by borders.[1] We also provide an overview of the external legal stressors that can compound in the reunification setting. Informants reported that getting used to cohabitation and in-person relationships with their parents or another sponsor was difficult initially but improved over time. Despite their biological, emotional, and financial bonds, minors had to learn how to relate to new authority figures and decide whether or how to follow their rules. Many of the youth we interviewed reported that they felt lonely and missed their grandmothers and other family members and friends left behind in their country of birth. The interviews open a window on intrafamily dynamics that are often overseen in discussions of the integration of immigrant children and youth into their new homes and communities.

This chapter focuses on furthering our understanding of the process of refugee and transnational family reunification—the primary reason why immigrant minors come to the United States from Central America. We describe how they position themselves within the new nuclear family as they go through the reunification process and, for many of them, await a decision on their asylum case. We also investigate how they view their interactions with the legal and immigration court systems. We specifically look at minors' response to house rules, their perceptions of their sponsors (parents or legal guardians in the

https://doi.org/10.7758/dvxg2393.3110

United States), and the impact of their interactions with those in their new homes and communities on their new lives in the United States.

## Legal Barriers Encountered during the Reunification Process

INTERVIEWER: Has your pending legal status affected the opportunities that you have had?

SEBASTIÁN (age eighteen, from El Salvador): A ton. It's affected me personally because I've come to feel less than the others. It's affected me a lot now because it's time to apply to university, scholarships, government assistance, and all that, and I've been very limited.

The children and young adults interviewed reported varying experiences with U.S. immigration authorities, both during procedures at the border and after they had been placed with sponsors or shelters. It is important to note that our sample of settled youth in the D.C. area, by definition, cannot include those who were unable to leave Central America, who were unable to make it to the border, or who were immediately sent back at the border or later deported from within the U.S. interior. All of the youth in our study had already been placed in the custody of their sponsors and thus had been allowed to stay at least temporarily in the United States. Many were working on obtaining a more permanent status. Some already had a green card or permanent authorization when they came; in this section, we focus on other youth among our interviewees who were looking to regularize their status and secure their ability to stay in the United States. This section on legal struggles precedes the later section on family reunification, which focuses on families with any legal status, so that we can first illustrate the different kinds of stresses that can inform the reunification process.

In general, these minors did not know very much about their cases; they would say that their parents were the ones who knew what was going on, even when they were preparing for a court date coming up soon. If they had lawyers who met with them frequently, then they generally felt that the lawyers were doing a good job and would get a fair outcome for them. Youth whose lawyers were less active reported having lower confidence levels.

## NAVIGATING THE U.S. IMMIGRATION SYSTEM AS A YOUNG ADULT

As explained earlier, immigrant youth who arrive at the border without a parent are classified as "unaccompanied alien children" and placed in the custody of the Office of Refugee Resettlement, where the sponsorship process begins. If they are with a parent upon crossing the border and the government pursues criminal charges against the parent, then the minor is also placed in ORR custody apart from the parent; otherwise, they are placed in a family shelter with their parents and released on their own recognizance (ROR). At this point they have several options, any of which would allow them to remain in the country with a sponsor (a parent, relative, or close family friend): they can apply for asylum, for special immigrant juvenile (SIJ) status, or for a T visa or a U visa. T or U status is for victims of trafficking and other crimes such as domestic violence; SIJ status is for children with one or both parents who have been found guilty of abuse, neglect, or abandonment. While youth have more options for attaining legal residency than adults do, they often find navigating this process unclear and confusing.[2]

Many immigrants come to the United States assuming that they will have access to jobs and education and will do well if they work hard.[3] Others are aware of the barriers encountered before the granting of citizenship. In her research, anthropologist Sarah Mahler finds that many Salvadorans find it worthwhile to migrate undocumented because work in the United States pays much better than it does at home.[4] Yet they still face innumerable challenges, and the economy has gotten tighter for all working people—working-class immigrants included—since the time Mahler wrote about in the early 1990s. For instance, many immigrants' children have dreams of going to college, a goal that is often drastically more fiscally challenging without citizenship, federal financial aid being unavailable to undocumented students and even to DACA recipients. Additionally, jobs that will pay enough to produce prosperity and savings in the United States, rather than just money to remit, are harder to come by without papers, underscoring the importance of pathways to legalization in the United States.

Some interviewees saw a lawyer frequently, and others hardly saw them at all. Daniella, an eighteen-year-old Salvadoran, said that she visited her lawyer fourteen to twenty days of the month and that, "for the time being, everything is going well. My papers are all in order. There are no issues right now. I just have to wait." However, not every youth we interviewed expressed as much confidence or awareness about their immigration cases as Daniella did about hers. Diana, age sixteen and also from El Salvador, said: "No, we go to the court, and then, they don't tell us anything. The lawyer said that they weren't going to give us anything, that . . . I mean, we didn't have hope, faith, that they would give us, I don't know, a permit [to stay]."

Overall, youth understood that they were under strict watch while their cases were being processed, whether they saw their lawyer frequently or not. Many reported that they had been told that anything they did could be used against them in immigration proceedings. Fifteen-year-old Carlos, who was from El Salvador, knew that he had to attend school, not work, and stay out of trouble. "I was in a migration center, but not the court. I understood the rules: I shouldn't miss school, I shouldn't work . . . mostly that."

Carlos had been nervous about the immigration system from the start. Once he was in ORR custody, he felt safe, but he said that at the border he was nervous because of how officials spoke to him and mistreat him: "In the center for minors, they treated me well. In the immigration center, they speak very angrily to you. I felt nervous because they spoke to me very angrily." Carlos understood the basics of what he needed to do to be able to stay in the United States, but he also felt that his family's lawyer was not helpful. His words echoed Diana's sentiments:

> One time I went with my father with that lawyer who has my brothers' cases, but he never tells them anything, and they have been here for three years already, and he doesn't say anything. He didn't help us that much. . . . I don't know anything regarding the decision on my case.

Lackadaisical or erratic attention from lawyers, unfortunately, parallels other instances of dysfunction within the larger system. Responsibility for providing care, information, and help during migrants' early days in the United States is split between CBP, the ORR, and sometimes the migrants themselves, a division of labor that can have disastrous consequences if the sponsor is not intentionally acting in the best interest of a child migrant. Nonprofit refugee resettlement and legal aid organizations were the largest sources of help for the migrants in our study. Some of these organizations were independent, and others were affiliated with the Catholic Church or the Lutheran Church, both of which often receive federal funding for this purpose. Seventeen-year-old Maria, who came from Honduras, was able to get help from the Catholic Church: "At the Catholic center, they gave us a pamphlet. They always call us, and we went to a few talks. We went to look for a lawyer there. And the lawyer is a very good lawyer. She helps us a lot because now we're only waiting for the residence permit for me and my brother."

While Maria's lawyer was attentive, this was too often not the case with other lawyers, for structural reasons. Many immigration lawyers and public defenders are overrun with cases and lack the time to meet with each client they are assigned. Manuel, a sixteen-year-old from El Salvador, said that he had never seen the lawyer working on his case. The lawyer was too busy to make the time. His parents had seen the lawyer for him, but Manuel himself did not seem to know what was going on with his case or have confidence that his lawyer was actually going to help him.

The implications and effects of the legal system go beyond having confidence or not in one's lawyers or gaining a permit to stay in the United States. All of those who are subject to its decisions are personally affected. Sebastián explained how being in court and having to deal with his immigration applications made him feel: "It has affected me personally because I've come to feel like I am worth less than others." He went on to explain the impact of not yet having a legal decision on other parts of his life: "It's affected me a lot now to apply to university, scholarships, government assistance, and all that, and I've been very limited."

For someone going through a life-course transition, not knowing if they will legally be able to remain where they are is both nerve-wracking and distressful. While many of his peers were applying to college, seeking scholarships and federal aid, Sebastián was stuck waiting to see if he would still be in the country in a year. Going to school and gaining skills would help him become the person he aspired to be as well as who the government allegedly wanted him to be. Migrants encounter these legal barriers in one way or another at all levels, during their K-12 years as well as when they are seeking post-secondary opportunities.[5]

Family life also complicated our interviewees' ability to attend appointments and respond to court orders—indeed, sometimes making it impossible—and the system grants little flexibility. Two respondents who were siblings explained that their younger sibling was born on the day they had court-ordered appointments, which they could not attend because of the birth. Francisco, age thirteen and from Honduras, said that, about a year before, "we didn't go to the court because my mom was giving birth to my little sister, who is a year old now, and that's why we didn't go to the court. My mom went the next day, but they told her no, that we all had deportation orders." Juana, Francisco's sixteen-year-old sister, said that she hid after missing that court date:

> Once we went to immigration because they didn't take us to court when we first came, and we had only gone once before. They gave us the appointment for February 2. But we couldn't go that day because my little sister was born that day, and we missed our court date. And we were like hiding [afterwards] because, if they arrest us, we'd be deported.

Francisco and his family eventually were able to clear their deportation orders. Nevertheless, the U.S. immigration system is often confusing and bureaucratic for youth and their families. These experiences—having to hide after unavoidably missing a court date and putting postsecondary plans on hold while an immigration application works its way through the system—shed light on some of the immigration system's structural issues that can inhibit the integration of young adults. For Juana and Francisco, entering the United States, being held, being released, and then obtaining asylum were not easy; then they had to meet several additional challenges to even be considered for any sort of permanent residency. They faced one of these challenges within the school system. In later chapters, we look at how youth integrate into school, as they struggle with their often liminal immigration status and continue to work through the trauma so many experienced on their immigration journey.

As discussed in chapter 3, many youth migrants who leave their home country have to make this decision on a moment's notice. Sometimes parents do not inform their children of their plan to send them to the

United States and keep it a secret from even their loved ones, fearing that gangs or the police in their community might discover their plan and thwart it. Some of interviewees knew that their parents had planned to send them to the United States, but even for them, concrete plans were usually not made until just before they started their journey. In numerous instances, parents handed a suitcase to their children and told them to pack because they would be leaving the country in one or two days. Although they may dream of immigrating to the United States, most young prospective migrants do not plan their life around migration, and they are neither versed in nor up to date on U.S. immigration law.

## Family Reunification: Struggles, Challenges, and Successes

Central Americans have been migrating out of necessity and sometimes are compelled to make a last-minute decision or a secret plan. In the migratory patterns we have seen, migrants tend to follow embedded social networks in the United States; family reunification remains a significant factor that motivates youth to migrate. Opportunity, economics, and education also remain among the top motives for the decision to separate a family and send unaccompanied children to the United States.

After traveling through Mexico and navigating the U.S. immigration system, youth must resume their day-to-day lives in the area around Washington, D.C., sometimes with a parent they have not seen in years and sometimes with a different family member or family friend. Even youth who are able to reunite with a parent often find a new stepparent or new siblings in the picture. Many parents who migrate when they are single will find a partner or spouse in the host country. In studying Central American mothers in the New York City area, Sandra Castro found that many of them found a romantic partner who provided love and companionship. However, due to legal liminality and financial stress, among other issues, some of these mothers felt stuck in a relationship that had become abusive.[6]

This stage has its own set of challenges for a youth migrant, who must integrate into a new family, community, school, and culture. It is certainly possible to meet these challenges, however, and after spending several years living in the United States and making these adjustments, many youth appreciate having access to more opportunities. Those in our study did not deny that immigrating had benefited them more than staying in their country of birth would have. At the same time, some acknowledged that the legal uncertainty they dealt with after arriving had been a source of stress.

Many families are separated for years, and both transnational parenting and family reunification can be difficult. There are other challenges when the sponsor is not a parent but another family member or a friend. Most of the children interpreted their position within their new family as one of the following:

1. They felt welcomed and gradually accepted as they were by family members.
2. They experienced friction at first with one or more members of the household but eventually improved those relationships.
3. They may have felt accepted but maintained a distance between themselves and all of the nuclear family members, including their sponsor.
4. They did not feel accepted and distanced themselves from their sponsor and family in the United States.

In any strong relationship, acceptance, communication, and understanding are three key aspects that affect the relationship between parents and children. In reunifying families, we found that, if the child felt heard and seen in their new family, even if they acknowledged differences between its members, they had happier relationships with their parents.

This chapter discusses how the circumstances of sponsor placement, reunification, and in-home context shape integration outcomes. Much of the existing literature on reunification describes the emotional and psychological impacts on youth—how they feel when they find themselves in a new nuclear family, often with family members they view as strangers.[7] We focus on how the migrants interact and position themselves within a new and often unfamiliar nuclear family and how they react to new situations, surroundings, and people in their lives. We find that, in general, those from more precarious financial backgrounds struggle more with new surroundings than their better-off counterparts. Some of the dynamics, however, are similar for all youth.

First, we briefly review some of the literature on family reunification and Central American youth. Then we report our findings and discuss their implications. In this section, we contribute to the overall literature on family reunification by discussing the integration process for Central American youth during the Trump administration in the U.S. capital area.

## Understanding Reunification, Family Separation, and the Idea of "Home"

We view family reunification as a process rather than a onetime event. Several factors that shape the family reunification process can have a massive effect on parents and children: the journey northward, the time spent apart (which sometimes can span more than a decade), and differences in life in the new country.[8] The length and efficacy of the reunification process thus depend on several factors: the amount of time spent separated from the parent(s); whether one or both parents left; the age of the youth at the time of the parents' migration; gender; sexual orientation; and parents' financial well-being and security.

Upon reunification, a young person may be excited to be with their parents or other sponsors, but as mentioned earlier, we must stress that youth often experience grief from leaving their caregivers in their country of origin.[9] Once these initial feelings fade, these minors—particularly adolescents and young adults—and parents alike report that "the long-term separation creates a sense of estrangement."[10] In previous research on Mexican immigrant youth adjusting to the United States, some described resentment because they felt the need to compete for their mother's time and attention with their new siblings or her new spouse.[11] Resentment contributed to an overall feeling of invisibility for many migrant children. Moreover, many young women and girls reported that their parents assigned them new responsibilities, such as doing domestic chores and taking care of siblings.[12] The work left them feeling physically and emotionally overburdened. The male participants often reported, however, that, even though they felt like they had a designated role, they felt "unburdened" compared to the female participants.

Furthermore, many minors reported that their expectations of their parents did not match reality.[13] In Ceres Artico's interviews with

Latin American youth undergoing reunification with their families, two common themes appeared: unmet parental expectations and feelings of loss or grief.[14] Artico stresses that youth may decide not to disclose some of these feelings. She argues that the children become their parents' emotional guardian, a position in which they lean into a "vow" of silence and secrecy around the emotions and challenges related to separation and reunification as well as to immigration status.

Carola Suárez-Orozco and her colleagues interviewed migrant youth from Central America, China, the Dominican Republic, Haiti, and Mexico who had been separated from their parents.[15] Their study focused on how the parent's migration impacted the migrant youth's psychological well-being once they were reunited with that parent. The authors interviewed migrants shortly after they arrived in the United States and once again after five years. They found an association between anxiety and depression levels and the amount of time separated from the parent. The youth who were separated for four years or more from their mother reported higher levels of anxiety and depression than youth who were separated for less than two years from their fathers or from both parents. It has also been found that some undocumented minors and U.S. citizens who have undocumented family members feel a lack of belonging.[16] Some also report feeling like they live in purgatory or limbo.[17]

Myrna Lashley describes the child's predicament: they miss their caregiver, they must adapt to a new household, and they acclimate to society through their peers.[18] The parents' predicament lies in getting to know their children anew, helping them adjust to a new country, and setting boundaries for them. Many parents have not seen their children in years. Similarly, Rousseau and her colleagues found similar predicaments emerging from their interviews with Congolese refugees in Montreal, Canada, about their families' reunification experiences.[19]

As Sonia Nazario chronicles, a young man named Enrique, after many attempts and long months, finally joined his mother in North Carolina. Nevertheless, once reunited, they would often fight. Enrique was full of rage and resentment about his mother's departure and would not obey her, saying that, since it was his grandmother who raised him, she was the only one who could reprimand him. His mother would often answer that, since she sent money to him, he owed her gratitude, credit, love, and respect.[20]

Artico had similar results from her interviews with parent-adolescent pairs. Immigrating often allowed parents to become relatively good providers of economic resources but constrained their ability, from the children's point of view, to provide emotional resources.[21] The reality is that parental migration is a crisis in the lives of children. The separation following migration is likely to alter the nature of the child-parent relationship forever; this relationship may be repaired and restored, but many children of migrants report feeling a void that cannot be filled. When a family member migrates, they may plan on returning, but no plan to return is ever made. There is no dated return ticket. Eventual return always seems possible in the minds of the migrant and the family, but more vivid to them is the absence.

These long absences are often caused by restrictive immigration policies that make border-crossing trips expensive and unauthorized; thus, it is incredibly difficult for many migrants to visit their families. Much like the families of soldiers at war, the families of immigrants must adjust to having one of their own away and not knowing when or whether they will return. The uncertainty of being separated from a family member for an indefinite time—what Pauline Boss has called "ambiguous loss"—can be more anxiety-provoking than mourning the final loss of a loved one to death.[22]

Families may first experience structural separation owing to economic need and then forced separation later on, after reunification, when a family member is deported.[23] Scholars have examined these separations by focusing on the resulting transnational families: family units in which one or more family members leave and the others stay in the home country.[24] Others have looked at those families who reunify later on, or become binational if they have permission to travel.[25] Joanna Dreby underlines children's agency in migration decisions.[26] Leisy Abrego reveals the variations in the ambivalence of youth left behind in El Salvador, depending on their resources. Youth who were struggling financially and emotionally were unclear about their future in the United States, while those who were more financially secure expressed a desire to stay in El Salvador.[27]

Researchers have noted some salient themes from reunification processes: overcoming challenges, finding strength, developing bicultural coping skills, increasing and improving communication between parent and child, parents empathizing with their adolescent children, and finding social support.[28] Other researchers make clear the connection between supportive families and the psychosocial health and well-being of resettled youth from refugee backgrounds.[29] Families and children can struggle internally and externally if they lack aspects of psychosocial health and strong communication skills, as can be the case during migration and family reunification. Youth experience various situations during the migration and reunification processes, and each possesses unique coping skills for handling them.

These aspects of reunification are inextricably tied to the experience of home in the context of migration. Researchers argue that "home" in migration is a culturally oriented experience tied to the interpersonal process of acquiring a sense of security, familiarity, and control.[30] In a migration context, a youth's departure is an upheaval from the old home and an arrival in a place that could become a new home but that may feel foreign for both them and their parents. In what is essentially a search for a sense of belonging and safety there can be consequences and successes that are not mutually exclusive. In Castañeda's conceptualization, feeling at home in a metropolitan area is an important sign of feelings of safety and belonging.[31] Thus, it is important that Central American youth feel at home, not only in their family home but also in the larger region that they inhabit, be it Washington, D.C., New York, Houston, or anywhere else.[32]

## Getting Used to a New Family

Karina shared that she was raised by her grandmother in El Salvador and did not meet her biological mother until she was ten years old. As a result, Karina did not have a strong maternal connection at age eighteen, when she was interviewed. As she said, "Building up strong family relationships after being separated for a long time is complicated. I left my grandmother, and I did all this sacrifice for something better, so I have to make it worthwhile." The pressure, obligation, and need to self-sacrifice that mothers feel when leaving their daughters behind is now carried by their migrating daughters for leaving their grandmothers behind. The emotional and psychological effects of migration are multigenerational.

Most people we talked to reported that getting used to a new relationship with their parents or other sponsor was difficult at first, though it improved over time. Samantha, age fifteen, had not seen her mother in years and was very little when she left for the United States. That made Samantha's first year in the United States challenging. She felt lonely and reported missing her grandmother and her sister, who had felt like a mother more than anyone else when she was still living in Honduras. Melissa (age fourteen), David (thirteen), and Sarah (eighteen) also reported that one of the greatest challenges of moving to the United States was leaving behind other relatives, like their grandmothers, who had raised them and felt like their mothers.

Fernanda, who migrated at age thirteen (though she had not wanted to), came by plane from El Salvador with immigration papers. She would find it difficult to integrate into her family in the United States.

> I felt that I really wasn't with my mother because I've always felt that my real mother was my grandmother, because she's been with me since I was little. She raised me since I was very young. She gave me everything I needed, like love. What I've always wanted is that my mother would give me, that she loved me.

Those who feel disconnected from their parents when they move may face even more challenges. Having spent her early years in El Salvador with her grandmother, Fernanda felt alienated from her new nuclear family. Everyone in the house got along with everyone else, though it seemed to her that her stepfather was never happy. Family reunification is not easy and can exacerbate old problems or create new ones.

Even as they struggled to adapt, however, many of our respondents reported that the benefits of family reunification were worth the struggles. For instance, Carlos's life changed in several ways when he migrated. With his father keeping a close eye on him and his siblings, Carlos gained a sense of safety and comfort that he did not have in his previous community. He did not mind his father keeping tabs on him. Similarly, Sarah reported that being back with her mother and having a better experience in school was a positive experience for her.

Having made drastic sacrifices to find a better life for their families and children, many parents harbored a significant fear of failure, whether financial, legal, or immigration-related, arising from a fear of what was going on in their home country. One mother, Ana, came to the United States with her children so that her family could escape the crime and poverty in her country of birth and achieve the American dream. She struggled financially in the United States as she worked to cover rent and legal fees and to pay off over $16,000 to the coyotes who brought her five children to the border. Ana, however, did not particularly fear ICE. By contrast, another mother, Karla, feared that either she or her children would be deported. She was afraid of the political and economic instability in El Salvador and did not want the family to have to go back.

Even if the children felt integrated and developed a sense of belonging in the United States, the parents would fear for their safety, even in the United States, and might not feel a sense of belonging themselves. Such fears might have affected the way that they parented. One mother we interviewed kept a close eye on her children and their whereabouts, saying, "This country is not theirs."

## Interpreting and Redrawing Boundaries

The youth varied in their responses to having household rules and in how they interpreted the rules. This variation was often related to the time they had spent apart from their parent(s), the presence of new family members, and the family's economic situation.

For some, the new home's rules and their importance were clearly spelled out; other youth found themselves in new homes where the rules were less clear. Still others might not have understood the rules or agreed with their parents on their importance. Isabela, a seventeen-year-old from El Salvador residing in Montgomery County, said that she understood her mother's rules to be in her best interest. Her trust and respect for her mother made it easy for her to obey the rules.

Elizabeth and Monica, however, found their parents' rules overly cumbersome. Elizabeth, a sixteen-year-old from Guatemala residing in Prince George's County, Maryland, detailed her mother's misgivings about her friends, which she did not understand. Her mother's attitude made her feel bad, and like any sixteen-year-old, she felt alienated from her mother because of it. As a result, she thought of her mother as "worse than a police officer." Likewise, Monica, a fifteen-year-old from Guatemala also living in Prince George's County, Maryland, had to ask for permission to go out. Her father's response was always no, she said, so she was always stuck at home.

Most respondents felt that the rules in their new homes were limiting—an indication of struggles between themselves and their sponsors related to communication, respect, and trust. All children and adolescents, immigrant or not, may have power struggles and differences with their parents, but the unique situations of immigrant youth significantly affect both rules and relationships in their lives. Immigrant youth balance two cultures as they learn the rules and requirements of their new household and country. Our data show that minors who were raised by someone other than the parent with whom they have been reunited may feel some resentment, distrust, and fear of a new separation that could get in the way of their relationship with their parents, as well as trouble understanding or agreeing with the rules set for them.

Other minors, especially older ones, reported that their new home had no rules per se but mentioned that their sponsors sometimes imposed basic limits on them or warned them about certain situations. Alexander, a twenty-year-old from El Salvador (who, importantly in this context, migrated at age seventeen), said that his mother had no specific rules for him but made general suggestions that he respected. For instance, when his mother thought that someone who was in his life was not a good influence, instead of forbidding him from seeing them, she would warn, "Be careful, this person is not good for you, because they are involved in things you shouldn't be." Alexander then did not need to be told that he was not allowed to do something. "I respect her opinion," he said, "because she knows more than us." Alexander seemed to have a strong relationship with his mother, bolstered by their mutual respect.

For Valentina, a sixteen-year-old from El Salvador residing in Montgomery County, the situation was similar. Valentina said that her mother "tells me to watch who I'm with and to not be a bad influence." Valentina even stated that she would be willing to follow any rules that her mother might put in place. After a certain age, mutual trust and respect emerge as keys to whether children and young adults are happy in their new homes.

Fernanda, age fifteen when she was interviewed and residing in Montgomery County, stated that she was still told what she was or was not allowed to do. Her mother neither allowed her to go out with friends nor let her friends come over. Fernanda inferred that her mother's disapproval came from her stepfather: "My stepfather is very grumpy. He doesn't like anyone coming over." At the time of her interview, she had been living in the United States for two years. As indicated by Fernanda's story, the struggles that come with having new stepparents and stepsiblings can compound the struggles of simply being a fifteen-year-old.

### Moving in with Biological Parents: "I Don't Call Her Mom, I Call Her 'Vos'"

This section details the dynamics of relationships between children and their mothers who are also their sponsors. Some appeared to have little trouble reintegrating with their mothers, but others seemed to be dealing with feelings of resentment or abandonment that stemmed from the time they had spent apart.

Seventeen-year-old Elizabeth, who lived with her grandmother before migrating from Honduras, described reunification with her mother as "nice": "With my grandma and with her, I have the same love because . . . I always maintained contact with her. And (*pause*) . . . in all honesty, I felt the same support." Even while her grandmother was raising her in El Salvador, she still felt connected with and loved her mother. Not everyone in her situation could say that.

Some respondents used first names to refer to their biological mothers, something that they would have not normally done had they been raised by them. Twenty-year-old Alexander, who was also looked after by his grandmother in El Salvador, described his understanding of and feelings toward his biological mother. He mentioned that she had been "attentive to all of us," but added, "I don't call her Mom, I call her 'Vos.'" He explained:

> I treat her like a friend because she tells us: "I know, I understand, because you all have grown up with my mother and from one minute to another you won't say Mom, or something . . . you all care more for my mom than me. And I know I have to understand, but little by little you will get used to me," she says. "Yes," I say, "but remember, we have spent a great amount of time with my grandma. We never forgot you, but we have spent more time with my grandma."

Many Salvadorans refer to their mothers using the formal "you," *usted*, out of respect. Salvadorans use *vos*, the informal "you," with individuals they know and are comfortable with (in the same manner as *tú* elsewhere). This usage has been adopted by Hondurans in the United States as well.[33] By referring to his mother as *vos*, Alexander acknowledged his comfort with his mother while upholding his grandmother's role as his primary caregiver, whom he talked to using *usted*. Alexander did not refer to his mother as "Mom" and acknowledged that he saw her as more like an older friend. Furthermore, his mother understood that, with time, Alexander and his siblings would slowly get used to her. He saw his mother as understanding and accepting their situation. Their mutual understanding may have helped Alexander respect and understand his mother's suggestions to him. For his sister Flor, however, the relationship with their mother was different.

Flor explained that her mother once had rules that she did not like, but as she approached eighteen, the rules seemed to stop being enforced. Her mother may have understood that she had done a good job educating her now legally adult daughter and that it was time for Flor to make her own decisions. Earlier, however, her Catholic beliefs had clashed with her mother's evangelical Christianity. When she first arrived, Flor recalled, "we went around the house arguing." Eventually, Flor said that she started to read the Bible to please her mother. Getting used to a new church during that time changed her relationship with her mother. Later, when she stopped attending church and became interested in reading other materials, her mother said, "You have drifted away from God." Flor and Alexander had different relationships with the same mother, perhaps owing in part to their genders, ages, or other characteristics.

Flor's relationship with her mother largely revolved around their differences in core beliefs, such as religion. Flor's experience illuminates that when a migrant leaves their home country, they do not just leave the country and its borders. They also leave their community, and trying to be part of a different and maybe unfamiliar community can be very lonely and difficult. Furthermore, youth and their parents experience these changes disjointedly and in different ways. For Flor, immigration did not draw her closer to religion, but it may have for her mother. When her mother saw her daughter struggling, she thought she was not close enough to God; Flor had a different perspective.

When Fernanda was still in El Salvador, she spoke with her mother regularly and felt close to her, so she thought that their relationship would stay that way when she was in the United States. However, when she arrived, she felt as though her mother was always angry. Adapting to a new setting and a new life can be hard for both the parents and children, and it can be challenging for the children to understand that their parents may be going through the same things they are. "Teleparenting" is a difficult endeavor that can create tension and lead to feelings of abandonment or resentment, even if social media allows members of a transnational family to stay on top of daily activities and get updates and permission for big decisions. Nelson said that he talked to his father in the United States every two hours when he was in Central America. Some jobs allow this level of communication, but many do not. Even frequent phone conversations do not create the tensions and frictions that daily cohabitation inevitably sparks once families are reunited. Many experience being together again as a rude awakening.[34] Moving in with a new person requires a lot of implicit negotiations and accommodations.

When Isabela listed the individuals who understood her, she mentioned her new friends, friends from her country of origin, and her godmother. When she was asked why she did not include her mother, she stated:

> Because I don't get along well with her, and to this day I don't know if she has won over my affection because she's only ever mad and blames my brother and me for everything. When my brother calls, all the anger, everything generated from that day, everything is taken out on us. She prefers a million times that man. He is not my dad; he is my stepfather. Sometimes she says it's our fault if they get separated. I would prefer a million times that she gives me up for adoption or return to my country, instead of her saying in the future, "Look, because of you I separated from my husband," because they're married. That's why I don't get along with her.

Isabela offered clear examples to show why she saw her mother as someone who did not understand her and why she felt hurt and distant from her mother, even after the physical distance was removed. She even expressed a wish to have been either adopted or allowed to stay in her home country, away from her mother. Some tensions and struggles are often inevitable, but individual relationships between family members often go fine from the start, or they improve over time. Just as the greater external context—the neighborhood and the city—matters to integration and placemaking, so does the internal context—who else occupies youths' new homes and is in their new lives.

Valentina described the change over time in her relationship with her father, who was not her sponsor but whom she was allowed to have a relationship with. When migrating, she was full of anticipation about seeing him, since she had only ever lived with her mother and sibling. Initially, she admitted feeling weird about being with and talking to him. She explained that at first her relationship with her father was "distant, I mean, like I didn't feel the same as when I was with my mom." Now she was used to him, and all three of them, Valentina and both her parents, spent time talking together. Valentina's initial feeling of distance from or unfamiliarity with her father grew into greater acceptance of him.

Similarly, Alexander described his relationship with his stepfather as pleasant, explaining that "he treats us well. He doesn't bother us, nor do we bother him. He has acted beyond well with us. The relationship is close. He is attentive to everything." Monica said that she had "normal" problems with her father because her mother did not live with them. She mentioned that she felt safe enough with him because her mother had advised her "that he is my dad, for me to have trust, all of that"; she disclosed, however, that she would have felt safer if her mother was with her. While Monica felt that she had only "normal" problems with her father and did not feel unsafe with him, she reported, something was still missing from her relationship with him.

Fernanda, by contrast, had difficulty getting along with multiple family members. She did not get along with her brother, her sister, or her mother. The only family members she did get along with were her younger sisters. Fernanda recognized that she was the only person in the family having a difficult time, since most of the others were "happy and get along well together," with the exception of her stepfather, who, she said, was "rarely ever happy."

### The Importance of Mutual Respect

The youth who said that they felt welcome and accepted in their new home were almost all sponsored by their mothers. They may have experienced this positive reception because they were rejoining their mothers in the United States rather than leaving their biological mothers behind or moving in with other relatives who culturally might have been expected to be not as warm as their mothers.

Isabela's recognition that she should obey her mother's rules because those rules would be good for her can be interpreted as a sign of Isabela's respect for her mother. Moreover, reunification with her mother appeared to have gone seamlessly. Isabela said that she had received the same support from her mother in the United States as she did from her grandmother in El Salvador, and in return, she had the same loving feelings for each of them. By describing her mother and grandmother as equals, Isabela was expressing how important both women were to her, regardless of the time spent separated from one or the other of them. With a mother and grandmother who, she felt, were equally loving to her, Isabela had one less change to adapt to than other minors adjusting to life in the United States.

Similarly, Valentina said that, though her mother did not have rules, she would have followed them if they existed. Her willingness to follow such hypothetical rules demonstrates Valentina's respect for her mother's decision-making and feeling that she was being looked after positively. Valentina also described the initial difficulties with integrating her father into their family, but later she embraced the new family member. Valentina thus found herself in a unique situation: as a new family member herself, she now had to welcome another family member. Kristina Lovato-Hermann describes the feeling among some youth that they had to compete for attention and time from other family members; perhaps Valentina found it hard to accept her father's presence in the family at first from a similar feeling of competition with him.[35] Isabella and Valentina respected their mothers as authority figures who could enforce rules. Each of these minors respected and was comfortable with her mother, and in their mothers' welcoming households, both were able to integrate more easily.

Alexander was the only participant who seemed to feel accepted into the new family but who remained distant from his sponsor. Like Valentina, he reported that his mother had no rules, but she did warn him about some people and gave him general guidelines within a covenant of trust between them. Alexander clearly respected his mother because of her knowledge, but still addressed her as "*vos*." Also exemplifying the comfort level within his family was how well his stepfather had treated Alexander and how attentive he was to him. Nevertheless, in spite of being accepted into the family by his mother and stepfather, Alexander could not immerse himself in the family completely. Although he did not say this himself, Alexander's inability to forget his grandmother may have been rooted in feelings of loss and grief, which would have been worsened by his inability to travel between his hometown in El Salvador and D.C.[36] Similar to Alexander, many immigrant youth fear that they may never see their grandparents again because they might die while they are trying to legalize their status in the United States. Such a fear creates an ambiguous loss and unending grief.[37]

For Elizabeth, Fernanda, and Flor, their relationship with their mother was a large source of conflict. On the other hand, Monica's mother was a source of relief from the estrangement between Monica and her father. For many youth migrants, a third party—often a stepfather, mother's husband, or an unfamiliar father—caused estrangement between them and their mother, or least complicated their relationship with her. Elizabeth felt that her mother preferred her husband over Elizabeth and her brother, and Fernanda was unable to go on outings with friends or have them over because of her stepfather's grumpiness. Monica's estranged relationship with her father drove her further away from him. Instead, she yearned for her mother, whom she used as a source of support because she did not trust her father.

## A New Life in a New Context

Ultimately a youth's integration into a new nuclear family is influenced by their sponsor's commitment to family reunification and the family's collective ability to be together again and make children feel at home, heard, and accepted. Some youth may feel fully integrated and accepted but still maintain reservations or completely distance themselves from their sponsor, but often a reunified family can make it work and move toward acceptance, trust, and healthy communication.

As minors integrate into their families, their structural integration is equally important. As they integrate into U.S. society, organizations and governments must provide resources for parents, sponsors, and their children to facilitate this process. The next three chapters discuss such resources, which include language learning, access to therapy, quality health care, and workplace protections for all workers.

Reunification is also complicated by traumas that migrant youth may have experienced before or during the migration trip, as well as by fears and uncertainty about their legal status, durable challenges faced in school, an uncertain future, and general acculturation. Symptoms of post-traumatic stress in particular can make adjustment to new households and schools more difficult, as we discuss in the next chapter.[38]

CHAPTER SIX

# MENTAL HEALTH AND IMMIGRATION: SYMPTOMS OF PTSD AND DEPRESSION

The situations, experiences, and lives described up to this point in the book would raise eyebrows among many non-immigrants and immigrants alike. Many people can hardly imagine the experience of living in a gang-controlled area, being unable to go to school or to travel to the United States, being hungry and having no food, being stuck in a bus near the Guatemala-Mexico border with the doors barricaded and someone threatening to burn down the bus with you and everyone in it, or being shouted at by locals when transported from one immigration detention center to another. Many would also struggle to imagine what it would be like to meet your mother in person for the first time at the age of seventeen. Such experiences, of course, can have significant effects on the individuals who have them.[1]

Previously, we discussed family separation and some of its effects. As is well known, one of those effects is on mental health. Research has shown that children from families divided across borders are more likely to experience separation anxiety, ongoing grief, and low self-worth.[2] Studies have also demonstrated the role of familial cohesion and stability in behavioral outcomes for immigrant youth.[3] Those cared for by their parents or relatives have better behavioral outcomes than those who do not experience familial supervision or guidance.[4] In addition, a caregiver's documentation status affects the well-being of the youth in their care; for instance, immigrant youth who live with an undocumented caregiver are more likely to be stressed.[5] Even though the parents may become stable providers of money, clothes, food, and toys, children often cannot comprehend parental separation as anything other

https://doi.org/10.7758/dvxg2393.2272

than abandonment.⁶ For children who eventually reunite with their parents in the United States, those feelings of resentment and abandonment may linger.⁷ Despite the parents' best intentions, those who experience family separation as a child often struggle to form close and trusting relationships in their adult lives, including with partners and children.⁸ The experience of long-term separation, hardships in their country of origin, and the trauma and stress of their own migration journey and their legal statuses will weigh on their mental health post-migration.

Family separation has immediate and everyday consequences, but it can also have traumatic consequences that can take years for youth to overcome. Adverse childhood experiences (ACEs), as defined by the Centers for Disease Prevention and Control (CDC), include experiencing or witnessing violence, abuse, or neglect, or witnessing an attempted or successful suicide. Importantly, ACEs also include "aspects of the child's environment that can undermine their sense of safety, stability, and bonding such as growing up in a household with substance misuse, mental health problems, or instability due to parental separation."⁹ These experiences can have lifelong consequences, including a higher likelihood of being a victim of violence, engaging in risk behaviors, and developing other health and social issues. Furthermore, such consequences of trauma can negatively affect students at home and contribute to higher school dropout rates.¹⁰

In 1995, sociologists Jo Phelan and Bruce Link argued that social conditions could be fundamental causes of disease and that socioeconomic status affects not only opportunities and life chances but also health outcomes.¹¹ This proven hypothesis has become known as the "social determinants of health" approach. Heide Castañeda, Seth Holmes, and their collaborators, among others, have shown that experiencing migration is also a social determinant of health.¹² Using the social determinants of health approach as a framework to understand mental health, we argue that the migration and integration processes present unique stressors that can shape mental health outcomes.¹³ Most of the literature on immigration and mental health focuses on either the negative effects or the positive health outcomes despite adverse social conditions in what is known as the "Hispanic paradox," which is often attributed to cultural differences. Here we argue that sometimes the change in social context and family reintegration brought about by international migration can lead to better mental health, especially if the length of separation is short.

## Social Determinants of Mental Health

To recap, the experience of migrating has a lasting effect on mental health, especially that of migrant youth traveling alone, who face an increased risk of undernutrition, dehydration, assault, kidnapping, and other forms of violence.[14] Such traumatic experiences put migrants at higher risk for psychological distress and disorders, which may cause obstacles to integration that create new stressors and accumulate into compounded traumas.[15]

How they enter the country shapes the lives of migrant families and their children. While qualified workers, refugees, and asylum seekers are often allowed to immigrate as family units, most other migrating families are often separated. These separations take several different forms, such as immigration without a child because options for legal migration are limited, or migration by unaccompanied minors. In addition, some migrants travel to the United States without their children so as not to expose them to the perils of the journey or because they plan to work abroad to send remittances only temporarily.[16] Other families are forcibly separated upon arriving at the U.S. border, or after they have made it across and established their new lives. Parents who leave their children behind operate under structurally constrained choices and are forced to sacrifice present needs for their children's future economic security.[17] When limited options force a family to separate, their decision ultimately comes down to what the family believes to be most beneficial in the long run.[18]

As Amanda Venta and Alfonso Mercado have documented, the mental health experiences of youth migrants are unique.[19] The work of other researchers has suggested that rates of PTSD are higher among asylum seekers and immigrant youth.[20] This increased risk for PTSD may be due to premigration trauma or traumatic migration experiences.[21] Also implicated are unaccompanied migration; higher acculturation stress for older migrants; prolonged family separation; threats of deportation and forced separation; and discrimination and hate crimes.[22] Furthermore, youth migrants may struggle to maintain healthy adult relationships in the future.[23] Because of these impacts on the social contexts that migrants travel from and settle into, migration is a social determinant of mental health for this population.

In certain contexts, PTSD prevalence varies by gender. One study reported that female immigrants from Latin America experience high levels of trauma from domestic, community, emotional, physical, and sexual violence. Some experience abuse at the hands of the relatives with whom their parents left them when they migrated. A minor of any gender could experience being left behind and forced to deal with neglectful or abusive caretakers as emotional violence.[24]

### Structural Violence and Multigenerational Trauma

On a plane flying to El Salvador in 2021, a teacher from El Salvador told Castañeda that she became very familiar with Mexican culture while growing up in Los Angeles. She noted the many similarities between Mexican and Central American immigration but also one significant difference: the general existence of multigenerational trauma among Salvadorans. This was not a surprising observation, given that, as we discussed in chapter 2, Guatemala, Honduras, and El Salvador have suffered civil wars, forced disappearances, state-led violence, and genocide against Indigenous groups. Many have been forced to forget these events, yet there are long-term effects of doing so.[25]

Besides political and domestic violence, natural disasters and climate change have also had devastating effects. As Marcelo Suárez-Orozco writes:

> Hurricane Mitch hit Central America in 1998, leaving more than 11,000 dead and 8,000 missing and displacing more than 2.5 million Hondurans. Many Hondurans began a massive exodus to a country to which they had not migrated before: the United States. The hurricane left a catastrophic environmental and psychosocial sequel. Data from the Brown University School of Medicine estimate that out of a total of 3.3 million adults (age fifteen or older) living in Honduras, more than 492,000 have experienced post-traumatic stress disorder due to Hurricane Mitch (Kohn et al. 2005). More recently, as Suro . . . notes, "To make a horrific situation worse, Central America experienced the most severe drought in decades during this period with relief agencies counting 3.5 million people in the region as food insecure at mid-decade" (Chishti and Hipsman 2016).[26]

In sum, events external to the individual and the family can also deeply impact material conditions, and thus the physical and mental health of prospective migrants and immigrants in the United States.

## Stressors after Arrival

After arriving in the United States, immigrants experience challenges associated with language, economic hardships, and discrimination. The lack of social support while trying to integrate into mainstream society can add to acculturative stress,[27] migration-related stressors,[28] and psychiatric disorders.[29] A study by Brian Karl Finch, Bohdan Kolodny, and William Vega found that as someone born outside the United States acclimates to their new home, their perception of discrimination slowly increases as they learn English and become familiarized with their environs.[30] This increased awareness of discrimination and acculturation stress significantly correlated with depression. One study found that Latin youth populations have the highest risk for depression among multiple youth ethnic groups. Furthermore, it found that the perception of discrimination among migrants significantly decreases self-esteem.[31] Even in diverse states like Florida and California, 55 percent of adolescent Latin individuals have experienced at least one form of discrimination.[32] Central American immigrants with high levels of acculturative stress are more likely to experience depression, suicidal ideation, and anxiety.[33] Joseph Hovey concluded that this might be because they feel caught between two cultures.[34] However, Marianne Dunn and Karen O'Brien report that, even though Latin immigrants feel pressure to learn English quickly, they experience lower stress levels assimilating into American society compared to other groups.[35]

Thus, preexisting traumas and subsequent mental illness influence immigrants' psychological well-being and integration experience in the United States. The mental health of immigrants is connected not only to the potentially traumatic experiences they may have faced before arriving in the United States but also to U.S. government policies, which have a long history of excluding Latin people and have become increasingly restrictive since the 1990s.[36] In addition to the hostile and xenophobic social and political environment often faced by immigrants and their children, policy changes over the past three decades have primarily targeted undocumented immigrants, who were previously not singled out and could go about their lives relatively undisturbed.[37]

None of this is to say that every migrant goes through traumatic experiences. For example, immigrants who make the journey by plane and enter the United States with immigrant visas or as tourists experience less violence and trauma on the journey. By contrast, those with legal recourse to immigrating through family reunification often take the journey over land, where they may endure life-threatening incidents with gangs, thieves, or human smugglers.[38] After arriving in the United States, many experience sexual and physical violence but feel that their immigration status prevents them from reporting it to authorities.[39] As all of these examples demonstrate, providing administrative avenues for immigration and family reunification would not only make migration a safer experience for all but have many mental health advantages. Instead, racist immigration policies that increase animosity against immigrants have heightened the fear of deportation and worsened immigrants' mental health.[40]

## Self-Disclosed Potentially Traumatic Experiences

Although traumatic experiences do not always predispose individuals to emigrate, nevertheless they are often part of the complex mosaic compelling someone to leave their home and seek a new one. The young adults and children we interviewed sometimes reported traumatic experiences and abuse. In addition to their stories about gang threats and violence and the often traumatic journey north, participants in the study reported that they had experienced traumatic life events before migrating, such as the death of a caregiver or a personal trauma such as being abused or witnessing abuse in their home. In this section, we describe some of these traumatic experiences, using quotes from the interviews with the minors to examine them in detail. These cases are not exhaustive but represent common experiences.

### THE DEATH OF A CAREGIVER GRANDPARENT

Jisel lived with her grandparents in Honduras. Her grandfather died when she was four years old, and her grandmother when she was ten. She then lived with her aunt and later joined her mother in the D.C.

area. Eighteen-year-old Juan's situation was similar. When asked who he lived with before coming to the United States, Juan explained: "With my grandma, but my grandma died, so I lived alone."

Many of the events discussed here would be traumatic to anyone. For immigrant youth, however, they have unique meanings. Beatriz, age thirteen, described what it is like when a caregiver dies:

> Because when I was born, they killed my dad, and later my mom came here and left me with my grandma. But my grandma died in 2015 and left me with my aunt, and well, it's not the same as with my grandma, because she raised me from when I was little. I wanted to go with my mom after not seeing her for ten years and those sorts of reasons.

Traumatic events in Beatriz's family had compounded. Given that her mother had already gone to the United States after the murder of her father, Beatriz felt that it was time for her to leave El Salvador too after her grandmother's passing and join her mother in the United States. The death of her main caregiver seems to have been a turning point in Beatriz's decision to migrate to be with her mother.

Moving in with extended family they have never lived with before after a grandparent's death can be difficult for teenagers and young adults. Sometimes they find themselves in an abusive situation that creates lasting trauma. For example, after moving in with her aunt and uncle, sixteen-year-old Elizabeth was abused by them: "Before living with my cousin, I lived with my mom's sister, then I moved away from that house because my aunt and uncle would hit me for things that I didn't do." When asked whether they had children of their own, Elizabeth replied, "Yes, three. They didn't hit them, just my brother and I."

## GENERALIZED VIOLENCE AND IMPUNITY AGAINST AGGRESSORS

Before coming to the United States at eighteen, Juan had lived his entire life in El Salvador. He described how he began to witness violence from a very young age:

> Violence in El Salvador started a long time ago. So, when I was like eight years old, I went out shopping—there the stores and bakery are close by—so that day, it was four in the afternoon, and I went to buy

French bread, and all of the sudden, when I was already heading back home, they were shooting, and the shooter came to my direction and then left running.

Even though Juan himself was not pursued or threatened after witnessing a shooting near his home, in a place where he often ran errands, this was the sort of potentially life-threatening event that could have led to symptoms of PTSD.

Others experienced threats and violence clearly directed toward them. Elizabeth described a harrowing event outside of her school:

I hung out with girls who really weren't . . . they weren't up to any good. One day they were hiding, and since we hung around with them often, the gang said that we were hiding the girls and that if they didn't find the girls, they would kill us. After that, they threatened me and everyone else at my school. The threat was general because most of us hung out with those five girls they were looking for . . . those girls were in the 18th Street gang. The rival gang had the custom of sending three people with a pistol, and they just told us that we had to turn in the girls if we didn't want them to kill us, and they started shooting in the air. It happened outside of the school. I was leaving school, and my cousin had just arrived to take me home.

For sixteen-year-old Manuel, a similar event when he was fourteen directly led him and his sister to leave El Salvador and migrate to the United States for their own safety:

MANUEL: What happened was that one time I went out with my sister and the gang members were interested in my sister like . . . they liked her. Since my sister wasn't interested in them, they told me that if I didn't hand over my sister, they were going to kill me. . . . They had come to the house and were watching us there. They threw stones. They got to the gate . . .

INTERVIEWER: Did you see them threaten anyone else in El Salvador with violence?

MANUEL: Um, yes. Some friends that they said they were going to kill because they were from opposing areas. In school, it was between two gangs. The school was like in the middle of two zones controlled by rival gangs. When someone from one of them, like from the zone where the 18th Street gang was, would come, and then other people from another area where MS-13 was from, then there would be problems at school.

INTERVIEWER: And were those friends that you saw get threatened your classmates or . . . ?

MANUEL: Yes. They didn't go to school anymore, they had already stopped going to school.

INTERVIEWER: After that they stopped going to school?

MANUEL: Yes. I also had cousins that weren't going to school anymore because they threatened them that they couldn't go anymore because if they went, they were going to kill them. They stopped studying.

Manuel's case exemplifies the conundrum in which many found themselves: going to school had become life-threatening. For many, the effect on them of premigration violence was likely to stay with them for life. Thankfully, Manuel and his sister could leave and be with their mother in the United States. Some of Manuel's contemporaries had to stop going to school for their safety but did not leave for whatever reason, be it poverty, lack of connections, or something else. How different would their lives have been if the U.S. government had not spent billions of dollars over the years on criminalizing immigration and spent those funds instead on immigrant integration programs? Gangs probably would not have formed in Los Angeles, nor would their members have been deported to Central America.

José, age seventeen, explained that he wanted to come to the United States to be with his mother and continue his studies, and also because he felt physically confined in El Salvador. He described instances of threats and acts of violence he had experienced from gangs and army police officers. Asked why he migrated, José answered:

> First of all, to be with my mom. I also wanted to continue my studies here, and have a better life, because there, I could go out anywhere, they'd just ask me where I was from and if I said where I was from and they were from the opposing gang, they'd kill me. Even if I was not affiliated with MS-13, just because of where I lived. . . . One time I went out to San Salvador with my girlfriend, and that time I made

the mistake of not asking my mom's permission. So I went, it was dangerous there, and I knew it was dangerous, but I went dressed pretty decently, with a shirt with long sleeves, all well dressed. And since the majority of people there were gang members, we had already started heading back to the house, waiting for the bus in the station, when a soldier stopped my friends and I. They confused us for gang members, and they hit me. They asked me some questions, but I didn't have any identification documents with me, that was when they got angry. And they asked me for the bus route. I didn't know it, since I don't know how to go out far, so I just said, "The ones that go towards San Miguel," but they got mad because I didn't know the routes, and that time they hit me and my friends too.

Like others in her community, gang violence had made Carmen, who was thirteen when she migrated from El Salvador, distinctly fearful about life there:

CARMEN: Because of crime, fear, because every time they killed people in the community, you lived with this fear, knowing that maybe you could be one of the next ones to die in that community. They killed two of my friends in the community, one who was older but who was a friend of the family. He lived in the same community. The other was my friend and was fifteen years old.

INTERVIEWER: And why did they kill them?

CARMEN: Well, the first was an accident, because the people from MS-13 arrived in our community, and in a store they had a shoot-out, and that guy was there, so . . . all of the gang members were there, but none of them were killed, but they killed someone who was shopping. It wasn't him that they had gone to kill, but the bullets killed him. He died, and the other was the following day, after they had killed the previous guy. The next day they were collecting money for the burial, for the wake for the other guy, and then all of a sudden, while they were walking, the gang members shot from a car. There were two guys in the car, and they shot him. So that guy, the smaller one, he had recently joined a gang. But I don't know if he knew that they knew that he was a gang member. Because they were going around killing any guy that looked like he was an opposite gang member.

Alexander, who was seventeen when he migrated from El Salvador, similarly explained that he wanted to come to the United States because of the gangs and because he had become anxious and apprehensive about going out in his neighborhood:

> Most of the time, our town is united; everyone knows each other. But there are times when people from other places come and try to see what is going on there and like to move there . . . just to bring trouble. And so, like always, we were playing sports in the field, and one night we went with my brother, we went out to buy something . . . a uniform I believe. We went out to shop for one for the team that we were playing on. And there was a car parked by our house. They asked us where we were from, and we told them that we lived there, and they asked if we knew some people, and we told them no and no and no, and they told us to leave because if we didn't they were going to kill us. "Get out of here because if not we're going to kill you." "But why, if we're not involved with anybody?" And they said, "Just get out of here, get out of here." When we were walking, we felt that they shot, and the bullets passed by my brother's head. And after that, we didn't go out because we always watched when unknown cars came into the town to be on watch or something.

Alexander also told us that several of his friends had been shot at, injured, or killed by gangs:

> INTERVIEWER: Did you see them shoot anyone else?
>
> ALEXANDER: Yes, friends of mine. They injured some of them, and some they didn't. They shot them because they didn't want to do what they ordered them to. They made things harder for them in that they were going to threaten them, and strongly, with their families and everything, so that they would join their gang. . . . So some of my friends whom I had grown up with, they killed them, and so, well, little by little they were disappearing from my life.

Eventually, Alexander's only options were to be killed by the gangs like his friends, to join a gang, or to flee the area. Internal migration is often not an option if no family members are established in other parts of the country or if there are no jobs waiting for them.[41]

We asked thirteen-year-old Beatriz if joining a gang was an option for her, and wisely for someone so young, she replied, "Well, no, because in the end, if it's not prison that's waiting for them, it's the grave." Knowing that most gang members either end up in prison or die young, she knew that the preferred option was to emigrate if possible.

Most youth respondents reported experiencing violence in their communities, often committed by gangs, before they migrated to the United States. Conflicts between rival gangs caused constant fear and uncertainty in their communities, forcing some to abandon school and stay home. They witnessed murders and gun violence close to their homes, and some had been victims of violence themselves. Even if such events had become normalized in their communities, they were no less harmful. Violence and threats of violence were thus a main motivation for migration. As discussed earlier, some young people were fleeing not only gang violence and poverty in their home countries but also unsafe living situations after their caregivers died or could no longer protect them.

### Difficult Experiences during the Immigration Journey

Respondents' migration experiences varied based on the types of transportation they took north. Experiences at the U.S. border were overwhelmingly negative for youths who traveled by land, who comprised most of the sample. Many recounted dangerous conditions traveling through Central America and Mexico and hostile treatment upon arriving in the United States. Respondents gave us particularly striking accounts of the final hours of their journey before entering the United States and the time they spent in detention at the border. As soon as they arrived, they were put either in a hielera (freezer), a large, cold room without proper amenities, or the *perrera* (dog pound), a room with cells. Those placed in a *casa hogar* (refugee house) for youth reported more positive experiences there. Youths who traveled by plane reported fewer troubles or none at all on the journey.

Miguel, who was twelve when he migrated from El Salvador, answered some of our questions a year later:

> INTERVIEWER: How did migration authorities treat you in Mexico? As in, did they offer you asylum in Mexico?

MIGUEL: When we arrived, they caught us. They asked the bus driver to stop, and as he was slowing down, we threw ourselves out of the bus. We fell on a wire fence and got scraped up. They grabbed me by the backpack, and when I tripped, they let go, I ran, and when they couldn't catch me, they threw a big rock at my foot, and I fell. Then he ran to catch me, and he couldn't catch me. Then my mom and I crossed another wire fence, and it cut up our backs. We got up from there and walked for around an hour, only uphill, and they looked for us and didn't find us. We came out in the early hours of the morning, and at like two in the morning, the migration car showed up. They caught us there...

INTERVIEWER: And how were the conditions of those detention centers?

MIGUEL: Umm... where they had us the first time, they gave us enough food, let us shower, gave us blankets and sleeping mats, we were all right there. But the second time we weren't because the bathrooms were horrible, dirty. We slept on filthy sleeping mats, and they gave us blankets, but they just chucked us dirty ones. They threw the food in through a window and said, "Whoever wants to eat, eat; whoever doesn't, don't." And they took us to a jail where the sleeping mats smelt like pee, they were wet, and all the blankets were full of kids' pee, and so filthy, horrible, and they gave us horrible food.

Miguel's description of these horrible conditions echoes what others have found in immigrant shelters, both formal and makeshift, at immigrant detention facilities in Mexico and Central America.[42]

Sarah, who was fifteen when she migrated from Honduras, responded matter-of-factly when asked whether she had any difficult experiences during her journey to the United States:

SARAH: Only when I crossed the river because I almost drowned. It wasn't for me but for a girl.

INTERVIEWER: Oh, you were trying to save another person?

SARAH: Yes.

After almost dying from rescuing someone else from drowning, Sarah described herself as lucky. And from what she had heard of others' experiences, she thought her own trip was relatively easy.

Carmen described what it was like being in U.S. immigration detention after immigration officials caught up with her:

INTERVIEWER:   And how did that happen for you?

CARMEN:   I crossed the river in a boat, with a guy and another person. And they just told us that we had to walk, that we had to go by ourselves from there. They left us there and said that we weren't their responsibility.

INTERVIEWER:   And what happened when migration caught you?

CARMEN:   Well, they just took us to a casa hogar. I was there for a while, like two weeks, and then they sent me here. First, they had me in a hielera for a day. There, just after arriving, they gave me a little bit of time to talk with my mom. After that, they put me in a place where . . . I became hopeless there. There I couldn't take it anymore, and I wanted to leave or go back or say, "Better that you'd send me back," because there's a ton of people; they had locked us up with a ton of people.

INTERVIEWER:   Can you describe where you were? That's the hielera?

CARMEN:   Yes, the hielera is where Migration takes you, then they just have you put on this plastic thing, like paper but plastic, and they give you bread, gross bread, to eat, and a juice. And the bathroom is there, and that's where all the people are; there are kids crying, women crying, disorder everywhere you look, and you don't know if it's night or day, or when they're going to come to take you, because there are also people there who were deporting people.

INTERVIEWER:   And how long were you there for?

CARMEN:   I was only there for a day.

INTERVIEWER: And after, you were in the casa hogar?

CARMEN: Yes, they brought me there afterwards.

INTERVIEWER: And how was the casa hogar?

CARMEN: Well . . . good, but I didn't feel good, because I didn't talk with my family. . . . I didn't feel, like, good. I missed my family, my sister . . .

INTERVIEWER: Do you know where the casa hogar was?

CARMEN: Yes, in Texas.

INTERVIEWER: How long were you there for?

CARMEN: Two weeks.

INTERVIEWER: And after you came here, where your mom was? How did you get to the D.C. area?

CARMEN: By plane.

INTERVIEWER: Who paid for the ticket?

CARMEN: My mom.

Carmen had access to her mother's phone number, and eventually she was allowed to contact her. Her mother paid for the travel expenses of sending Carmen to her. Other times, immigrant sponsors fly to the detention center for bittersweet reunions.

As we mentioned in chapter 4, Valentina, who was sixteen years old when she emigrated from El Salvador, was traveling with her mother and brother. They crossed Mexico in a pickup truck. Once at the border, they crossed the river in a small raft. The Border Patrol agents encountered everyone they were traveling with as soon as they crossed the international boundary. Then they were taken into custody and then into the ICEboxes. Valentina and her mom were separated from her brother, who was ten years old. We interviewed Valentina the same year she arrived in the United States.

INTERVIEWER: About how long were you there for?

VALENTINA: Like a day and a half.

INTERVIEWER: And in that day and a half what happened? Did they give you something to eat? [Did they] interview you?

VALENTINA: Yes, they interviewed us, and for the three meals they just gave us a sandwich and a fruit juice. Just that.

INTERVIEWER: And what did they ask you? Did they interview you with your mom or separately?

VALENTINA: No, they interviewed me by myself, they just asked me where I came from, how old I was . . . from there they asked my mom all of the questions.

INTERVIEWER: And after you left the hielera, what happened?

VALENTINA: Well, from there, they took us to a place called la perrera, it was a place like this, super-big, and it was divided by . . . by those fabrics like that they put in the . . .

INTERVIEWER: Like wire mesh? Like they put in the windows?

VALENTINA: No, it was like an, I don't know, it was like this long, and had some big holes. Like what they put in fences. And they had the kids on one side, they separated me from my mom, and they had them together, my brother and her were together and they separated me.

INTERVIEWER: Did this place have cells, made with that mesh?

VALENTINA: Yes, they put me with other girls. Just girls. There were mats, and just one of those things, it wasn't so cold, but they gave us a gray thing, it was like . . . like what you wrap food in.

INTERVIEWER: Like aluminum foil?

VALENTINA: Yes! Like that, for us to wrap ourselves in, so we'd keep the heat inside. And then they gave us snacks, like lunch, they gave us bread, a sandwich, a drink, and a piece of candy.

INTERVIEWER: Could you leave that cell?

VALENTINA: No. Inside it the whole time. I was there less than a day. Then we left for Casa Hogar.

INTERVIEWER: And what was Casa Hogar, like a refugee house?

VALENTINA: Yeah! Something like that.

INTERVIEWER: And the three of you went with your mom?

VALENTINA: Yes, the three of us together, we stayed together the whole time. Almost ten days . . . five days.

INTERVIEWER: What was Casa Hogar like?

VALENTINA: Well, there I felt good because we were studying, we were in school, we watched TV, we slept, it was great. And we had everything, breakfast, lunch, and dinner all the time. Supergood. The three of us were together in a room.

INTERVIEWER: When you were in la perrera and they separated you from your mom, how did you feel?

VALENTINA: Well, I felt kind of sad, honestly, because I didn't know anyone, I felt sad and lonely.

These experiences predate the Trump administration's policy of separating families encountered at the border, sometimes keeping the children at ORR facilities and deporting the parents, thus creating international orphans. Nonetheless, even temporary separation during detention is painful and traumatic, so much so that some commit suicide during detention. Nelson, who was eleven when he migrated from Guatemala and twelve when interviewed, explained what happened when he and his family arrived at the border:

INTERVIEWER: Who are they?

NELSON: The ones . . . the ones that watch the border there. And they caught us and brought us there and they began to inspect everything. And from there they brought us inside.

INTERVIEWER: Inside?

NELSON: To . . . like a room.

INTERVIEWER: And what happened in that room? Were you with your mom that whole time or had they separated you?

NELSON: No, they had separated me.

INTERVIEWER: And how did you feel?

NELSON: Sad.

INTERVIEWER: Why did you feel sad?

NELSON: Because I wasn't close to her.

INTERVIEWER: And were you ever scared?

NELSON: No.

INTERVIEWER: Just sad.

NELSON: Mhmm.

INTERVIEWER: So they separated you and brought you to this room. And what happened there?

NELSON: There were more kids there.

INTERVIEWER: Kids your age?

NELSON: Yes. And after three or five days, they took us out and brought us to another area. . . . There they took us to shower, and they gave us clothes. We had been in the same dirty clothes for three days, and after we showered, they gave us those clothes. We were there for like four more days. After they brought us like that we could go out to another house, like apartments.

INTERVIEWER: Okay, and were you still alone or with you mom?

NELSON: No, I was already with my mom.

INTERVIEWER: When did you get back together with your mom?

NELSON: In the last house we went to.

INTERVIEWER: Do you remember how long it had been when Migration caught you until you got back to being with your mom?

NELSON: Like . . . twenty-eight days.

INTERVIEWER: You were without your mom for twenty-eight days?

NELSON (*nodding*): Mhmm.

These experiences of being separated from a parent, split apart from those who were raising them, and being threatened by gangs or witnessing gang violence firsthand were all potentially traumatic. Moreover, these experiences could inform and affect the processes that lay ahead, not only journeying north but also reuniting with parents, settling into a new home, trying to find happiness and stability, and maybe eventually returning to their home country.

## Mental Health Measurements

In addition to informal conversations, field observations, and interview questions, our data include participants' answers to the validated Patient Health Questionnaire (PHQ-9), modified for children, and the Child PTSD Symptom Scale (CPSS). These scales were included alongside interview questions in which we asked participants to self-report the presence or absence of mental health problems, sadness, anxiety, or stress before and after migration. We use mixed methods to explain the impact of accumulated discrete experiences and the social environments in which they occur on the mental health of young migrants from Central America. We find that Central American youths' self-reported mental health improves after migrating to the United States, but that they remain at risk of further trauma exposure, depression, and PTSD. We find that they were disproportionately likely to have lived through traumatizing experiences that blocked their integration by putting them at higher risk for psychological distress and disorders. Difficulty integrating, in turn, may create new stressors that exacerbate PTSD, depression, and anxiety. These conditions can be minimized through programs that aid immigrant integration and mental health.

These mental health scales and diagnostic tools can be used to determine if a child or teen has depression or suffers from PTSD. While we can compare population averages at a certain point in time, they are also valid when talking about the effects and existence of PTSD among the interviewees discussed here.

## "DESCRIBE YOUR HEALTH STATUS BEFORE AND AFTER MIGRATION"

We anticipated that respondents' mental and physical health status would change after migration. To track such changes, question 8 of the survey asked respondents to "describe your health status prior to migration" by checking "yes" or "no" to the following mental health–related conditions: constant stress, anxiety (defined as "unease or excessive concern"), and depression. Respondents were given these options in Spanish: *estrés constante, ansiedad* ("*intranquilidad o preocupación excesiva*"), and *tristeza*. At the end of the survey, they were asked the same question about their health after migration.

Only three out of fifty-eight responded that they experienced "mental health problems" before migrating to the United States (figure 6.1). After migration, none of the respondents reported experiencing "mental health problems." However, many reported having had feelings of sadness, worry, and restlessness, both before and after migration. About 60 percent of youth reported feeling sad before and after migration. While feelings of sadness decreased post-migration, the change

**Figure 6.1** *Respondents' Self-Reported Mental Health before and after Migration*

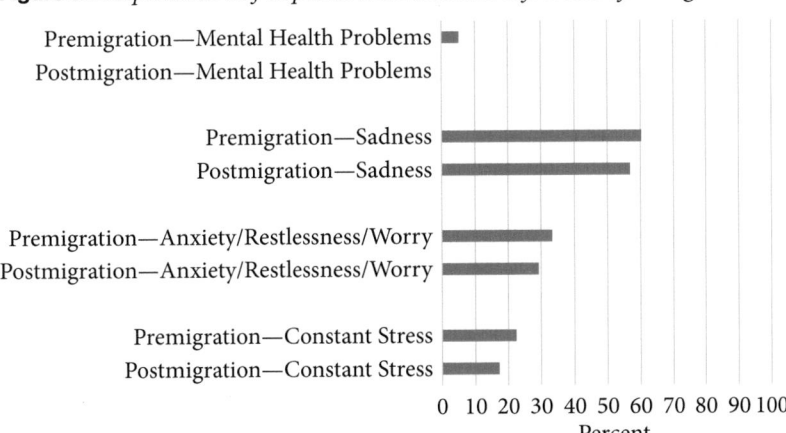

*Source:* Authors' compilation.

was slight, at less than 3 percent. About one-third of youth reported feeling anxiety, worry, and restlessness both before and after moving to the United States.

That some Central American immigrant youth in our sample reported a decrease in constant stress after migrating suggests that it was experiences in their home countries, the migration journey, or both that had caused their exceptional stress. Furthermore, many had traumatic experiences. We do not display these data to show population prevalence rates but to report results from our sample and to contrast the mental health self-reported by participant minors with the results from both the scales and the traumatic experiences shared during the same meetings with them.

Those who answered in the affirmative for any of the pre- and post-migration mental health conditions were not always the same individuals. There were no statistically significant differences in these self-reported concerns before migrating (through recollection) and at the time of the interview. No statistically significant differences were found based on gender. However, the three individuals who self-reported mental health problems before migrating were all males. Their self-reported mental health slightly improved after migration.

Even though our respondents reported feeling sadness, anxiety, and stress and experiencing traumatic events (figure 6.1), they did not think of themselves as "having mental health problems." Such self-assessment could be framed as either resilience or lack of awareness about mental illness. However, an important finding is the discrepancy in self-reporting between "mental health problems" and other aspects of mental health. Young people may not consider their anxiety, depression, or constant stress a mental health problem, and they also may experience these feelings without directly identifying them as such. Our findings related to symptoms of PTSD also tell us that respondents may be having mental health problems but simply do not conceptualize their symptoms as part of a larger whole. One reason for this discrepancy may be their internalization of the widespread stigma around mental health. Additionally, adolescents generally have more difficulty than adults do in understanding their emotions and identifying healthy adaptive emotion regulation strategies.[43] A lack of emotional awareness, coping skills, and mental health information might account for some participants' tendency to report negative emotions but not mental health problems. We also acknowledge that, by using the term "mental health problems," our study addresses issues that a mental health professional has not formally diagnosed.

Our qualitative results also tell us that those in our sample faced many challenges throughout their lives. Children and parents often struggle to understand one another after reuniting in the United States—there can be unspoken tension, recurrent feelings of abandonment, and struggles getting to know one another (again or for the first time). Respondents reported that getting used to the relationship with their parents or other sponsors was hard, though it improved over time. Youth often must also get to know a new stepfamily in addition to their own blood relatives, and the dwellings that house immigrant families may be small and cramped and offer little privacy or space.

Many of the migrants discussed in this book are likely to be safer in the United States than in their country of origin, but preoccupations about deportation and their documentation status can impact their mental health.[44] Many are afraid of returning to a place where they feel less safe. A minor's immigration status can contribute to their anxieties about immigration authorities and the possibility of being sent back to an unsafe environment. Children might fear making friends because no one will understand their situation; in a worst-case scenario, children may fear that another child will notify authorities of their or their family's presence.[45] Their feelings of abandonment, the separation from their parents, and the possibility of being turned over to the authorities can all contribute to feelings of isolation.

The experience of being forcefully separated from their parents at the border by government agents may contribute to mental health difficulties for Central American minors. Children who are separated from their parents by Border Patrol agents, immigration judges, or prison guards witness those they love the most being humiliated and taken away from them. Seeing the helplessness of those who made them feel safe is likely to have a profound and lifelong impact. Similarly, the later deportation of a parent can also lead the child to experience depression, insecurity, and loneliness.[46]

In the open-ended and follow-up questions, the participants talked more about the sources of their worry before and after migration. Table 6.1 summarizes the types of worry and stressors most often cited.

**Table 6.1** *Sources of Respondents' Mental Health Worries and Stressors before and after Migration*

|  | Premigration Sources of Worry | Postmigration Sources of Worry |
|---|---|---|
| Constant stress | · Wanting to see and reunite with parent(s)<br>· Gang presence<br>· Living alone<br>· Planning the trip | · Having to stay indoors and being bored<br>· Work |
| Anxiety | · Future dreams<br>· The trip to the United States<br>· Violence affecting friends<br>· Gang violence<br>· Need for parental support<br>· Inability to afford school supplies<br>· Inability to study around delinquency<br>· Payments to gangs or coyotes | · Missing and worrying about family in their home country<br>· The new U.S. president (Trump)<br>· Possible deportation of family<br>· Future life<br>· Exploitation at work<br>· Bullying |
| Sadness | · Leaving friends and family<br>· Being prevented from getting out by gangs<br>· Lacking things that others had<br>· Missing a parent<br>· Not knowing their mother; wanting to meet their mother<br>· Death of grandmother<br>· Death or disappearance of friends<br>· Alcoholic caregiver | · Family separation<br>· Missing friends in the home country |
| Mental health problems | · Frustration<br>· Aggression<br>· Headaches | · None |

*Source:* Authors' compilation from a draft by Noemí Enchautegui-de-Jesús and Aida Romero for the "Household Contexts and School Integration of Resettled Migrant Youth" study.

**Table 6.2** *PHQ-8 Scoring Guide to Severity of Depression Symptoms*

| Scoring | Severity |
|---|---|
| 0–4 | No or minimal depression |
| 5–9 | Mild depression |
| 10–14 | Moderate depression |
| 15–19 | Moderately severe depression |
| 20–24 | Severe depression |

*Source:* Kroenke and Spitzer 2002.

## THE DEPRESSION SCREEN

Respondents filled out a PHQ-9 modified for teens in Spanish to screen for depression symptoms minus the questions related to suicidal ideation, also known as PHQ-8.[47] This scale has been validated in English and Spanish and is used by psychologists and clinicians internationally.[48] The instrument asks if respondents experienced individual depression symptoms in the previous two weeks on a scale of 0 (none, *ninguno*), 1 (various days, *varios días*), 2 (more than half the time, *mas de la mitad de los días*), or 3 (almost every day, *casi todos los días*). We scored as indicated in table 6.2.

Using the modified PHQ-9 for teens, referred to as PHQ-8, we were able to examine the severity of depressive symptoms among participants in the study. Although 31 percent of participants reported that they had not struggled with any depressive symptoms within the last two weeks, 79.3 percent scored between 0 and 4 on the PH8-scale, indicating the presence of no or minimal depression, and around 20 percent exhibited symptoms of mild or moderate depression (table 6.3). In one of the follow-up questions, not to be used for scoring, respondents were asked if they felt sad or depressed most days in the last year. Contrary to their other answers, 38 percent responded "yes." We did not ask about suicidal ideation, nor did we follow up with a formal diagnosis by a clinician, so the depression scores may be on the conservative side.

In 2019, 2.8 percent of adults in the U.S. population experienced severe symptoms of depression, 4.2 percent experienced moderate symptoms, and 11.5 percent experienced mild symptoms in the previous two weeks.[49] Before the pandemic, depression among U.S. teens (ages twelve to seventeen) had risen from 8 percent in 2007 to 13 percent in

**Table 6.3** *Respondents' Symptoms of Depression as Determined by the PHQ-8*

|  | N | Percentage |
|---|---|---|
| No or minimal depression | 46 | 79.3 |
| Mild depression | 8 | 13.8 |
| Moderate depression | 4 | 6.9 |
| n | 58 | 100.0 |

*Source:* Authors' compilation.

2017; the rate among girls in 2017 was 20 percent.[50] Depression was disproportionately high among our sample, with more than 20 percent of respondents stating that they had felt sufficient depressive symptoms at least some of the time in the last two weeks to have scored in a mild or moderate category for depression (table 6.3). Almost 40 percent of the respondents answered "yes" to the question, "Have you felt depressed or sad in the past year most days, even when you feel good sometimes?" These results support our key finding that one-third of our sample may have struggled with moderate to severe PTSD, as depression is a common PTSD comorbidity.[51]

### THE CHILD PTSD SYMPTOM SCALE

Respondents filled out a Spanish version of the Child PTSD Symptom Scale (CPSS), a version of the PCL-5 used by the Cognitive Behavioral Intervention for Trauma in Schools (CBITS), a school-based trauma program designed to screen for post-traumatic stress disorder in children and adolescents.[52] The instrument is routinely used to provide services and was translated into Spanish by the Los Angeles Unified School District. It is a self-reporting checklist assessment utilizing the DSM-IV's definition of symptoms apparent in those with PTSD. The CPSS assesses PTSD symptoms and diagnoses in children ages eight to eighteen based on three items: reexperience of trauma, avoidance, and arousal.[53] The seventeen-question assessment asked respondents to report and rate symptoms they experienced in the previous two weeks. They were asked to choose how often they experienced symptoms by selecting 0 (not at all, *nunca*), 1 (once in a while, *ocasionalmente*), 2 (half the time, *el 50 por ciento del tiempo*), or 3 (almost always, *prácticamente en todo momento*). Following CBITS scoring guidelines, we

**Table 6.4** *Respondents' Symptoms of PTSD as Measured on the Child PTSD Symptom Scale*

|                    | N   | Percentage |
|--------------------|-----|------------|
| Zero               | 7   | 12.3       |
| Low                | 31  | 54.4       |
| Moderate to severe | 19  | 33.3       |
| n                  | 57  | 100.0      |

*Source:* Authors' compilation.

tallied all points for each of the seventeen questions to obtain a total for each respondent. We used a cutoff of fourteen points or higher to indicate moderate to severe symptoms of PTSD. We purposely did not use a checklist of traumatic experiences in order to avoid triggering study participants and making participation itself traumatic. If they felt comfortable doing so, respondents were invited to talk about their feelings and symptoms, self-report mental health conditions, and disclose their traumatic experiences.

Based on the CPSS, 66.7 percent of youth showed low to no symptoms of PTSD. However, 33.3 percent of youth did show symptoms that could indicate moderate to severe PTSD symptoms. Although answers to this assessment are not usable as stand-alone criteria to measure or diagnose PTSD, they allow researchers to assess individuals preliminarily, monitor present symptoms, and examine whether symptoms indicate PTSD.

The results shown in table 6.4 are heterogeneous: 12.3 percent reported no symptoms of PTSD, 54 percent reported a few symptoms, and 33 percent scored above the cutoff of fourteen points. However, eleven of the forty-seven participants who answered scored between 20 and 28. Notably, two individuals had very high scores, 42 and 45, close to the maximum possible score of 51. As a comparison, a meta-study found that 15.9 percent of children and adolescents exposed to a traumatic event develop PTSD.[54] In that study, the incidence of PTSD is higher among girls than among boys.

One-third of respondents had moderate to severe symptoms of PTSD. Meanwhile, 12 percent of respondents reported no symptoms of PTSD as assessed by this scale. Those who reported no symptoms may have had extremely intense symptoms that they coped with by disassociating. A dissociative state is caused by denial and avoidance and is part of the trauma sequelae of PTSD.[55] Part of surviving trauma is often forgetting that it happened.[56] Nevertheless, the results show that the lives of Central Americans cannot be reduced to possibly traumatic experiences. Some young immigrants may have no PTSD symptoms at all, many others may have some, and a few may have many symptoms. All young immigrants with PTSD symptoms, however many or few, can be helped by adequate and accessible mental health services and a network of nonprofits helping this population, as many do in the D.C. metropolitan region.

## Mental Health, Migration, and Data Collection

Carlos said that the gang violence in his home community inhibited his ability to study, move around, or take advantage of opportunities outside of school. Once he settled in the D.C. area, he said that he felt very safe and cared for because his father kept a close eye on him and his siblings. For Carlos, uncertainty about whether he would be allowed to stay with his father in the D.C. area when he turned eighteen or instead would be sent to El Salvador, where he had no safe place to stay, was probably a persistent source of anxiety, as is often the case for those with liminal legal status.[57] Carlos was having difficulty in school because of language barriers, but like other youth in our study, he had been able to develop friendships among classmates who were also still learning English. Importantly, Carlos now could imagine doing more than he could in El Salvador. Being in his father's care enabled him to start seeing the possibility of a better life for himself.[58] Carlos's post-migration experience underscores the importance of family reunification and family support in supporting mental health and immigrant integration.

Furthermore, a minor who witnesses violence or is surrounded by violence in their home community, is separated from family, and makes a notoriously dangerous journey northward can be traumatized for far longer than is visible. For instance, multiple participants reported that, when they were very young, one or both of their parents were killed by gangs. The other struggles described here, some but not all involving violence, can also play a role in different forms of mental strife.

Our findings surrounding mental health are mixed. While the sample's mental health was positive by some measures, it was negative by others. This nuanced result can be seen even within responses from the same individual. Diana reported that she wanted to come to the United States because she knew the educational opportunities were better and she was determined to become a doctor and return to El Salvador. However, she also reported that she sometimes felt isolated and sad. Despite the strong support system of faculty and peers at her school, she felt that she might never achieve her dreams. We do not aim to directly attribute such feelings to migration—many people, migrant or not, may harbor similar desires and feelings—but we do hope to place our respondents' experiences in context with the descriptive data earlier and other qualitative data reported throughout the book.

Samantha spoke about feeling safer in the United States than in Honduras. However, she also experienced the loneliness that Diana described, felt tired, and had little energy to do anything beyond the minimum of what everyday life required. Her mental strife could have stemmed from never feeling safe in Honduras and constantly fearing for her immediate physical safety on the journey from Honduras to the United States. As demonstrated here, Diana and Samantha had both experienced complex traumatic situations and subsequent feelings of isolation. Their feelings of loneliness may also have been due to prior trauma, such as being left behind when their parents migrated to the United States. Immigrants parents often attempt to compensate for distance through "teleparenting" and by sending advice, admonitions, money, clothes, and toys from afar.[59] Nelson, who was eleven when he left Guatemala, said that his father would call him every two hours most days, but this level of contact is not realistic for many parents working in the United States. Thus, many children in our sample reported feeling ungrateful for what their parents understood to have been the sacrifices they made for the benefit of their offspring. A parent's immigration leaves both the child and the parents sad and uncertain about the future.[60]

The youth in the study had all made it to the border and been placed with a sponsor. Therefore, this sample includes relatively privileged individuals compared to those who could not make or complete the trip and those who were returned at the border. Additionally, because we recruited some of our participants through after-school programs, counselors, and social and legal service providers, many of them were privileged in that they were more likely to be enrolled in school than the overall Central American youth population in the Washington, D.C., metro area. Other qualitative findings in the study show that schools were instrumental in developing friendships. With an *n* of fifty-eight in our study, our findings probably understate the pressures faced by the larger population from whom they were drawn. Nevertheless, our data about immigrant youth allow us insights into recent cohorts of unaccompanied Central American youth, about whom little is generally known. Our survey data and instruments can also be used for individual-level analyses.

Given the self-reported format of the survey, these results may be underreporting negative mental health outcomes. The vocabulary related to mental health conditions used in the survey may have been unfamiliar to some of our respondents, or it may have been understood differently in Spanish than in English.[61] Cultural differences in interpretations and stigmas concerning mental health might have caused respondents to downplay, exaggerate, or hide information or experiences.[62] Indeed, studies on mental health stigma and self-concealment have documented the wariness of individuals about disclosing their mental health status or seeking out services.[63] Latin Americans with mental or psychosocial disabilities may experience employment discrimination; therefore, revealing a mental health problem could impact them financially.[64] Furthermore, youth who had not thought or spoken openly with us about their feelings, especially younger ones, may have misinterpreted or struggled to understand the survey questions, but were able to elaborate further on such topics in the follow-up open-ended answers. Emblematic of possible underreporting were the negative answers of most of our respondents when asked if they struggled with "mental health problems." Many reported suffering from anxiety, depression, constant stress, or sadness. Although we cannot define negatively perceived emotions and stress alone as "mental health problems," they could be indicative of mental health disorders.[65] These responses are especially important when considered alongside the finding from the Child PTSD Symptoms Scale that one-third of the Central American minors included in the data may have been struggling with moderate to severe PTSD. This gives us reasons to believe that the actual values are much higher for both our sample and the Central American immigrant youth population at large.

Another limitation was that the answers regarding premigration circumstances were based on recollection rather than on two different measurements in a longitudinal study. These findings further show the limits of self-reported physical and mental health data, particularly for people with little access to health care.[66] They also show the importance of conducting direct measurements during the study and triangulating self-reported questions, validated scales, open-ended questions, and the qualitative data they generate.

No equivalent census, phonebook, or neighborhood is available from which to create a randomized sample of this hard-to-reach population—a further indication of the vulnerability of the people missing from the interviews who travel accompanied but without papers, or those who are Indigenous and not Spanish-speaking. Their situation only got worse under Trump administration policies and with the closing of the border, even to asylum seekers, after the onset of the COVID-19 pandemic under Title 42. Therefore, the results presented here undoubtedly understate the situation of young Central American migrants between 2018 and 2023.

Given the conditions in their countries of origin, the difficulty of the passage through Mexico, the militarized international borders, and the criminalization of immigration and asylum-seeking throughout the world, we assumed that all participants had been exposed to many or at least one traumatic event during their lifetime. We did not verify this assumption through a trauma exposure checklist, however, because doing so could have been too upsetting for them to complete.

## The Social Determinants of Immigrant Mental Health for Central American Youth

A repeated sentiment throughout the interviews was that young migrants had few or no opportunities in their sending communities owing to the power and violence of gangs or the inadequacies of local schooling and labor markets. Leaving the only home one has ever known, the notoriously dangerous journey to the United States, and the challenges of immigrants' circumstances upon arriving are all possible sources of PTSD symptoms.[67] Although self-reported mental health measures are not iron-clad ways of understanding an individual's feelings, these measures showed a clear trend among our respondents of improving slightly after migration. These measures showed that being in the United States improved mental well-being perceptions for some, but not all. In other words, mental health concerns did not worsen postmigration when measured by any of the scales or questions used. For participants, emigration reduced some risks but brought new challenges around familial and societal integration.

This chapter has shown the complex situations that immigrants face after arriving in the United States.[68] Even when their outcomes improved after coming to the United States, our findings show that one-third of our respondents may have been suffering from PTSD or depression. In line with the literature, we conclude that changes that allow better access to social services, education, health care, and employment are needed to improve mental health outcomes and prevent further trauma exposure. Mental health is not the simple result of individual-level experiences or predetermined neurochemistry alone but is deeply affected by environmental factors, including poverty, inequality, and immigration policies, as discussed in the next chapter.

CHAPTER SEVEN

# IMMIGRANT INTEGRATION INTO SCHOOL ENVIRONMENTS

The social and educational aspects of the holistic process of integration are just as important as others. Schools and social service organizations are critical for enhancing minor immigrants' sense of belonging and their structural integration into their new communities. Small acts can make a big difference, as when a teacher works to deliberately include migrant children in all educational activities. Bilingual programs, Spanish-speaking PTA groups, message boards, and WhatsApp groups, mentoring of immigrant children, and after-school programs for members of reunited families are all examples of ways to support immigrant youth as they learn English, finish high school, apply to college, and find jobs.

Many families with children who migrated on their own underwent years of family separation, with notable consequences for youth in school, in their behavior, and in their emotional well-being.[1] These impacts coalesce and interact in a way that can make integration a lofty goal. Migrants must accustom themselves to new physical surroundings, new people, a new language, and a new school. At the same time, they also need to learn, understand, and adapt to their new familial surroundings, with make-or-break effects on their integration and feelings of belonging. Schools are the main avenues of integration for minors in the United States since there are so few programs welcoming immigrants and asylum seekers.

https://doi.org/10.7758/dvxg2393.1134

**Table 7.1** *Respondents' Relationships with School Staff at Their D.C. Area School*

| In school, you have a teacher or an adult who ... | Percentage |
|---|---|
| Cares about you | |
| Not true | 14.55 |
| A little true | 10.91 |
| Fairly true | 14.45 |
| Very true | 49.09 |
| Will notice if you are not in school | |
| Not true | 7.27 |
| A little true | 27.27 |
| Fairly true | 0.00 |
| Very true | 65.45 |
| Listens to what you have to say | |
| Not true | 7.27 |
| A little true | 3.64 |
| Fairly true | 34.55 |
| Very true | 54.55 |

*Source:* Authors' compilation.

## Relationships in School

Overall, youth respondents feel happier in the United States. They were making friends, appreciated being able to go to school, and felt safe in their communities. Safety and friendship are two ways to measure a sense of belonging, as well as good measures of integration. These positives outcomes were often related to respondents' age at the time of arrival, having the legal right to remain in the country, feeling physically safer than in their home country, being comfortable in their new family home, and being able to navigate both school and language by making friends with other youth who spoke Spanish. Respondents answered questions about their relationships in school with teachers and friends. Half of those in our study said that they had an adult in school who cared about them, 65 percent responded that they had a teacher or other adult who would notice if they were not in school, and 54 percent said that they had an adult in school who listened to what they had to say (see table 7.1).

This shows that a majority of those surveyed had strong relationships with adults in school and that even more had at least fairly strong relationships. Having someone who listened to them, cared about them, and noticed them when they are not present were all key pieces of feeling a sense of belonging in a school and feeling more at home there.

## Relationships with Peers

The sociological literature documents the importance of measuring and comparing adolescent interpersonal ties.[2] Peer relationships are also important in generating a sense of belonging, and they can extend outside the school building and into the home and community. Having someone around their age to whom immigrant youth could relate was important for settling in and developing a sense of belonging. Results from the questions about peer relationships are shown in table 7.2.

**Table 7.2** *Respondents' Relationships with Peers in the D.C. Area*

| You have a friend around your age who . . . | Percentage |
|---|---|
| Cares about you | |
| Not true | 34.55 |
| A little true | 18.18 |
| Fairly true | 9.09 |
| Very true | 38.18 |
| You can talk with about your difficulties | |
| Not true | 34.55 |
| A little true | 18.18 |
| Fairly true | 23.64 |
| Very true | 23.64 |
| Can help you with your problems | |
| Not true | 7.27 |
| A little true | 3.64 |
| Fairly true | 34.55 |
| Very true | 54.55 |

*Source:* Authors' compilation.

Some respondents reported having strong relationships with peers, but many had no peers to talk with about their difficulties (35 percent). Additionally, the only "very true" response from this category chosen by over 50 percent of these minors was having a peer who could help with their problems, coming in at 54 percent. The other categories were much more evenly distributed around the four possible answers. However, in every case, a majority answered that the statement posed in each category was at least "a little true." These findings were replicated in the open-ended answers (discussed later).

Interpersonal relationships are of great importance for maintaining positive mental health and, in turn, social integration. Having friends and other people to turn to has immense positive effects on mental health for adolescents. One study found that adolescents who have been maltreated or abused are more "buffered" from symptoms of depression in adulthood when they have higher levels of perceived support from friends and family.[3] Other studies have shown that how high-quality friendships are associated with adolescents' improved self-esteem and subjective well-being.[4]

Respondents reported that being in school was hard at first, but that after some time they felt more like they belonged there and were excited to attend. They consistently reported that language was one of their biggest struggles in school and a barrier to their performance and happiness. By making friends and speaking in Spanish with Latin students who were native to the United States, immigrant youth were able to feel more at home and a part of their community. Therefore, the ability to communicate with others in Spanish became an important determinant of enjoyment in school. Other Central American migrants understood what newer migrants were going through, and frequently the Spanish language was able to bring a variety of such students together. Unfortunately, there were also reports by school practitioners and staff running after-school programs that some second-generation students would bully the new migrants in school. Program staff have a chance to intervene to remedy this behavior and support bullied students.

Besides the support of other youth, the high level of support services available to youth through their school helped them to integrate. Melissa, age fourteen, reported that she felt welcome and had a good institutional support system in the United States, from free public school to language and integration support programs and the presence of many students in her school to whom she could relate because their situations were similar to her own.

David, who was fourteen when he arrived, quickly felt integrated into his new school. He did not feel discriminated against there and was hopeful about going to college eventually because he felt like he could do well in school, especially among the many other students willing to help him. He felt like a major strength of life in the United States was the provision of services to help parents and provide free medical care in school. Of course, the social services infrastructure in the D.C. region may not be replicated in many other places in the United States.

Older students often struggled more, felt more discriminated against, and had more issues at school and home because they struggled more to learn English and feel respected. They were also tempted to leave school and start earning money, especially given that plenty of relatively well-paying jobs are available in the D.C. area. Diana, age sixteen, described her initial struggles from not knowing any of the course content because she did not learn enough in El Salvador. She was nervous that there would be no one she could relate to in school. However, she found the contrary to be the case: there were many people in her school to help her academically, and she was able to make friends there:

> It was very taxing. At first, I did not want to go out. I was afraid of people who I thought did not speak Spanish. I don't know, I thought they would say, "Go, you aren't from here," things like that. And I didn't want to go to school, I felt sad. But after the first day I went to school, I made friends, and then I didn't even want there to be a weekend. I only wanted to be in school. Because we played. And although some classes/subjects were difficult for me, like math—because let me tell you, in El Salvador they barely had taught me how to add. I didn't know how to multiply, I didn't know how to divide, I didn't know anything! I only knew how to read, but I didn't read very well. And here they taught me in Spanish. They are teaching me how to read better. And I am interested in school here. They have a lot of programs to help us, for the students at our school.

Eighteen-year-old Daniella reported that her school experience was good but also hard for her because of the language barrier. When asked whether she had friends in school, she responded that she had many friends and that they encouraged her to stay in school—that is, to not drop out of school. She and her friends had a strong bond, and the group made decisions collaboratively—such as to skip class every now and then to get food.

INTERVIEWER: Do you have friends in school?

DANIELLA: Yes, many.

INTERVIEWER: Many? Great! How?

DANIELLA: From my classes. We know each other well.

INTERVIEWER: And do your friends motivate you to stay in school or ditch/skip?

DANIELLA: To stay. But if more than one says, "Let's go eat," if we ditch school, I believe that the decision that is made, we make it together.

These friends gave Daniella a reason to come to school every day, and her group helped each other with their problems and supported each other. Although her school could provide language training and opportunities to socialize with other youth and adults, it was her friendship group that made Daniella feel integrated into her school whether or not she was in the building.

Many others echoed Daniella in reporting that having friends their age in school was massively beneficial in making them feel at ease, despite other issues in school. For instance, Maria, age seventeen, said that even though she had problems in school with the language and was bullied by some because she did not wear designer clothing like other students, the other Latin friends she had made and the warm and celebratory environment created by her school and her teachers helped her feel comfortable and enjoy being at school. Maria had experienced many hardships prior to migration. Before she was even born, her father had left her family. Gangs had kidnapped her older sister after that, and then her mother went to the United States. Her grandmother raised Maria until she was old enough to leave Honduras and the family had enough money to send her to be with her mother in the United States.

MARIA: I wanted to have a better future here, and there it's difficult.

INTERVIEWER: Why?

MARIA: Because it's riddled with gangs and they're everywhere. They even threaten students, and even try to recruit them, and I didn't want that to happen to me.

INTERVIEWER: What would they say to you?

MARIA: They didn't say anything to me, mostly to others. I was scared, and I wanted to be with my mother.

INTERVIEWER: Was your mother already in the U.S.?

MARIA: Yes.

In their new schools, respondents felt most like themselves and had opportunities for identity formation and making friends. Schools are not only a place of socialization but also of socializing, and both are necessary for the integration of youth. Respondents enjoyed school if they felt supported and welcomed by teachers and could find others their own age to whom they could relate. These positive relationships helped to create a feeling of belonging and integration for them. Furthermore, school often seemed to have fewer expectations than their homes. The school was a place where they could be themselves rather than, for example, the devoted daughter or the independent son.

Schools helped migrant youth access diverse social networks and accumulate cultural and social capital, two of the various forms of capital other than economic capital described by sociologist Pierre Bourdieu. Briefly, "cultural capital" refers to place-specific knowledge—for instance, understanding and being familiar with idiomatic phrases or the movies and TV shows that the people around you watch. "Social capital" refers to connections and networks—knowing people who help you navigate school, teach you cultural knowledge, or help you find a job, for instance. It is clear that children and youth develop these types of capital in schools.

## Insights from Interviews with Local and School Officials

Youth often faced both external and internal structural barriers to integration. External barriers arose in school and community contexts, while internal barriers were related to their ability to integrate into their families and begin healing from past traumas. In addressing students' social, emotional, and academic needs, school officials and service providers used some proven ways to deal with structural barriers to integration and education.

School system registration, immigration status, technology access, and follow-through from the ORR can all affect how easily youth and families can engage with available resources and register in the school system. The Fairfax County Public Schools system has adapted by establishing the systemwide Immigrant Family Reunification Program, which provides social services and helps with procedures like registration. Registering minors in school can be a lengthy process depending on whether their sponsor is a parent. During that process, in an effort to anticipate future issues, Fairfax County schools have nonmandatory informal meetings with sponsors to both screen for structural barriers to education and address issues around students' integration, such as housing, food security, and transportation needs. They also connect families with the resources they need to navigate both social services and the school system.

The manager of a school-based mental health program at Mary's Center in D.C. has called attention to a disconnect in access to federally provided mental health services for youths after they have been released from government custody. Minors are referred to Mary's Center by schools to receive clinical mental health services if they are depressed, suicidal, or exhibiting behavioral issues in school. The center's services are reimbursable on a billable model that makes it easy for its clinicians to see anyone with health insurance but difficult to see those without insurance. Every student in D.C. is covered by Medicaid, but many sponsors are either unaware of that or do not want to put their name on a Medicaid application and thus have been unable to arrange insurance coverage for their children. It may also be that Medicaid administrators and the intake centers of mental health services providers like Mary's Center are not making applicants for these services aware of the availability of insurance coverage through Medicaid.

The ORR has similar issues with access to the federally funded services it provides. An international student counselor notes that migrant students have a wide array of possible problems that the school district cannot exactly know or catalog for each one: "Sure, I'd like to interview every single kid about the experiences that happened to them when they come in, but number one, it's not appropriate. Two, it's probably not even possible." She noted that some youth—usually those who are younger and have had intensely traumatic experiences—are identified through ORR and given a social worker, but they may be a minority of students. Even within the ORR, she said, there are problems:

One of our obstacles is we don't get enough information from them, ORR. And the thing is, they might give this packet to the family, but first of all, I can tell you one thing: nobody's going through all those papers, and it's very confusing for the family, for the legal services, for any kind of services. And I can tell that some of them have done a super job orienting the families, but most of the time it's just like, "Here's this packet of stuff."

Almost all new immigrants feel isolated and lonely at first, and maybe anxious about what the future may hold in a new place. A D.C. area program director noted that, like immigrants, young or old, all youth may experience these feelings in school. Some schools are also experiencing rapid demographic change due to the influx of migrant youth into the D.C. area. Thus, there are several reasons why school contexts vary widely. Is the school prepared to support migrant youth? What is the school's culture like? Does the school have gang issues?

One D.C. area school whose student body historically was predominantly African American had become 60 percent Hispanic within only a few years, and of that 60 percent, most were immigrants. The program director described the challenge for schools undergoing this type of demographic change:

> You have to hire people who can speak the language... [and] you have to develop just a general cultural sensitivity. I've certainly met plenty of people who don't speak Spanish who are extremely sensitive.... But I've certainly also met social workers who look at those students and say, "They're not my students. I can't speak to them." And so our staff end up being really overloaded at that school. And so I think administratively that's probably something the principal would tell you, that "I can't find people who speak Spanish. We have so many of these kids. I need a culture shift at this school."

In line with our findings that youth integrate better when they can communicate with peers, it makes sense that the ability of teachers and social workers to communicate with youth and their parents is also important. Teachers and social workers at the school must be culturally sensitive to migrant students' situation and communicate with them and their parents. One way this can happen is through ESOL programs, which teach fluency in English. However, this type of program takes time, so there still is a need not only for effective ESOL programs but also for Spanish-language support in schools.

## Youths' Past Lives and Structural Barriers

In addition to language intervention programs, schools and organizations operate family reunification and integration intervention programs. Mary's Center has worked with schools to organize reunification counseling and family therapy, but differing work schedules can make these and other types of meetings hard to organize. Sponsors have jobs, and often the youth do as well. Besides support groups, some schools have also successfully organized events like post-election meetings with the community and with sponsors of unaccompanied youth.

Echoing what many reported in this study, the experts we interviewed noted that youth are coming to the United States for many reasons. A family may have been threatened by gangs. Maybe the person responsible for caring for the child when they were five does not want to or is unable to take care of the teenager that child has become. Or the parents may finally be able to pay for their children to join them. Some children do not want to leave the family they have been living with in their home country, and moving away from their caretaker can arouse feelings of grief and loss similar to those evoked by the original family separation as they begin the process of reunification with a new family.

Students' life experiences, unresolved trauma, and unmet socio-emotional needs can affect their performance in school. The program director noted that there is wide variation in migrant youths' academic needs. Many who received inconsistent schooling before arriving in the United States are designated as students with interrupted formal education (SIFE). When Central American migration to the D.C. area first began, many schools dealt with SIFE students by putting sixteen-, seventeen-, and eighteen-year-old students in classrooms with fourteen-year-olds. Robin Hamby, an expert on the topic who formerly worked on these issues with the Fairfax County Public Schools in Virginia, notes that this ultimately cannot work owing to the gaps in maturity level and life experience between youth of different ages. Another problem is that some youth not only are not fluent in English but have low levels of formal literacy in their native language.

One way that Fairfax County dealt with these issues was to create a transitional high school specifically for the seventeen- and eighteen-year-old migrants. Its program begins with a curriculum in Spanish and ends with adult education and planning a path to the next step, whether high school graduation, a GED, trade school, community college, or a career. In Prince George's County, Maryland, educators observed lower academic achievement in an area with more migrant youth and lower academic achievement for English Language Learners (ELLs) throughout the district. To remedy this, they started working on two new high schools specifically for ELL youth. Each school will have no more than four hundred students to keep the student-to-teacher ratio small. Their goal is language learning through all content areas, and they model the school so that "you have maybe a student who is a newcomer in the same math class as a kid who's been here three years and might be more English proficient than other students."

This model has proven successful in New York and California, demonstrating once again that youth tend to do better when they are around students with whom they can identify. The ELL schools have added a weekly social justice class that gives students a chance to work with questions that will help them process their lives and circumstances, such as: What does it mean to be an immigrant? How does race play into the different spaces I navigate as a student?

### "I'm Smart in Spanish, but I'm Stupid in English"

Robin Hamby and Ligia Diaz, who worked for Fairfax County Public Schools' Immigrant Family Reunification Project, mentioned that many sponsors are confused that the migrant youth now living with them are not happy and do not feel like they belong, even after a year. Diaz noted that schools in the United States are very different from those in Central America, where a school may be just one room and students are expected to stay quiet and listen to lectures rather than ask questions, as is expected in U.S. schools. Students' language struggles, as frequently mentioned by the youth interviewed for this study, were echoed by Hamby, who noted that some ELL students say things like, "I'm smart in Spanish, but I'm stupid in English." Many were good students in their home country but now are genuinely struggling in the new school and are scared to ask questions or advocate for themselves.

School, family, language learning, mental health, and integration are all interconnected. Academic struggles related to language learning and home life can lower the self-esteem of children and adolescents, and parents can find it challenging to understand what is going on. "Learning Together," another Fairfax County Public Schools program, attempts to engage parents in the school process while giving them resources to bring back to their homes to use regularly with their children. These resources include workshops on improving communication skills with their children and understanding their rights as parents in schools. This program also conducts learning experiences, such as arts and crafts, martial arts, or robotics classes, that engage the parents, showing them the value of an education and helping them understand their children and their experiences in the American school system. At two education conferences per year, the facilitators continue to discuss pressing issues with parents, such as social and emotional health, understanding report cards, and resources for accessing college information for their children.

Fairfax County Public Schools has set up parent support groups that could also serve as a model for districts nationwide. Parents meet in one group and children in another to discuss their fears, hopes, anxieties, self-esteem, and aspirations. Then they all come together to discuss their findings in a large group and with a professional facilitator. The adults work together as a group on a topic while the youth do the same, and then the groups make presentations to one another. Furthermore, these sessions allow for several hours of family togetherness and community building.

Students feel less alone when they know others that they can relate to in school. Likewise, families can feel less alone when they are invited to talk about their struggles, which they may have felt were unique to their family but discover are shared by others. The hardest part for all family members may be managing expectations versus reality, which turns on whether youth and parents or other sponsors can gain the ability to collectively come to terms with their reality and foster understanding between one another. One of the program facilitators states: "We're not saying, 'You're going to love your dad,' or 'You might not ever love your dad.' Not all families react to that well. But we're saying, 'We want to come to a place where your dad supports you, and you support your dad, in terms of you understanding what he's trying to do.'"

## School and Other Key Institutions That Can Facilitate Integration

Social integration to the United States happens through a successful family reunification experience and integration to local institutions such as schools. Whether youth successfully integrate into their new schools depends on various factors, within the school context and beyond. When support systems are in place for refugee and immigrant students to help them succeed and feel supported in the classroom, they can thrive. Success at school helps immigrant students feel a sense of belonging in their own countries and thus in the United States as well. When schools, government programs, and nonprofit organizations set out to meet the needs of immigrant youth, they are likely to find that, in doing so, they are also supporting non-immigrant students at risk.

Many interviewees enjoyed and did well in school, a finding that echoes the work of sociologist Roberto Gonzalez, who showed that K-12 schools are "havens" for minors who are waiting to adjust their legal status and have yet had "to learn to be illegal" in the labor market or when applying to college.[5] Interviews with the counselors and local authorities who interface with these families show that parenting and youth programs in the places of settlement can intervene effectively to improve relations between recently reunited children and parents. Improved relations, in turn, can help students with scholastic achievement and thus eventual socioeconomic advancement and structural integration.

Respondents reported that overall, they felt safe and comfortable in their host community, especially when compared to their previous place of residence. Carlos, age thirteen, mentioned that he felt much safer in the United States and therefore could perform better in school. He and several others told us that increasing gang activity was a factor in their decision to leave their Central American community, or that they generally felt safer in the United States.[6] Their main challenge was figuring out how to handle social dynamics and personal relationships in their homes and schools—places where they could also learn to flourish.

## How Can Schools and Communities Help?

For the migrant youth we interviewed, teachers, administrators, and other children were all involved in growing their school into a place of support, community, and belonging. Many interviewees who were longing for family left behind in their birth country while simultaneously adjusting to a new school reported that being in school had been hard at first. They told us that contending with English-language instruction hampered their performance in and enjoyment of school initially, but as their sense of belonging improved, they became excited to attend school. This improvement, which came about as they made friends and were able to speak in Spanish with other Latin students they met, allowed them to feel more at home and part of their community. We concluded that opportunities to communicate with others in Spanish can be an essential determinant of school enjoyment.[7]

Interviewees also benefited from support networks comprised of friends, bilingual counselors, and community organizations offering support to their families as well. Melissa, age fourteen, reported that she felt welcome in her school and received sound support from being able to attend a free public school, participate in language and integration support programs, and come to know many students in situations like her own. The efforts undertaken by schools and communities to support youth migrants can make all the difference for them during what is often a distressing period of integration. To truly become welcoming and supportive institutions, schools need more language support, staff who speak Spanish, and more social workers. School systems should ensure that explicit training is provided to all school officials in working with Central American immigrants and students with a history of traumatic experiences.

Overall, the benefits of family reunification are worth the struggle. Interviewees, both youth and adult, repeatedly reported that, while the experience could be incredibly challenging, they were now more comfortable in their day-to-day lives and felt that they were working toward a better future. Family services for refugees, asylees, and immigrants can make a considerable difference in the lives of immigrant families. School systems that establish family support programming, or provide grants for community organizations to do so, give youth and their families more opportunities to process their past, reimagine and plan for the future, and work with support toward achieving health and happiness.

CHAPTER EIGHT

# FAMILY-PROPELLED MIGRATION AND IMMIGRANT INTEGRATION

Since 2015, tens of thousands of unaccompanied minors have arrived in the United States and been placed across the country with sponsors who may be their parents, other family members, or friends. Many of the young people among these migrants who are from El Salvador, Guatemala, and Honduras are motivated to leave by the increasing violence and economic and political instability in their countries of birth, as well as a desire for reunification with their parents. Of this group, over 20,000 have moved to the Washington, D.C., region, where they face barriers to integration in their neighborhoods and cities. Their difficulties include overcoming traumatic experiences, family separation, inconsistent or interrupted schooling, and language barriers in their new schools.[1]

In the previous chapters, we discussed the impact of migrating, issues surrounding legal status, home life, and school dynamics on Central American immigrant youths' structural integration, mental health, and well-being. In this concluding chapter, we discuss these issues in tandem as we review the findings of our study, compare the empirical reality to the assumptions that policymakers try to tackle, and recommend urgently needed policy changes.

## The Challenges and Opportunities Faced by Resettled Youth

Young immigrants enter a new country facing different challenges than those confronting adult immigrants. It is clear that any immigrant who wants to integrate into a new country and find a sense of belonging there

https://doi.org/10.7758/dvxg2393.1770

**Table 8.1** *Challenges and Facilitators to Integration*

| | Challenges | Facilitators |
|---|---|---|
| Immigration and legal system | · Anti-immigrant policies<br>· Lack of time, attention from lawyers<br>· CBP conditions<br>· Inability to legally migrate<br>· Fear of deportation for self, family, friends<br>· Legal status barriers to work opportunities, funding | · Ability to legally migrate, with papers in order prior to migration<br>· Weekly meetings with a lawyer |
| Home life | · Family reunification<br>· New siblings, stepfamily<br>· Tight surroundings<br>· Inflexible rules | · Mutual trust and acceptance |
| Schools | · Language acquisition<br>· Interrupted education in sending country<br>· Lower educational level in sending country<br>· Lack of peers and teachers who support them<br>· Systematic registration issues<br>· Bullying | · ESOL programming<br>· Bilingual classrooms<br>· Teachers trained in cultural competence<br>· Supportive peer friendships<br>· School administration able to take on culture change in schools |
| Community | · Fear of police and ICE<br>· For a few, continued gang presence | · Welcoming community<br>· Sport leagues<br>· Public parks and events |

*Source:* Authors' compilation.

has multiple hurdles to jump—understanding new surroundings and a different language, learning new cultural norms, and making connections (see table 8.1). These challenges, however, only skim the surface.

## The Legal System: Cruel and Counterproductive Policies That Criminalize Migration

The Trump administration's many immigration policy changes made it increasingly difficult for asylum seekers, immigrant youth, and their families to gain legal immigration status in order to stay in the country.

Some of those policy changes are listed in the following timeline of zero tolerance policies:

**2017**
- February: Memo is issued increasing the use of expedited removal and expanded detention.
- March: DHS contemplates using family separation as a deterrent.[2]
- June: Prolonged detention. U.S. Immigration and Customs Enforcement (ICE) and the Office of Refugee Resettlement (ORR) share information, targeting sponsors of UACs.
- August: The Central American Minors (CAM) program is rescinded. It allowed certain minor nationals of El Salvador, Guatemala, and Honduras, as well as some of their family members, an opportunity to apply for refugee status and resettlement in the United States.
- September: Rescission of DACA is attempted. The program is soon after upheld by the courts, but no new people can register for it.

**2018**
- April: The Trump administration's zero tolerance policy is announced.
- June: Obtaining asylum becomes more difficult for those fleeing domestic and gang violence.[3] The new family detention policy decreases family detention but increases prolonged family separation as family members are held in different detention centers for women, men, and children, including babies of breast-feeding age, rather than as family units or a parent and young child unit.
- The scope of the Flores Settlement Agreement is narrowed.

**2019**
- January: The migrant protection protocols (MPPs) program, also known as "Remain in Mexico," is introduced. Asylum seekers entering the United States to make their asylum case and wait for their court date begin to be metered and sent back to Mexico with no information about when to return to file for asylum.

**2020**
- March: The CDC is ordered to invoke Title 42 to stop taking in asylum seekers owing to public health concerns around the COVID-19 pandemic.
- April: MPP hearings are postponed.[4]

**2022**
- August: The Biden administration's 2021 termination of MPPs is allowed by the courts.

**2023**
- May: Title 42 ends. The Biden administration announces new programs to schedule asylum appointments, parole programs for Haitians, Venezuelans, Cubans, and Nicaraguans, and announces a more comprehensive family reunification program for Salvadorans.

Fear impacts immigrants' mental and physical health, and much of that fear stems from policies that could be changed. Over the last fifty years, there has been a noted rise in the number of undocumented people (a status that is artificially produced through inadequate immigration laws) and in the construction of "legality" as a moral compass, as well as rising inflexibility in not only the U.S. immigration system but other immigration systems around the world. These trends started before Trump, and they have continued after Trump. The Illegal Immigration Reform and Immigration Responsibility Act of 1996 (IIRIRA) established a "bar of inadmissibility" for five to ten years of undocumented immigrants who overstayed their visas, and it allowed for deportation without counsel or legal representation.[5] Additionally, the IIRIRA increased resources for immigration enforcement agencies such as Customs and Border Patrol. The IIRIRA was not the only discriminatory policy passed at this time. The Personal Responsibility and Work Opportunity Reconciliation Act of 1996 (PRWORA) restricted undocumented immigrants' rights to social services, including access to food stamps, health care, and Social Security.[6] These acts removed the federal government's responsibility to grant aid to immigrants and allowed state governments to limit or exclude immigrants from federal and state programs with the justification that they had not been in the United States long enough to be entitled to such services.[7] These policies played a critical role in increasing the risk of mental health disorders in immigrant children, including PTSD, anxiety, and depression, by restricting their access to mental health care.

Besides IIRIRA and PRWORA, state laws, such as Arizona's Support Our Law Enforcement and Safe Neighborhoods Act (Arizona SB 1070) of 2010, subjected immigrants to additional perils. Arizona SB 1070 empowered law enforcement agencies to detain anyone who was suspected of being an undocumented immigrant. Anyone detained who was not carrying a legal residency document would be charged with a misdemeanor. The primary goal of Arizona SB 1070 was to reduce the number of undocumented immigrants, to encourage self-deportation, and to discourage new immigrants from entering Arizona. In practice, this law criminalized people simply for appearing to be Hispanic and thus assumed to be undocumented.[8] Another study showed the unfavorable impacts of racial profiling on high school–age Hispanics, who showed a higher probability than Black and White students of reporting feelings of sadness. Hispanic students were also slightly more likely than others to have suicidal thoughts and to have made suicide attempts.[9]

Much has changed since late 2016 and early 2017, when we conducted interviews. Even though former president Trump had already been elected and taken office as many of the interviews were conducted, his immigration policies had yet to take effect. Many who were surveyed had resided in the D.C. region for a long time and may have already had their cases sorted out, but court proceedings were interrupted for others' cases as executive orders and administrative changes altered the rules. Trump's campaign and rhetoric had demonized people who appeared Hispanic; he conflated them with supposedly criminal, "illegal" Mexicans, and his rallying cry urged the United States to build a wall on the southern border.[10] Trump also attacked Central America specifically, making the argument that immigration systems were not secure enough and that gang members—specifically MS-13 members—were supposedly coming in large numbers. Later, the public profile of immigration from Central America and Mexico was turned into spectacle by some observers when the caravans of migrants journeying north highlighted and accelerated immigration from this region.[11]

The Trump administration had a tangible effect on the general atmosphere of immigrants' homes, communities, and schools and sometimes affected the immigration cases of those interviewed. Sixteen-year-old Valentina explained that Trump's rise to power had changed things for her in migration court: "Well . . . I feel that the new laws are being very unfair to immigrants. With the [Trump] government." Gloria, who was nineteen and, like Valentina, from El Salvador, had been in the United States with her family since 2014. She spoke in-depth about the issues that arose after the 2016 election in her interview on June 20, 2017—well into the first part of the Trump administration:

> We went to immigration court before the election, we won the case for residency with the judge, but then when the new president [Trump] entered, they delayed everything, and they asked for more evidence and paperwork. So the lawyer says that we still have until September [2017] to see if they'll—if . . . that is, it goes well with the case or not, or they deny the petition, we don't know.

Indeed, the Trump administration wrote a slew of executive orders and memorandums that rolled back many immigrant protections, including those for children, even unaccompanied children. In July 2017, CBP piloted the practice of separating families from Central America in the El Paso sector. In April 2018, the Trump administration announced the zero tolerance policy vis-à-vis immigration, which was implemented by the Department of Homeland Security and the Department of Justice (DOJ). Under this policy, each and every migrant, including asylum seekers, attempting to cross the U.S. border anywhere other than at an official port of entry was to be detained and criminally prosecuted. As a consequence, migrant children were separated from the adults accompanying them. After public outcry in June 2018, Trump announced that the government would no longer separate families arriving at the border. Yet the separated families were not speedily reunited.[12]

Later in 2018, other policies began to roll out that targeted migrant children: children were transferred to ICE detention immediately after their eighteenth birthday; ORR shared sponsor information with ICE, which used that information to detain undocumented sponsors; the definition of "asylum" (Matter of A-B-) was narrowed; and regulations were proposed that would provide minimal protections for children in federal immigration detention and decimate the protections outlined in the Flores Settlement Agreement. Then, in the beginning of 2019, the Trump administration began implementing the migrant protection protocols (MPPs) program, also known as "Remain in Mexico." Under MPP, individuals who arrived at the southern border and asked for asylum were given notices to appear in a U.S. immigration court and then sent back to Mexico. Though unaccompanied minors were exempt from this program, some were reportedly caught in the policy as well. In conjunction with MPP, the Trump administration also created a process called "metering," whereby after reaching an informal daily quota CBP officials turned asylum seekers away without processing them or providing any specific date or time for when they could return. In conjunction with the MPP program, on July 16, 2019, the Trump administration announced and put into effect a ban on asylum, also known to some as "Asylum Ban 2.0," which made all individuals who entered, attempted to enter, or arrived in the United States across the southern border ineligible for asylum if they transited through at least one country outside of their country of origin and had not applied for protection in that country.[13]

Despite the public controversy over its intentional separation of immigrant families, the Trump administration continued to execute policies that affected the lives of children coming to the United States. On March 20, 2020, the administration invoked a public health law, Title 42, to restrict border crossings for public health reasons. These restrictions initially were also applied to children, and under Title 42, more than 8,800 children were expelled from the United States. The first danger for children who were being processed under Title 42 was that it took away the protections granted to unaccompanied migrant children under Title 8 of the U.S. Code §1232 ("Enhancing Efforts to Combat the Trafficking of Children") and the Trafficking Victims Protection Reauthorization Act (TVPRA) of 2008. Because children no longer had the protections that they were previously afforded, they were no longer being processed and detained through ORR. Instead, they were secretly being held in hotels and eventually expelled from the United States. Unlike licensed ORR shelters nationwide, the hotels were not inspected by child welfare agencies to ensure that the children were being given adequate care. Furthermore, because little information about these hotels was available, the children did not have access to legal counsel there and thus could not be screened for eligibility for protection and legal relief. Since then, litigation stopped the detention of minors in hotels and has allowed them to enter the United States and be processed under Title 8.

The Trump administration did everything in its power to push its anti-immigrant agenda and strip children and adults of the humanitarian protections they deserve. Thus, *some of the people interviewed for this study may have since been deported or denied asylum.* Importantly, future administrations and policymakers need to institute a more humanitarian refugee, asylum, and immigration policy.[14]

## Home Life: New and Old Family Relationships

The youth surveyed in this study reported that getting used to the relationship with their parents or other sponsors was hard at first, though it often improved over time. For instance, thirteen-year-old Diana shared that she was raised by her grandparents and had not met or had a relationship with her parents before migrating. She had talked to them a few times, but had no knowledge of them outside of understanding that they were her parents. When asked about leaving El Salvador, she said: "I felt good, on the one hand, but also sad. I felt good because I was going to meet my parents and have more opportunities to study. And sad too, because I was going to leave my grandparents, who would be staying there, as well as my friends."

Sofia (age sixteen), Luis (nineteen), Nelson (twelve), and Manuel (sixteen), who went from living with other relatives in their countries of origin to living with their parents in the United States, reported that those whom they considered to be their family or who supported them the most were now the farthest away. When asked who he thought of as family, Manuel, who was fifteen when he migrated, said, "Just my grandparents." Luis said that learning how to have relationships with those who are family by title but not by experience can be a long and difficult process.

Overall, the benefits of family reunification are worth the struggles—but those struggles do not have to exist. Ending practices of separation and regularizing the legal status of individuals and families who are in the United States would be a major start. Family service organizations, which are constantly pursuing outreach efforts to refugees, asylees, and immigrants, can make considerable differences in the lives of immigrant families. Jurisdictions around the country could create their own programs or award grants to community organizations to scale up their school and family support programs, protected from federal changes that could take place in funding, to help immigrant families process their past while overcoming barriers to health and happiness in their new lives and building for their future.

## Schools and Education

Foreign educational credentials and other forms of human capital do not always translate into better work opportunities and higher pay, even though the predominant schools of thought in economics argue that they do. Juan wanted to finish his technical training before coming to the United States, but it was interrupted when he needed to move on a moment's notice. Even if he had finished his training, Juan would probably have needed other credentials on top of what he had learned in his home country if he was to find technical work in the United States. In addition, finishing his technical training before migrating would not have brought him the social capital—connections to people—that he would need. He was likely to encounter hiring managers who preferred workers who spoke perfect, unaccented American English. For example, Juan mentioned that he still struggled in English-only spaces, such as when he tried to ride a bus and could not understand what the driver was telling him. Even if he spoke English well, he might be profiled as uneducated by those screening him for work.[15]

One of the most prominent struggles that schools have in welcoming and accommodating young adults is the language barrier. Immigrant minors are often enrolled in programming for students with interrupted formal education (SIFE) and in English for Speakers of Other Languages (ESOL) and English Language Learners (ELL) programs. Those in our study reported that low proficiency in English was a barrier to their performance and happiness in school, but that after they made friends and found other Latin students with whom they could speak Spanish, they felt more at home. Thus, the ability to communicate with others in Spanish was an essential determinant of school enjoyment. Bilingual staff were invaluable, as were the many dual-language immersion programs in the area.

## Institutional Responses to Trauma

We found that school districts and families need more support within our region from schools and other public institutions. Against a backdrop of economic anxiety and food insecurity, especially during the COVID-19 pandemic, food pantries, school-based food programs, and school-based counseling and family services have been welcoming and lifesaving. Many of these benefits were opened up to everyone, not means-tested, and did not require any particular legal or employment status. These efforts should continue to be supported, celebrated, and expanded.

## Community Support: Aspirations and Hopes

Although every immigrant's circumstances are different, broadly speaking, integration is often successful when immigrants achieve the freedom to meet their physical, social, and emotional needs. Many of the youth we interviewed had been victims of or witnessed violence at a young age. Many also carried the memories of a notoriously dangerous journey north and detention by Customs and Border Protection. Others were leaving family members who raised them and entering an unfamiliar household with parents they may have never known, and some were now living with their new stepfamilies. They also harbored dreams and ambitions: a desire to learn English; a hope that they, like any other student, would make friends in school; the goal of following a particular career path; and for many, a desire to return to their home country one day.

A common problem is that families and youth may not be aware of the full breadth of the federal, state, and other services available to them. This problem could be alleviated with more resources for local organizations to make more contact with parents to ensure that they know about these services for them and their children. Local schools and districts could provide more extensive bilingual and immersion programs that provide this information, and they could institute "deliberate integration." For instance, Prince George's County has opened new high schools designed explicitly for getting unaccompanied immigrant youth where they need to be regarding SIFE and ESL. Public youth programming, such as park district teams, local youth soccer leagues, and afterschool and summer programs, should conduct outreach to enroll more immigrant youth whose parents are not fluent in English.

## The Social Process of Family Reunification

In the following section, we provide a quick summary of findings, which sometimes do and sometimes do not confirm points in the literature and popular discussion of who youth migrants from Central America are, why they are coming, and what their presence means for the greater society.[16]

### VOLUNTARY VERSUS FORCED MIGRATION

There was consensus among several service provider respondents that country of origin functions as a reliable predictor of youths' primary motives for migration. Around 2016, Guatemalan youth and families were typically framed as economic migrants, in contrast to their Salvadoran and Honduran counterparts, who were often characterized as refugees fleeing situations of untenable violence and persecution. This notion was based on service providers' knowledge of youths' migration histories and the reasons for their interrupted formal education.

Salvadorans, Hondurans, and many Guatemalan youth consistently cited economic reasons for leaving school, such as having to work to augment the family income, in some cases even when the family received remittances. Some felt a need to work because they did not have enough money to afford school uniforms, supplies, or transportation. Youth migrating at age sixteen saw themselves more as workers than as students, given that they already fulfilled many responsibilities in their families, including contributing to family income. Salvadoran and Honduran youth also frequently reported being unable to attend school in their hometown owing to community security issues, including gang recruitment along routes to school and school closures prompted by gang activity in and around schools. What motivated these youth to migrate, however, were aging caregivers becoming unable to care for them financially, the desire to be reunited with their parents, and different kinds of threats, from gang violence to climate change affecting crops and natural disasters, such as Hurricane Mitch, destroying their houses.

Salvadoran and Honduran youth whose education was interrupted dropped out of school closer to the time of their departure for the United States; as a result, they seemed to have accumulated fewer educational deficits than their Guatemalan peers. Our youth interviews support these providers' perceptions of education. In at least a few instances, Salvadoran and Honduran youth respondents abandoned school only weeks or months before migrating. Although Salvadorans outnumber Guatemalans throughout the Washington, D.C., metropolitan area, this is not the only reason they outnumbered Guatemalans in our study. The tendency of Guatemalan youth to forgo schooling in order to enter the labor force full-time—first in their native country and then in the United States—could partly explain the disproportionately low number of Guatemalan students referred to our study by our school-based service providers. Furthermore, their limited formal education in Guatemala may have posed a barrier to persisting in their studies in U.S. schools and perhaps even to enrolling in the first place.

### U.S.-BASED FAMILY MEMBERS: THE KEY INITIATING AGENTS AND FACILITATORS OF YOUTH MIGRATION

Whether or not their children were the ones to push the idea, in most cases parents in the United States took responsibility for coordinating the logistics of their children's journey, including hiring and paying for a coyote. They also provided the contact information that the youth would need to present to immigration authorities once apprehended at the southern border. This finding speaks to the central role of family reunification in consideration of the resettlement destination for migrant youth. However, it does not contradict our finding that more immediately compelling circumstances, such as forced recruitment of youth by gangs, a caregiver's poor health, or the death of the caregiver, frequently make reunification the only alternative. In other words, while family reunification is a long-term goal of most transnational families, the emigration of Central American minors seems to be further motivated by violence and insecurity in the home community.[17] We conceptualize that decision-making process in terms of cumulative risk, hypothesizing that once a threshold of adversity is reached, no viable alternatives remain outside of migration.

Drawing on interviews with Mexican families who had migrated together to North Carolina, Krisa Perreira and her colleagues frame immigration as a "parenting decision" motivated by parents' determination to act in their children's best interests—for example, to obtain a better education for them, secure a better economic future for them, have them grow up in a safer environment, or reconnect them with family.[18]

### SPONSORING AGENCIES: THE KEY TO EFFECTIVE DETERRENCE-BASED STRATEGIES

As a corollary to the previous finding, the most effective deterrent to youth and family migration from the region has proven to be fear and uncertainty around immigration enforcement policies and practices among family sponsors in the United States. Referencing the political climate in 2016 and 2017, around the time Donald Trump was elected president, family members we interviewed routinely expressed reluctance to send for other children or relatives still living in their country of origin and serious concern for the few youths in our sample who had opted to migrate since the beginning of the Trump administration.

This finding is corroborated by the 54 percent drop in the number of unaccompanied minors apprehended at the southern border during the first six months of 2017 compared to the same period in 2016. We see a further decrease in 2020, largely caused by the COVID-19 pandemic but also by the continued outsourcing by the United States of some of its immigration enforcement activities to the Mexican government to stop international immigrants en route to the border.[19] The decrease in the number of minors apprehended at the border does not indicate, however, that zero tolerance policies work in the long term; moreover, there are serious issues with the effects of such policies in the short term as well. Violence, more costly attempts, longer family separations, and an increase in danger along the land routes are some of the highlighted long- and short-term effects of such policies.

### OBTAINING DOCUMENTATION FOR YOUTH MIGRANTS

Not all Central American youth reuniting with their families arrive without documents or asking for asylum. Indeed, 18 percent of newcomer youth enrolled in our study arrived in the United States with documents; in all cases, derivative beneficiary status had been secured via a relative's petition. In approximately half of the cases, the sponsoring relative was a father or grandfather, and in the other half a stepfather was the sponsoring relative.

Even though Guatemalan and Honduran youth accounted for over half of our youth respondents, documented youth in our study were exclusively of Salvadoran origin. One plausible explanation for this finding is the higher rate of naturalization among Salvadoran immigrants nationwide: around 34 percent for Salvadorans, 28 percent for Guatemalans, and 23 percent for Hondurans.[20] Higher rates of naturalization translate into increased eligibility to sponsor immediate family members abroad. Another possibility is that relatively higher levels of community organization and solidarity among Salvadoran immigrants in the United States facilitate greater awareness of and access to petitioning processes and resources.

## THE DECLINING HEALTH OR DEATH OF A PRIMARY CARETAKER IN THE HOME COUNTRY

Many family members we interviewed mentioned the failing health or death of a grandparent as the precipitating event in the emigration of minors in the family. This finding points to a new stage in the transnational family life cycle: parents emigrated for largely economic reasons in the 1990s and early 2000s and left their children in the care of grandparents; in the 2010s and 2020s, those caregivers are now well into *la tercera edad* (old age) and finding themselves unable to take care of their adolescent grandchildren. In at least a handful of cases, the poor health of grandparents (uniformly referred to as *mami/mamá* and *papi/papá*) remained a serious cause of anxiety for their grandchildren now residing in the United States.

## THE ROLE OF MISINFORMATION

Premigration awareness of the legal protections that shield unaccompanied youth from immediate deportation was mixed among respondents. When youth indicated that they had intentionally presented themselves to Border Patrol officials, assuming that they would eventually be placed with family members in the D.C. area, that assumption was usually based on familiarity with the similar experiences of friends or family rather than on knowledge of any specific legal provision. Sponsors' perceptions that an amnesty was in the works may have been created by the Obama administration's executive actions around Deferred Action for Childhood Arrivals (DACA) and Deferred Action for Parents of Americans (DAPA), which were indeed introduced by the executive because of Congress's reluctance to pass another amnesty.

Meanwhile, at the height of the so-called border crisis in 2014, numerous reports emerged of migrant smugglers disseminating false information regarding recent and pending U.S. immigration policies in order to expand their Central American client base.[21] Respondent accounts of how coyotes were contracted, coupled with our finding regarding the protagonist role of U.S.-based family members, suggests that migrant smugglers' marketing efforts centered more on selling their record of success to potential clients than on conjuring up partially erroneous expectations among Central American households concerning the prospects of amnesty. Although no doubt capitalized on by smugglers, those expectations had probably already been raised prior to the summer of 2014 and were enduring as accounts of resettlement following apprehension at the border spread throughout sending communities. Nonetheless, family dynamics and situations on the ground remain a larger driver of migration than changes in U.S. policies or administrations.

## "HEROIC" VERSUS "INDIFFERENT" MIGRANTS

After nearly two decades of largely remittance-driven migration, the most recent Central American migrants forced from their region appear to have changed the migrant profile, calling into question the widely held assumption that they represent the self-sacrificing heroes of their society. Without turning a blind eye to migrants' fortitude and resilience, we have the impression that youth are less often motivated by courage or a desire to be counted among their community's and family's remittance-sending heroes than by direct threats of violence or a wholesale lack of opportunities that compel them to leave. They are further spurred on by the hope and faith that they will be exempt from the dangers of the migration journey itself (despite public awareness campaigns funded by the U.S. Department of State and United States Agency for International Development) and the hardships of living in a foreign country.

That said, some youth, even though they were like all the other youth respondents in wanting to remain in the United States, could be characterized as content bordering on indifferent. They had been uprooted from social circles in their home countries but continued to engage with friends and family through social media. A majority of them reported not missing anything beyond family and, occasionally, food. Nonetheless, they would be fine with returning to their countries of birth if security and economic conditions improved.

### CHILD ABUSE OR HOUSEHOLD VIOLENCE REPORTED BY YOUTH RESPONDENTS

Based on interviews with over three hundred unaccompanied Central American youth between the ages of twelve and seventeen conducted in 2014, the UN Refugee Agency (UNHCR) found that almost one in five (23 percent) of Guatemalan children reported some form of abuse in the home, as did 24 percent of Hondurans, 20 percent of Salvadorans, and 17 percent of Mexican children.[22] This finding was not mirrored in our study: around 11 percent of our respondents reported physical abuse at home. There are several possible reasons for this discrepancy. First is the difficulty in eliciting such sensitive information coupled with children's reluctance to share shame-filled experiences. Also, UNHCR used a broad definition of "abuse" that included physical, emotional, and sexual abuse, sibling violence, and intimate partner violence, not all of which were explicitly asked about in our study. Finally, youth may fail to recognize their experiences as abusive, a point also raised in the UNHCR report.

For example, Sebastián, a young Salvadoran man, recounted the routine use of severe corporal punishment in what he otherwise reported as a loving, supportive home. It is unclear whether he considered that kind of discipline action abusive at the time when he was the target of it or whether he came to identify it as such only after migrating. If the latter, his experience would speak to differing cultural norms between sending and receiving communities around the role of corporal punishment in child-rearing. Other notable reports included one case of physical abuse, two cases of sibling violence, and at least one report of forced labor.

Related to the question of household violence were reports from a handful of mother sponsors citing an abusive relationship as one of the principal reasons for their decision to migrate to the United States and leave their children in the care of grandparents or other relatives. Domestic abuse was less prevalent in the lives of the mothers who recently accompanied their children to the United States. Less than half of newly arrived migrant mothers reunited with their children's biological father residing in the D.C. metropolitan area.

## COPING WITH GENERALIZED SOCIETAL VIOLENCE

Widespread societal violence did not appear to correlate with heightened levels of stress or anxiety experienced by youth in their country of origin. Participants displayed diminished and blunted emotional responsiveness to the violence they had experienced. On several occasions, a young interviewee impassively narrated an account of the disappearance of friends and non-immediate family members. Respondents spoke of the ubiquity of gangs—expressed most commonly in terms of restricted movement within their neighborhoods and between rival gang territories—as simply a reality to be managed—that is, until becoming a target for gang recruitment or retribution. Thus did the deeply entrenched forms of societal violence manifested in brutalities and terror at the community level become normalized as everyday violence, including but not limited to extortion payments, curfews, staying home from school, and shoot-outs in the street.

Youth respondents were considerably more likely to reference an overall climate of violence than an imminent threat to their own personal safety as one of the reasons behind their decision to migrate. There were, of course, multiple exceptions, but often they had opted to migrate before they were directly persecuted themselves, whether by a gang or by others threatening violence. Youth tended to experience generalized violence in particular areas of Central American countries as a major push factor rather than as purely individual-level persecution, with its implications for their eligibility for legal status. Although youth and sponsors alike were aware of the consequences of waiting until it was too late, it could be inferred from many of the sponsor interviews that many were unaware of the fact that indiscriminate violence did not constitute sufficient grounds for an asylum claim in the United States at the time.

### INTERNAL RELOCATION: NOT AN OPTION

There were practically no accounts of respondents attempting to relocate within their country of origin prior to leaving for the United States. We can infer that relocation was not viewed by respondents as a feasible option based on at least a few factors. One was a lack of family members or other potential caregivers living elsewhere in the country, or in a safer place. Another factor was the systemic nature of the factors that contribute to social exclusion; that is, relocation from a rural area to an urban center does not guarantee optimal insertion into the new labor market or government provision of basic services, including but not limited to security. Finally, and perhaps most importantly, gangs have sophisticated networks that monitor citizens' movements, precluding their ability to escape detection by gang members. Nonetheless, because this surveillance is weaker in the United States, U.S.-based family members are better able to facilitate youth migration.

### Family-Propelled Immigration

Central American immigration is ultimately driven by social networks and familial connections. We call this idea "family-propelled migration." This is not to say that there is no violence, instability, and poverty in the region causing people to migrate; in fact, that is very much the case. However, only those lucky enough to have the connections, money, and sponsors to come to the United States are able to make it out. Someone who was in as bad a situation as those experienced by many of our informants but who did not have the connections abroad and the access to money that they did would have had to stay or migrate as an indentured servant, forced to work, even if they were a minor, to pay their migration costs.[23]

### Helping Minors and Their Families at the Border by Integrating Them into Our Communities

The desire of children and teenagers to reunite with parents abroad from whom they have been long separated has fueled their migration in recent decades. Given that family-propelled migration is common, we argue that the current increase in immigrant arrivals at the U.S.-Mexico border is largely driven by: (1) the long-term family separation of transnational families; (2) U.S. interventions in Central America and the legacy of the Cold War, which made the parents and grandparents or recent minor arrivals settle in the United States; and (3) the war on drugs, the criminalization of youth gangs, and their jailing in the United States and deportation to Central America, further fueled by the war on drugs in Mexico and the increased power and impunity of organized crime in Mexico and northern Central America.

Since the 1980s, Central Americans have immigrated to the United States in high numbers and by now have integrated into communities across the country, from Los Angeles to Washington, D.C. Additionally, Central Americans are now the primary source of high-demand labor at the lower end of the pay scale in the United States because Mexican migration has decreased to net zero since 2008. With that in mind, the best way to help Central American minors and their families and to rebuild the American economy after the economic and public health devastation wrought by the COVID-19 pandemic is to welcome them to our communities. Research shows that communities that welcome and support immigrants are stronger ones. Instead of focusing on preventing immigrants and asylum seekers from arriving at the border or expelling them if they make it that far, a nation that receives many immigrants should focus on integration. In particular, we should focus on improving mental health by providing a safe and welcoming context that is respectful of immigrants' rights and cultures and creates a feeling of belonging. A large part of that is ensuring that everyone living in the country has food, shelter, and safety.

At the beginning of the Biden administration in early 2021, some questioned whether there was a "crisis" at the border. There was certainly a humanitarian crisis in El Salvador, Guatemala, and Honduras, however, brought on by issues such as lack of clean water, climate change, natural disasters, and the lasting legacies of U.S. interventions that have led to corruption, violence, and instability in this northern part of Central America. Today we are seeing minors arrive at the border unaccompanied hoping to reunite with their families, family units as a whole seeking survival, and single adults trying to ensure economic security for their families or fleeing gang threats and partially failed states. As climate change progresses, some of the issues in Central America may only worsen. Countries that were victims of imperialism, extraction, and interventionism face numerous challenges to safe and stable governance. Ultimately, then, the role of a perpetrator of interventionism and former colonizer on the global stage is to equitably and expediently accept migrants and provide a structure to help them integrate and belong. Attacking the root causes of these problems to ensure safety and stability is the way to go, but it will take time. Furthermore, only Central American countries themselves can do this work, with outside support as needed, and with other countries accepting immigrants abroad.

There are several reasons why the number of migrants arriving at the U.S. southern border were higher than usual in 2021. First, there are seasonal increases and lulls in migration related to the weather, and with the high temperatures of the desert in northern Mexico, it can be more dangerous to travel in the heat of the summer; the cold nights of the winter are also a dangerous time to traverse the desert. People argued in 2022 and early 2023 that there were historical highs in the number of migrants because of the increase in CBP encounters with them. This increase, however, was due to an almost complete closing of the southern border under the Trump administration at the beginning of the COVID-19 pandemic; with the border virtually closed, unaccompanied minors were unable to enter to seek asylum. Furthermore, and contrary to international refugee law, some asylum seekers were made to wait for their court hearings in Mexico.

In recent times we have seen caravans moving from Central America to the U.S.-Mexico border, but the current arrivals are not traveling in large caravans for the most part. Most are children and family members joining a mother, father, uncle, or grandparent already living in the United States for a decade or longer. Whether they arrive at customs and immigration desks alone or with parents is sociologically unimportant. They are part of a transnational family—that is, some of their family members work in the United States and others live in Central America. Many of them have been part of a transnational family for over a decade, or even their entire life. Their migration to the United States is almost entirely about family reunification.

What should the authorities do with new minor arrivals as well as with the minors who were separated from family members by the Trump administration who still have not been reunited with their families?

- The best option is to release minors to family members or approved sponsors. This process takes time because the family members have to be located, their identities must be confirmed, and they need to be vetted to make sure they will take proper care of the children. Some of them may be living undocumented in the United States; others were captured when reporting to pick up minors during the Trump administration and later deported when reporting to pick up minors. So some potential caregivers are now reluctant to step in. There is also now a possibility that the adult family members they traveled with are still stuck in Mexico.
- The Biden administration should speed up the asylum process, for which it will need personnel with adequate cultural and linguistic knowledge. All of these are lacking in the Department of Homeland Security inherited from the Trump administration, which mainly invested only in Border Patrol agents and theatrics around the border wall. Such activities are not helpful in dealing with minors and asylum seekers.
- The asylum process needs to be made clearer and more humane as part of an expanded legal migration system. It also has to be better explained to the wider public.

Defending himself from anti-immigrant critics, Alejandro Mayorkas, the Biden administration's secretary of homeland security, said early in 2021, "We keep the kids, we expel the families."[24] He did not mean that the Biden administration is separating families, as the Trump administration did, but that minors were being given priority for asylum case dates and single adults and families were being sent back to Mexico or sometimes flown back to their country of origin. Initially, the new administration was accepting requests for asylum in the United States from minors traveling alone (unaccompanied minors) as well as from family units with children younger than six years old. Processing the asylum cases of people older than eighteen was not a priority. Priorities change by the day, however, and now some adults who were being held in U.S. facilities are being released into the United States to make room in shelters and immigration detention facilities. At the same time, Mexico is taking longer to process the arrival of noncitizens in its territory.[25] It is likely that asylum policy will continue to be an ever-changing patchwork of processes and priorities for many years after this book is published, though it is our hope that the arguments we make here for a simpler and more compassionate system will resonate with policymakers.

Those arguments are based on these premises: Deporting any adults and families prior to an asylum hearing is both inhumane and against the principles of international law. Mexican-side border camps are unsafe. The border must be open to adult asylum seekers.

## WHAT TO DO

Much of the immigration discourse does not mention some basic facts. The first and most important is that many of the youth coming to the border already have a parent living in a community in the United States where they live, work, and contribute to society. Second, conditions in the areas that youth are coming from can be violent, economically disadvantaged, or both, and they are fleeing for their safety and health and to reunite with their families. Youth and their families want to stay in their home country but often feel as though they have no choice if they are to survive. Youth should be allowed to pass through the border and reunite with their families.

The best way to address the pressures that we see at our southern border would be to begin by strengthening and expanding the legal migration system. This would work in various ways. First, if the Senate approved a pathway to citizenship for those living in the United States undocumented or with temporary protective status, the asylum cases of many Central Americans would be settled through the legal process of family reunification, thus speeding up processing times for those cases.

The Biden White House's move in this regard should be lauded. On April 27, 2023, the Homeland Security Department and the Department of State announced new programs "creating family reunification parole processes for El Salvador, Guatemala, Honduras, and Colombia, as well as modernizing the longstanding Haitian Family Reunification Parole process and the Cuban Family Reunification Parole process."[26] These new programs are absolutely steps in the right direction. Time will tell how efficacious they are.

Second, having a system for applying for preapproved asylum and family reunification in the United States while remaining in one's country of origin could help those who do not need to leave immediately. It would also help those who face active gang threats plan a safer passage to the United States. State and Homeland Security have also moved to make migration safer and more efficient for migrants by allowing them to process applications away from the border and the U.S. interior and instead in offices in Latin America and on the CBP One app; the results of this innovation, however, remain to be seen.[27] Nevertheless, like many Afghans, some Central Americans—including dozens of young Central Americans we interviewed—need to escape sudden and credible death threats, and expecting them to follow this procedure would be inhumane and impractical.

Third, connecting Central Americans to agricultural work visas could help the unemployed in Central America and those facing the negative effects of climate change and natural disasters; it would also relieve the pressure on the asylum system and lessen the exploitation of many agricultural workers, who have no power in the workplace owing to their immigration status.

The solution to migrant "crises"—which includes expanding work and immigrant visa programs that treat families as the unit of migration and not the individual—is actually not that hard. The real problems are found in the many durable inequalities that create and maintain structural family separation alongside precarious work conditions and low pay for migrants. Gradually creating a global safety net by rethinking international aid aimed at reducing global inequality and producing sustainable development globally to reduce climate change could also reduce the economic incentives of those living in the Global South to move abroad by creating economic opportunities for them. Development aid should go to projects that the governments and populations of El Salvador, Honduras, and Guatemala see as useful, worthwhile, and capable of providing long-lasting support for those who live there.

The public and politicians should drop their mantra of "do not come" and instead embrace the value of migration while simultaneously acknowledging the harm that the United States has done to create geopolitical and economic situations that necessitate migration for many who face hardship, poverty, or persecution. Non-precarious legal status and protections need to be more readily available to those who are already in the United States and those who come here to work; clearly, there is seldom a shortage of work in the United States, and making immigration easier reduces risk across the board. The current system upholds a restrictive process that puts prospective migrants in danger during the migration trip, at the border, and in the communities where they settle. It is an informal and underground immigration system that sends children to travel alone on a dangerous journey, often on hazardous transport like La Bestia, and subjects them to traumatic situations. No one should have to experience such a journey, let alone children. In the United States, labor policies and enforcement are needed that would help everyone from the bottom up, such as raising the minimum wage for everyone, regardless of immigration status.

Our work has distinctive and important implications for social policy that are not restricted to immigration, youth, and families. It also points to the ways in which poor families are often left to fend for themselves and must depend on a labor market that systematically underpays them and provides no avenue for learning and career growth. We also make a clear connection between parents' inability to be the parents they want to be and the low wages and weak labor protections for not only immigrants but also the greater American public.[28] There is no reason for confining these findings and connections to immigrants; rather, they show us the importance of a well-functioning social democracy for *everyone*.

School access, public health care, and legal protections in and out of the workplace affect everyone. For instance, our findings show clearly that the more well-resourced traditional public school districts we have, the better off students and families are. Based on our research, we definitively find a somewhat obvious conclusion—that free and low-cost community health care and free or low-cost health insurance improve the health of children and families in every way—socially, emotionally, and physically.

We find many signs of Central American youth integrating successfully into the area of D.C., Maryland, and Virginia. With a better national immigration policy environment, more general education that addresses wrong stereotypes of immigrants, and social programs that benefit everyone living in the United States, the societal integration of these minors is more likely to be indistinguishable from the integration and belonging of children in White families that have been in the United States for many generations.

Finally, being intentional in welcoming new immigrants, refugees, and asylum seekers will go a long way in securing the success of those who have chosen to participate in the future of the United States, not only in how we greet them at the border but also in how we support our communities and schools. Investing in public parks, schools, and national safety nets benefits immigrants and locals alike. We would do well to remember that immigrants do not threaten the U.S. economy or U.S. culture but maintain and strengthen them—and will continue to do so as they and their children live in the country that welcomed them.

# APPENDIX: NOTES ON METHODS AND INSTRUMENTS

## Semistructured Interview Guide for Local Officials and School Administrators

Please answer these questions specifically as they relate to newly arrived unaccompanied youth from Central America.

1. What are the main challenges that unaccompanied migrant youth face in enrolling and integrating into school?
2. What social, emotional, and academic needs do these youth have? (*Depending on the role of the respondent, the following questions may be answered in terms of the entire school district, a specific school, or both.*)
3. What administrative or structural challenges do schools face in servicing this population?
4. What new programs or additional resources have been allocated to meet these youths' needs?
5. What services are available for these youth to prevent dropout?
6. What services are available for these youth to prevent mental health problems?
7. What services are available for these youth to treat mental health?
8. What services are available for these youth to prevent substance use?
9. What services are available to promote the engagement of these youths' caregivers?
10. What resources are needed to better meet the needs of these youth?

https://doi.org/10.7758/dvxg2393.6387

## Encuesta a Menores Migrantes No Acompañados (Survey of Unaccompanied Migrant Minors)

Hola, mi nombre es _____. Como parte de este proyecto estamos entrevistando jóvenes migrantes que por razones políticas o económicas han emigrado de su país de origen. No hay respuestas correctas o incorrectas, sólo queremos aprender de sus experiencias.

Todas las respuestas serán confidenciales. No le preguntaré su apellido u otra información personal. No tiene que responder a todas las preguntas. Usted tiene el derecho de contestar o no contestar cualquier pregunta. Solo tengo que informarle que si usted hiciera mención en particular sobre violencia domestica, o pensamientos suicidadas o homicidas tendré que informarle a las autoridades.

Las respuestas obtenidas en esta entrevista serán comparadas con las respuestas de otras 100 personas entrevistadas y no usaremos su nombre al reportarlas. ¿Podría entrevistarlo(a)? Sí me lo autoriza, grabaré la entrevista en audio. En cualquier momento puedo dejar de grabar si usted me lo solicita.

Muchas gracias por su participación. ¿Tiene usted alguna pregunta antes de iniciar?

### INTRODUCCIÓN

1. ¿De qué país es usted?
2. ¿Cuántos años tiene?
3. ¿Cómo te identificas? ¿Hombre, mujer u otro (*especifique*)?
4. ¿Con quién vivía antes de migrar?
5. ¿En donde dormían usted y su familia? Es decir, ¿cómo se acomodaban las personas para dormir? (*si necesita aclarar*) ¿Varias personas dormían en una misma habitación? ¿En una misma cama?]
6. ¿Cómo se llevaba la familia antes de migrar?
7. ¿Iba usted a la escuela?
   (*si sí*) a. ¿En qué nivel o grado estaba la última vez que fue a la escuela?
   (*si no*) b. ¿En qué año dejó de estudiar en su país de origen?

8. Describa su estado de salud antes de la migración. (*solicite que explique y sondee las siguientes condiciones*)

|  | Si | No |
|---|---|---|
| Estrés constante | | |
| Ansiedad (intranquilidad o preocupación excesiva) | | |
| Tristeza | | |
| Problemas de salud mental (*especifique*) | | |
| Problemas médicos (crónicos, infecciosos, y otros) (*especifique*) | | |
| ¿Consumía alcohol (licor)? | | |
| ¿Fumaba o usaba productos de tabaco? | | |
| ¿Usaba drogas ilícitas (ilegales)? (*si sí*) ¿Qué droga? | | |

9. ¿Cómo describiría su situación económica antes de migrar?

### EXPOSICIÓN A VIOLENCIA/ AMENAZAS EN EL PAÍS DE ORIGEN

10. ¿Alguna vez fue amenazado en su país de origen? ¿Vio que alguien más en su país de origen fuera amenazado con violencia?
11. ¿Alguna vez fue golpeado en su país de origen?
12. ¿Era usted maltratado en su país de origen?
13. ¿Usted o alguien fue atacado con un cuchillo?
14. ¿Fue alguna vez atacado con un arma de fuego?
15. ¿Vio a alguien a quien le dispararan?
16. ¿Había pandillas donde usted vivía?
17. ¿Conoce a alguien que forme parte de una pandilla allá?
18. ¿Hubo alguien que alguna vez le pidiera unirse a una pandilla?
19. ¿Sintió que debía unirse? (¿Me puede explicar?)
20. ¿Fue usted o su familia víctima de extorsiones o secuestro allá? (*si sí*) ¿De qué tipo? ¿Con qué frecuencia?
21. ¿Alguna vez tuvo hambre pero no tenía dinero para comprar alimentos? (*si sí*) ¿Con qué frecuencia?

### VIAJE A LOS ESTADOS UNIDOS

22. ¿Por qué salió de su país?
23. ¿Cuándo salió de su país?

24. ¿Cuántos años tenía cuando salió de su país? ¿Salió o emigró usted solo(a) o acompañado(a)?
    a. *(si fue acompañado[a])* ¿Quién lo acompañó? ¿Viajó con amigos o familia?
    b. ¿Están ellos también en el área de D.C. ahora?
25. ¿Quién de su familia estaba viviendo en los Estados Unidos antes de que ud? Llegara? (*si tenia familia en E.U.*) ¿Estaba usted ya en contacto con su familia en Estados Unidos antes de salir de su país de origen? (*si sí*) ¿Con cuál de ellos estaba usted en contacto?
26. ¿Por qué fue usted ubicado en D.C.?
27. ¿En qué año llegó usted a este país?
28. ¿En qué año llegó usted a esta ciudad?
29. ¿Qué sucedió cuando usted cruzó la frontera de los Estados Unidos?
30. ¿Cuánto tiempo se tardó en llegar a la frontera después de que salió de su lugar de origen?
31. ¿Cuánto tiempo pasó entre el momento en que cruzó la frontera y llegó a D.C.?
32. ¿Tuvo que pagarle a alguien para que le ayudara con el viaje a los Estados Unidos? (*si sí*) ¿Quién pagó? o ¿Está aún pagando?
33. ¿Con qué recursos contaba usted para emigrar? (*Explore financieros, redes sociales, empleo, beca, familia, ninguno.*) Traía dinero? Sabía si lo esperaba un trabajo? Estaba en comunicación con personas en EUA a través de redes sociales?
34. ¿Se sintió seguro viajando por México o cualquier otro país por el que haya pasado? (¿Me puede explicar?)
35. ¿Fue víctima de algún tipo de violencia mientras viajaba por México o cualquier otro país por el que haya pasado?

### DINÁMICA FAMILIAR

36. ¿Cuándo fue la última vez que vio a su mamá?
37. ¿Cuándo fue la última vez que vio a su papá?
38. ¿Fue usted criado por alguien diferente a sus padres, por ejemplo, sus abuelos o un amigo de la familia?
    *(si sí)* a. ¿Dónde viven?
    b. ¿Cuándo fue la última vez que los vio?

39. ¿Tiene hermanos o hermanas?
    *(si sí) a. ¿Son mayores o menos que usted?*
    *b. ¿Dónde viven?*
    *c. ¿Alguno de ellos ha hecho este viaje a los Estados Unidos antes, con, o después de usted?*
40. ¿Quiénes forman parte de su familia hoy en día? (*Explore si hay dolor emocional, soledad, felicidad, melancolía, pérdida, distanciamiento, contrastes del antes y después.*)
41. ¿Cómo se lleva su familia hoy en día? (*Explore si hay dolor emocional, soledad, felicidad, melancolía, pérdida, distanciamiento, contrastes del antes y después.*)
42. Describa cómo se sintió cuando se separó o dejó su hogar en su lugar de origen. (*Explore si hubo tristeza, temor, melancolía, paz u otros.*)
43. Describa cómo ha sido su experiencia estableciendo un hogar en esta región. (*Explore cambios positivos, negativos o no cambios y razones.*)

### PATROCINADOR

44. ¿Es su patrocinador...
    *a ... uno de sus padres, hermanos, otro pariente o amigo?*
    *b. ... una persona que ya conocía o que le habían presentado antes?*
45. ¿Dónde vive en este momento? (*Explore si vive con su patrocinador en este momento.*)
46. ¿Cuántas personas viven con usted?
47. ¿Cuántos de ellos son familiares suyos?
48. ¿Cómo se llevan?
49. ¿Su patrocinador(a) trabaja?
50. ¿Qué tipo de trabajos tienen las personas que viven con usted?

Califique las situaciones que voy a leerle usando la siguiente escala: (0) totalmente en desacuerdo; (1) en desacuerdo; (2) ni de acuerdo ni en desacuerdo; (3) de acuerdo; (4) totalmente de acuerdo.

51. La gente con quien vive ahora le ayuda mucho.
52. La gente con quien vive ahora se lleva muy bien.
53. La gente con quien vive ahora es muy unida.

Califique con qué frecuencia la gente con quien vive ahora realiza las siguientes actividades juntos usando la siguiente escala: (1) nunca; (2) rara vez; (3) a veces; (4) a menudo; (5) muy a menudo.

54. Ver televisión juntos.
55. Comer juntos.
56. Jugar dentro o fuera de la casa juntos.
57. Visitar a familiares o amigos juntos.
58. ¿Considera que está bien que su patrocinador tenga reglas sobre dónde, cuándo y con quién puede usted pasar el tiempo?
59. ¿Cuánto tiempo pasa sin la compañía de personas adultas cuando está . . .
    a. . . . *fuera de la casa?*
    b. . . . *en su casa?*
60. ¿Con qué frecuencia habla con su patrocinador acerca de lo que usted hace cuando no está en casa?
61. ¿Con qué frecuencia su patrocinador le pregunta sobre lo que hace en su tiempo libre?
62. ¿Con qué frecuencia necesita usted tener el permiso de su patrocinador para estar fuera de la casa más tarde de lo habitual?
63. ¿Qué lo hace sentir seguro en su casa/comunidad?
64. ¿Qué lo hace sentir inseguro en su casa/comunidad?
65. ¿Hay crimen en donde usted vive? (*si sí*) ¿Lo ha afectado el crimen local aquí? ¿Cómo?
66. ¿Le gustaría quedarse en los Estados Unidos?
67. ¿Cree que los Estados Unidos lo trata justamente?
68. ¿Alguien lo ha hecho sentir mal o lo ha molestado a causa de su raza, color de piel, o por el lugar dónde nació?
    *(si sí)* a. ¿*En casa?*
    b. ¿*En la escuela?*
    c. ¿*En dónde vive?*
69. ¿Cómo esperaba que fuera los Estados Unidos? ¿Ha sido como usted lo esperaba?
70. ¿Va usted a la iglesia? (*si sí*) ¿Dónde?
71. ¿Ha buscado asesoramiento o asistencia de un padre o un pastor de la iglesia? (*si sí*) ¿Cómo le han ayudado?

72. ¿Ha recibido o está recibiendo algún tipo de orientación, asesoramiento o terapia? Especifique cuál. ¿Dónde?

## CORTE DE INMIGRACIÓN

73. ¿Estuvo en una corte por temas relacionados con su estatus migratorio o por alguna otra razón?
    *(si sí)* a. *¿Cree que entendió los procedimientos judiciales?*
    b. *¿Cree que fue tratado de forma justa por la corte?*
74. ¿Ha hablado con un abogado?
    *(si sí)* a. *¿Cómo encontró un abogado?*
    b. *¿Cuándo fue la primera vez que vio a un abogado?*
    c. *¿Con que frecuencia y cuando ha consultado a un abogado? ¿Es el mismo abogado?*
    d. *¿Su abogado le proporciona el apoyo que necesita?*
    e. *¿Está su abogado solicitando alguna forma específica para evitar su deportación, por ejemplo, asilo o Estatus Especial para Jóvenes Inmigrantes?*
75. ¿Se ha tomado alguna decisión sobre su caso de inmigración?
    *(si no)* ¿Cuándo espera que el caso sea resuelto?

## ESCUELA

76. ¿Trató de inscribirse en una escuela aquí?
    *(si sí)* a. *¿Cómo supo a cuál escuela debía tratar de inscribirse?*
    b. *¿A qué lugar fue para entrar en el sistema escolar?*
    c. *¿Qué pasó cuando intento inscribirse?*
77. ¿Se inscribió a una escuela?
    *(si sí)* a. *¿A qué nivel o grado?*
    b. *¿Era ese nivel o grado el adecuado para usted?*
78. ¿Ha estado en más de una escuela? *(si sí)* ¿En cuáles?
79. ¿Está usted yendo a la escuela en este momento? *(si no)* ¿Por qué no está yendo a la escuela?
80. (*Si estaba yendo a la escuela y dejó de ir*)
    a. *¿Cuándo dejó de ir a la escuela?*
    b. *¿Algún empleado de la escuela intentó contactarlo a usted o a su patrocinador para ayudarlo a volver a la escuela?*
    c. *¿Por qué decidió dejar de ir la escuela?*

81. (*Si está en este momento yendo a la escuela*) ¿Con qué frecuencia va?
82. ¿Cómo ha sido o fue su experiencia en la escuela? ¿Cómo se siente o se sintió?
83. ¿Ha hecho o hizo amigos en la escuela?
    *(si sí)* a. ¿Sus amigos la/lo han ayudado a quedarse en la escuela? ¿Cómo?
    b. ¿Sus amigos lo/la motivaron a no dejar la escuela?

Califique las situaciones que voy a leerle usando la siguiente escala: (1) no es cierto; (2) un poco cierto; (3) bastante cierto; o (4) muy cierto.
¿Tiene usted un amigo de casi su misma edad . . .

84. . . . que realmente se preocupa por usted?
85. . . . con el que puede hablar acerca de sus problemas?
86. . . . que lo ayuda cuando usted está teniendo dificultades?

En la escuela, hay un profesor o un adulto que . . .

87. . . . se preocupa por usted.
88. . . . se da cuenta cuando usted no está en la escuela.
89. . . . lo escucha cuando usted tiene algo que decir.
90. ¿Conoció a un profesor/a o empleado de la escuela que le ayudó? (*si sí*) ¿Cómo le ayudaron? ¿Le ayudaron mucho o poco? ¿Cómo?
91. ¿La escuela demostró que quería que (los estudiantes/usted) tengan éxito? ¿Cómo demostraron que querían que (los estudiantes/usted) tengan éxito? ¿A su escuela le importa que usted sea exitoso?
92. ¿Su escuela ofrece algún tipo de programas especiales para estudiantes recién llegados de otros países?
93. ¿Es usted bilingüe? (*Explore si lo es en inglés o español.*)
94. ¿Habla usted alguna otra lengua? (*si sí*) ¿Cuál?
95. ¿Su escuela ofrece clases en español?
96. ¿Ha tenido alguna clase para aprender inglés?
97. ¿Ha tenido dificultades para comunicarse en su primera y/o segunda lengua? (Explore si ha sido discriminado(a) por su

acento o lengua que habla, o ha sido rechazado(a) o ha tenido acceso a clases de segundo idioma.)
98. ¿Tiene contacto con otros estudiantes que están en su misma situación?
99. ¿Cuántos niños en su escuela cree usted que están en una situación similar a la suya? ¿Cuántos niños son como usted o son de su mismo país? ¿Diría que la mayoría; algunos; muy pocos; ninguno?
100. ¿Está involucrado en actividades extracurriculares? ¿Está en algún club, equipo deportivo, o algo similar? (*si sí*) ¿En cuáles? ¿Cómo se enteró acerca de ellos?
101. ¿Ha establecido contacto con algún tipo de grupo social, comunidad de apoyo u organización en esta ciudad? (*elabore*)
102. ¿Piensa terminar la escuela secundaria? ¿Qué planes tiene para terminar?
103. ¿Qué quiere hacer después de terminar la escuela secundaria? ¿Espera ir a la universidad después de terminar la escuela secundaria?
104. ¿Su calidad de vida mejoró o empeoró como resultado de la migración? (*Explore y obtenga ejemplos.*)
105. ¿Qué cambios culturales, en costumbres o valores, ha tenido como resultado de la migración? (*Explore el tipo de cambio y solicite ejemplo[s].*)

### TRABAJO

106. ¿Está usted trabajando?
    *(si sí)* a. *¿En qué trabaja?*
    b. *¿Cómo encontró este trabajo?*
107. ¿Está tratando de buscar (un trabajo/otro trabajo/un segundo trabajo)?
108. ¿En qué gasta el dinero que gana en el trabajo?
109. ¿Qué tipo de trabajo le gustaría tener cuando sea adulto?

### SALUD EN EL PRESENTE

110. Describa su estado de salud después de la migración. (*Solicite que explique y sondee las siguientes condiciones.*)

|  | Sí | No |
|---|---|---|

Estrés constante
Ansiedad (intranquilidad o preocupación excesiva)
Tristeza
Problemas de salud mental (*especifique*)
Problemas médicos (crónicos, infecciosos, y otros) [Especifique]
¿Consume alcohol (licor)?
¿Fuma o usa productos de tabaco?
¿Usa drogas ilícitas (ilegales)? (*si sí*) ¿Qué droga?

111. ¿Ha estado en alguno de los siguientes lugares en los últimos seis meses?
    a. Clínica u hospital      Sí____ No____ NR____
    b. Albergue      Sí____ No____ NR____

    Descripción_____

    c. Centro de detención      Sí____ No____ NR____
    d. Centro de atención mental/emocional    Sí____ No____ NR____
    e. Centro de rehabilitación por adicciones    Sí____ No____ NR____
    f. Otro      Describa_____

Ver página siguiente para más preguntas.

## Una Encuesta de Parte de su Proveevor de Cuidados de Salud (PHQ-8 Modified for Teens)

*Instrucciones:* ¿Qué tan a menudo ha sentido cada uno de los siguientes síntomas durante las dos ultimas semanas? Por cada síntoma escriba una "X" en el cuadro que mehor describe como se siente.

**Durante las últimas 2 semanas,** ¿qué tan seguido ha tenido molestias debido a los siguientes problemas? (Marque con un "✓" para indicar su respuesta)

|  | (0) Ninguno | (1) Varios Días | (2) Mas de la Mitad de los Días | (3) Casi Todos los Días |
|---|---|---|---|---|
| 1. ¿Se seinte deprimido, irritado, o sin esperanza? | | | | |
| 2. ¿Poco interés or placer para hacer cosas? | | | | |
| 3. ¿Tiene dificultad para dormirse, quedarse dormido, o duerme demasiado? | | | | |
| 4. ¿Poco apetito, perdida de peso, o come demasiado? | | | | |
| 5. ¿Se siente cansado o tiene poca energía? | | | | |
| 6. ¿Se siente mal por usted mismo-o siente que es un fracasado, o que le ha fallado a su familia y a usted mismo? | | | | |
| 7. ¿Tiene problema para concentrarse en cosas tales como tareas escolares, leer, o ver televisión? | | | | |
| 8. ¿Se mueve o habla tan lentamente que las otras personas pueden notarlo? ¿O al contrario-esta tan inquieto que se mueve mas de lo usual? | | | | |
| 9. ¿Pensamientos que estaría mejor muerto o de hacerse daño usted mismo de alguna manera ? | | | | |

*(Table continues on p. 222)*

|  | (0) Ninguno | (1) Varios Días | (2) Mas de la Mitad de los Días | (3) Casi Todos los Días |
|---|---|---|---|---|

¿En el año pasado se ha sentido deprimido o triste la mayoría de los días, aun cuando se siente bien algunas veces?

[ ] Si     [ ] No

Si usted esta pasando por cualquiera de los problemas mencionados en este formulario, ¿qué tan difícil estos problemas le causan para hacer su trabajo, hacer las cosas de la casa, o relacionarse con las demás personas?

[ ] No difícil     [ ] Un poco difícil     [ ] Muy difícil     [ ] Sumamente difícil

¿En el mes pasado hubo algún momento donde usted pensó seriamente en terminar con su vida?

[ ] Si     [ ] No

¿Alguna vez en su vida, trato de matarse o trato de suicidarse?

[ ] Si     [ ] No

*Source:* Spitzer et al. 2010. Translated by the Asian/American Center of Queens College with funds provided by the Queens Borough President Helen Marshall. Modified with permission by the GLAD-PC team from the PHQ-9 (Spitzer, Williams, & Kroenke, 1999). Revised by PHQ-A (Johnson 2002) and the CDS. DISC Development Group, 2000).https://sa1s3.patientpop.com/assets/docs/142048.pdf.

## Trauma Exposure Checklist: Part B

A continuación incluimos una lista de problemas que los jóvenes posiblemente tengan luego de vivir una experiencia estresante, como estar en un accidente grave, padecer de una enfermedad grave, estar separad por más de un par de días de uno de tus padres o de alguien del cual dependías, estar amenazado o golpea estar presente cuando alguien le ha atacado a otra persona con un cuchillo o le ha pegado un tiro o cualquier otra cosa.

Piensa en el evento estresante que más te ha molestado. Marca con un círculo a las palabras que describ con mayor exactitud la frecuencia con la que estos problemas te han molestado en LAS ULTIMAS DOS SEMANAS.

|   | 0 | 1 | 2 | 3 |
|---|---|---|---|---|
| 1. ¿Has tenido pensamientos o imágenes sobre el evento que invaden tu mente indeseadamente? | Nunca | Ocasionalmente | El 50% del tiempo | Prácticamente en todo momento |
| 2. ¿Has tenido sueños desagradables o pesadillas? | Nunca | Ocasionalmente | El 50% del tiempo | Prácticamente en todo momento |
| 3. ¿Has estado comportándote o sintiéndote como si el evento estuviera volviendo a suceder (por ejemplo, oyes algo o ves una imagen al respecto y sientes como si estuvieras viviendo la situación nuevamente)? | Nunca | Ocasionalmente | El 50% del tiempo | Prácticamente en todo momento |
| 4. ¿Te has sentido alterado cuando piensas u oyes sobre el evento (por ejemplo, te has sentido asustado, enojado, triste, culpable, etc.)? | Nunca | Ocasionalmente | El 50% del tiempo | Prácticamente en todo momento |
| 5. ¿Has sentido emociones en tu cuerpo cuando piensas u oyes sobre el evento (por ejemplo, comienzas a sudar, el corazón te late más rápidamente)? | Nunca | Ocasionalmente | El 50% del tiempo | Prácticamente en todo momento |

*(Table continues on p. 224)*

|  | 0 | 1 | 2 | 3 |
|---|---|---|---|---|
| 6. ¿Has tratado de no pensar sobre el evento, de no hablar o de no sentir al respecto? | Nunca | Ocasionalmente | El 50% del tiempo | Prácticamente en todo momento |
| 7. ¿Has tratado de evitar actividades, de evitar a la gente o a sitios que te hacen recordar el evento (por ejemplo, has sentido que no quieres jugar afuera o ir a la escuela)? | Nunca | Ocasionalmente | El 50% del tiempo | Prácticamente en todo momento |
| 8. ¿Te ha pasado que no puedes recordar una parte importante del evento? | Nunca | Ocasionalmente | El 50% del tiempo | Prácticamente en todo momento |
| 9. ¿Has perdido interés o no quieres hacer las cosas que te gustaba hacer? | Nunca | Ocasionalmente | El 50% del tiempo | Prácticamente en todo momento |
| 10. ¿Te has sentido distante de las personas que te rodean? | Nunca | Ocasionalmente | El 50% del tiempo | Prácticamente en todo momento |
| 11. ¿Te ha pasado que no puedes sentir emociones intensas (por ejemplo, no has podido sentirte muy feliz)? | Nunca | Ocasionalmente | El 50% del tiempo | Prácticamente en todo momento |

|  | 0 | 1 | 2 | 3 |
|---|---|---|---|---|
| 12. ¿Has estado sintiendo que tus planes o deseos para el futuro no se harán realidad (por ejemplo, no asistirás a la preparatoria, no conseguirás un trabajo, no te casarás, no tendrás hijos)? | Nunca | Ocasionalmente | El 50% del tiempo | Prácticamente en todo momento |
| 13. ¿Te ha resultado difícil quedarte dormido o dormir? | Nunca | Ocasionalmente | El 50% del tiempo | Prácticamente en todo momento |
| 14. ¿Te has estado sintiendo irritado o has tenido arranques de ira? | Nunca | Ocasionalmente | El 50% del tiempo | Prácticamente en todo momento |
| 15. ¿Te ha resultado difícil concentrarte (por ejemplo, no puedes seguirle el hilo a un relato en la televisión, te olvidas lo que lees o no puedes prestar atención en clase? | Nunca | Ocasionalmente | El 50% del tiempo | Prácticamente en todo momento |
| 16. ¿Has sido demasiado cauteloso (por ejemplo, quieres estar al tanto de quién o qué te rodea)? | Nunca | Ocasionalmente | El 50% del tiempo | Prácticamente en todo momento |
| 17. ¿Has estado nervioso o te has sobresaltado (por ejemplo, cuando alguien se acerca a ti desde atrás)? | Nunca | Ocasionalmente | El 50% del tiempo | Prácticamente en todo momento |

*Source:* Translated by the Los Angeles Unified School System Translations Unit.

## Guía de Encuesta Semiestructurada para Patrocinadores

Hola, mi nombre es _____. Como parte de este proyecto estamos entrevistando padres u otros familiares de jóvenes migrantes que han emigrado de su país de origen. No hay respuestas correctas o incorrectas, sólo queremos aprender de sus experiencias. Todas las respuestas serán confidenciales. No le preguntaré su apellido u otra información personal. No tiene que responder a todas las preguntas. Usted tiene el derecho de contestar o no contestar cualquier pregunta. Solo tengo que informarle que si usted hiciera mención en particular sobre violencia domestica, o pensamientos suicidadas o homicidas tendré que informarle a las autoridades.

Las respuestas obtenidas en esta entrevista serán comparadas con las respuestas de otras 100 personas entrevistadas y no usaremos su nombre al reportarlas. ¿Podría entrevistarlo(a)? Sí me lo autoriza, grabaré la entrevista en audio. En cualquier momento puedo dejar de grabar si usted me lo solicita.

Muchas gracias por su participación. ¿Tiene usted alguna pregunta antes de iniciar?

1. ¿En dónde nació? (*Preguntar por el país de origen.*)
2. ¿Cuánto tiempo ha vivido en los Estados Unidos?
3. ¿Cuál es su parentesco o relación con el menor?

(*Si el patrocinador es el padre o la madre del menor, realice las preguntas que se encuentran a continuación [4–7] y luego proceda a la Pregunta [9].*)

Si no es padre or madre proceda a la pregunta 8. (¿Qué tan bien conocía al menor antes de que llegara a vivir con usted?)

4. ¿Alguna vez fue separado de su hijo/a? Si la respuesta es sí, ¿por cuánto tiempo?
5. ¿Con quién vivió su hijo/a mientras estuvieron separados?
6. ¿Cuánto contacto tuvo con su hijo/a antes de que él/ella llegara a los Estados Unidos? (*Preguntar: ¿un día, una semana, dos veces por semana, una vez al año?*)
7. ¿Qué tan bien conocía a su hija/hijo antes de que llegara a vivir con usted?

Si no es padre or madre:

8. ¿Qué tan bien conocía al menor antes de que llegara a vivir con usted?

(*Todos los patrocinadores responden a las siguientes preguntas:*)

9. ¿Con quién vivía el menor antes de venir a los Estados Unidos? (*Preguntar: ¿el padre y la madre, solo con la madre, otro familiar, alguien fuera de la familia?*)
10. ¿Cuándo llegó su hijo/familiar a los Estados Unidos?
11. ¿Cuáles fueron las razones principales por las que su hijo/familiar vino a los Estados Unidos?
12. Desde que llegó a los Estados Unidos, ¿cuáles considera que han sido los mayores desafíos o dificultades que su hijo/familiar ha tenido que afrontar? (*Preguntar por desafíos o dificultades en la casa, la escuela, el trabajo, etc.*)
13. ¿Está su hijo/familiar inscrito en la escuela? Si la respuesta es sí, ¿Dónde y en qué nivel o grado?
14. ¿Está involucrado en la educación de su hijo/familiar? Si la respuesta es sí, ¿Cómo? Si la respuesta es no, ¿Por qué?
15. ¿Tiene su hijo/familiar un trabajo fuera de la casa?
16. Desde que llegó a los Estados Unidos, ¿Le ha preocupado que su hijo/familiar haya sufrido episodios de tristeza intensa, ansiedad, irritabilidad u otros síntomas notables que parecen afectar el bienestar del menor? (*Si la respuesta es sí, preguntarles al padre o la madre cuales son los síntomas, con qué frecuencia se presentan, la fuente o la razón que genera el estrés, etc.*)
17. ¿Cómo maneja o lidia su hijo/familiar con estos desafíos o dificultares? (*Preguntar: ¿Al menos ve a algún consejero o asesor? ¿Con quién habla?*)
18. ¿Existe algún tipo de servicios que considera serían de ayuda para su hijo/familiar? (*Preguntar por servicios que ellos consideren que puedan ayudar con el proceso de transición.*)
19. ¿Cuáles son sus mayores preocupaciones con respecto a su hijo/familiar? (*Preguntar por lo que le preocupa a los padres o al cuidador, incluyendo el estatus legal del menor, su salud mental, abuso de sustancias, etc.*)

20. ¿Cuántas personas viven con usted?
21. ¿Cuántos de ellos son familiares suyos?
22. ¿Cómo están relacionados con usted?

*Respuestas usando una escala:* Califique las situaciones que voy a leerle usando la siguiente escala: (0) Totalmente en desacuerdo; (1) en desacuerdo; (2) ni de acuerdo ni en desacuerdo; (3) de acuerdo; (4) totalmente de acuerdo.

23. Su familia se ayudan mucho (unos a otros).
24. Su familia se lleva muy bien.
25. Su familia es muy unida.

*Respuestas usando una escala:* Califique con qué frecuencia su familia realiza las siguientes actividades juntos usando la siguiente escala: (1) Nunca; (2) Rara vez; (3) A veces; (4) A menudo; (5) Muy a menudo.

26. Ver televisión juntos
27. Comer juntos
28. Jugar dentro o fuera de la casa juntos
29. Visitar a familiares o amigos juntos
30. ¿Tiene reglas sobre dónde, cuándo y con quién su hijo/familiar pasa el tiempo?
31. ¿Cuánto tiempo pasa su hijo/familiar sin la compañía de personas adultas cuando él/ella está fuera de la casa? ¿Cuándo él/ella está en su casa?
32. ¿Con qué frecuencia habla con su hijo/familiar sobre lo que él/ella está haciendo cuando no están en casa?
33. ¿Con qué frecuencia le pregunta a su hijo/familiar sobre lo que él/ella hace en su tiempo libre?
34. ¿Con qué frecuencia su hijo/familiar necesita su permiso para permanecer fuera de la casa más tarde de lo habitual?

Ya estamos finalizando la entrevista. Solamente tengo dos preguntas más.

35. Recuerde que tiene derecho a no contestar si así lo prefiere, ¿Cuál es su estatus legal?
36. ¿Hay alguna otra cosa que quiera decirme o compartir con nosotros sobre los temas de los que hemos hablado hoy?

# NOTES

## Preface

1. Rose 2022.
2. We use "Latin" as a gender-neutral adjective and sometimes use "Hispanic," when citing studies or statistics that use that term, as synonymous. For more details, see Castañeda 2019, chap. 1.
3. But see Dudley 2020.

## Introduction

1. Scholtes and Ethridge 2014.
2. Godlasky 2022; Holmes and Castañeda 2016; Sajjad 2022.
3. Castañeda 2019.
4. Menjívar and Perreira 2019.
5. Chiodo and Meliza 2014; Jalongo 2010.
6. Boss 2002.
7. Calhoun 2010; Tilly 2010.
8. Czaika and de Haas 2015, 3; Castañeda 2022a; Castañeda 2020b; International Organization for Migration 2022.
9. Xiang and Lindquist 2014, 124.
10. Alba and Nee 2003; Foner 2022; Ignatiev 1996.
11. Although W.E.B. Du Bois studied the internal migration of Black people in the United States around the same time, he has not been widely considered as a contributor to the migration canon.
12. Stone and Harris, 2017.
13. Gans 1992.
14. Castañeda 2019.
15. Jiménez 2010; Telles and Ortiz 2008; Telles and Sue 2019; Tilly 1998.
16. Osuji 2019.

17. Alba and Nee 2003, 270.
18. Bohrt and Itzigsohn 2015, 361.
19. Haller, Portes, and Lynch 2011; Portes and Rumbaut 2014; Portes and Zhou 1993.
20. Haller, Portes, and Lynch 2011, 736.
21. Zapata-Barrero 2015.
22. Ruoxi 2020.
23. Castañeda 2018a; Castles and Davidson 2000; Chaudhary 2018; Foner and Simon 2015; Rumbaut 2005; Ruszczyk 2019; Stepick and Dutton Stepick 2009; Yuval-Davis 2006.
24. Boccagni 2017; Castañeda 2018a, 2020a; Duyvendak 2011.
25. "Integration" here is used differently than it was used to discuss the upward mobility options of African Americans post-emancipation, which would be equivalent to immigrant assimilation or subordination to the culture of White elites.
26. Alba, Kasinitz, and Waters 2011; Alba and Nee 2003; Perlmann and Waldinger 1997.
27. Alba, Kasinitz, and Waters 2011, 764.
28. Alba, Jiménez, and Marrow 2014; Itzigsohn 2009; Kasinitz, Mollenkopf, and Waters 2004; Kasinitz et al. 2008; Okamoto 2003, 2006.
29. Groger and Trejo 2002; Bean and Stevens 2003; Telles and Ortiz 2008.
30. Castañeda 2019.
31. Castañeda 2018a; Gowayed 2022; Hendriks and Burger 2020; Nesterko et al. 2019.
32. Zapata-Barrero 2015.
33. Bohrt and Itzigsohn 2015, 361; Massey 2018. For a problematization of the term "underclass," see Wacquant 2022.
34. Abrego 2014; Heidbrink 2020; Menjívar 2000; Menjívar, Abrego, and Schmalzbauer 2016.
35. Castañeda et al. 2019; Gonzales, Terriquez, and Ruszczyk 2014; Kreisberg and Hsin 2021; Nicholls 2013; Rendón 2019; Valdivia 2020.
36. Evans, Perez-Aponte, and McRoy 2020; Suárez-Orozco et al. 2010.
37. García 2019; Wilson 2020.
38. Boehm 2012; Castañeda and Buck 2011, 2014; Dreby 2010; Oliveira 2018; Parreñas 2005.
39. Castañeda 2018a.
40. Ibid.
41. Hamlin 2021.
42. Galli 2023; Ruehs-Navarro 2022; Olivares 2022.
43. Gonzales, Terriquez, and Ruszczyk 2014; Menjívar 2017.
44. Gonzalez-Barrera and Krogstad 2019.
45. Gonzalez-Barrera 2015; Gonzalez-Barrera and Krogstad 2019; Wassink and Massey 2022.
46. Torres et al. 2022, 1.
47. Cheatham 2021.

48. We thank the second reviewer for some of the insights presented in this subsection.
49. Castañeda 2019.
50. Soboroff 2020; Olivares 2022.
51. Abrego et al. 2017; Menjívar and Abrego 2012.
52. FitzGerald 2020.
53. Ganster 2008.
54. Ngai 2004.
55. Muchowiecka 2013.
56. Hayes 2014, 352.
57. Stokes 2022.
58. Brubaker 1992; Falcke and Vink 2020.
59. Bucerius 2014.
60. Sayad 2004, 2006.
61. Lilly López 2021, 3.
62. Ibid., 26.
63. Suárez-Orozco 2019, 2.
64. Ibid., 2.
65. FitzGerald 2020.
66. UNICEF Mexico, n.d.
67. Heidbrink 2020, 39.
68. Duruiz 2019.
69. DeParle 2019, 161.
70. Ibid., 171.
71. Boccagni 2012; Solari 2017.
72. Cohen 2004; Hondagneu-Sotelo 1994; Massey et al. 1987; Parreñas 2005; Sayad 2004.
73. Massey, Goldring, and Durand 1994, 1499–1550.
74. Tilly 2005, 2007; Tilly and Brown 1967.
75. Portions of the text in this section are adapted from Castañeda and Buck 2011.
76. Nazario 2006.
77. U.S. Customs and Border Protection 2023.
78. Castañeda 2022c.
79. UNICEF Mexico, n.d.
80. Lic. Ortencia Ayala Díaz MAS Guerrero, interview with Castañeda, August 2005, Huamuxtitlán, Mexico.
81. Castañeda 2018a.
82. Sayad 2004; Smith 2006.
83. Suárez-Orozco, Todorova, and Louie 2002.
84. Hondagneu-Sotelo 1994, 62.
85. Grinberg and Grinberg 1989, 23.
86. Akhtar 1995.
87. Moya et al. 2016.
88. Castañeda and Buck 2011.

89. Heymann 2006.
90. Artico 2003.
91. Boss 2002; Suárez-Orozco, Todorova, and Louie 2002.
92. Suárez-Orozco, Todorova, and Louie 2002, 627.
93. Dreby 2006, 3; Foner 2000.
94. Parreñas 2005, 162.
95. Castellanos 2007a.
96. Brennan 2010.
97. Stinchcomb 2020.
98. Chacón 2010.
99. Chauvin and Garcés-Mascareñas 2014.
100. Galli 2020; Holmes et al. 2021; Moffette 2014; Ticktin 2011.
101. Heidbrink 2014.
102. Boehm 2012; Boehm and Terrio 2019; Terrio 2015.
103. Abrego 2014.
104. Moore 2023.

## Chapter 1: What We Know and What We Set Out to Find

1. Massey et al. 1987; Durand 2007.
2. Massey 1990; Tilly and Brown 1967.
3. Castañeda 2013; Massey, Durand, and Pren 2014.
4. Burawoy 1976.
5. Sassen 2001.
6. Castañeda and Buck, 2011, 2014; Dreby 2010; Oliveira 2018; see also Abrego 2014; Boehm 2016; Boehm and Terrio 2019; DeParle 2019; Parreñas 2005.
7. Castañeda 2013; Schmalzbauer 2004, 2008.
8. Terrio 2015.
9. Canizales and Diaz-Strong 2021; Canizales 2022.
10. Hamlin 2021.
11. Galli 2020, 2023.
12. Rathod, Hershberg, and Stinchcomb 2017; Stinchcomb 2020; Stinchcomb and Berger Cardoso 2018; Stinchcomb and Hershberg 2014.
13. Ruehs-Navarro 2022.
14. Abrego 2014; Castañeda and Buck 2011; Dreby 2007; Lovato-Hermann 2017.
15. Suárez-Orozco, Bang, and Kim 2011.
16. Boehm 2012.
17. Dreby 2007.
18. Dreby 2015.
19. Abrego 2014.
20. Boehm 2012.
21. Castañeda 2013; Gonzales 2016.
22. Office of Refugee Resettlement 2022.
23. U.S. Department of Health and Human Services 2020.

NOTES    233

24. Berger Cardoso et al. 2019.
25. Menjívar, Agadjanian, and Oh 2022.
26. Ward and Batalova 2023.
27. Scallen 2019.
28. Mahler 1995; Menjívar 2000.
29. Stinchcomb and Hershberg 2014; Castañeda 2014.
30. Soboroff 2020.
31. Mangual Figueroa and Barrales 2021.
32. Boehm and Terrio 2019; Terrio 2015.
33. Rung 2020.
34. Heidbrink 2020; Frank-Vitale 2021.
35. Dreby 2010.
36. Castañeda and Smith 2022.
37. Let's recall that much of the data used in social science publications comes from collectively gathered sources—including census data, large national surveys, political polls, and the Mexican Migration Project. All of these databases are built from the efforts of large research teams whose PIs do not interact with all participants directly. There are benefits, in terms of time and speed, to doing so with qualitative and smaller-$N$ studies as well, especially in studies like this one in which interviews are recorded and can be revisited multiple times by the PIs. Recent notable examples of works based on qualitative data collected by others include Streib 2020 and the *Russell Sage Foundation Journal of the Social Sciences* special issues featuring open qualitative science.
38. Castañeda et al. 2021.
39. These surveys and instruments can be found at the end of the book. See Castañeda 2021.
40. Castañeda, Morales, and Ochoa 2014; Creswell and Clark-Plano 2007; Rumbaut 2005; Small 2011; Zamora-Kapoor and Castañeda 2014.
41. We use what Pawel Kaczmarczyk and Douglas S. Massey (2019) call "ethnosurveys": detailed specific questions along with opportunities to share migration trajectories, experiences, and views. Because this is a mixed-methods study, we sometimes use the words "interviews" and "surveys" interchangeably.
42. Canizales and Diaz-Strong 2021; Diaz-Strong 2021.
43. Zamora 2022; Lovato 2020.
44. Luiselli 2017, 2019.

## Chapter 2: A Brief History of El Salvador, Honduras, and Guatemala: Historical Contexts and Drivers of Migration

1. Alec Singer helped to draft parts of this chapter.
2. Segovia 2021.
3. Mahler 1995; Nevins 2016.
4. Chomsky 2022, 460.
5. Enríquez 2022, 8–9; Foxen 2020, 29–38; Heidbrink 2020, 37.

6. Coe 2012.
7. Wikipedia 2022.
8. Chomsky 2022, 10.
9. Ibid., 35.
10. Ibid., 13.
11. Garrard-Burnett 2008.
12. Lokken 2013.
13. Garrard-Burnett 2008; Lokken 2013.
14. Sedgewick 2021.
15. Lindo-Fuentes, Ching, and Lara Martínez 2007.
16. Anderson 1992.
17. Lovato 2020.
18. Veytskin, Lockerb, and McMullen 2009.
19. LaFeber 1993.
20. Haggerty 1988.
21. Fish and Sganga 1988.
22. LeoGrande 2008.
23. Kroc Institute for International Peace Studies, n.d.
24. Moslimani, Noe-Bustamante, and Shah 2023; O'Connor, Batalova, and Bolter 2019.
25. Mahler 1995.
26. Scallen 2019.
27. Ibid.; Castañeda, Danielson, and Rathod 2023.
28. Menjívar 2006.
29. Mahler 1995.
30. Ibid.; Scallen 2019.
31. Austermuhle 2019.
32. Mahler 1995; Scallen 2019.
33. Vine 2021.
34. Nevins 2016.
35. Ibid.; Rivera 2015.
36. Rivera 2015.
37. Moslimani, Noe-Bustamante, and Shah 2023.
38. Blanchard et al. 2011.
39. Rivera 2015.
40. Ibid.
41. Enríquez 2022, 8–10.
42. Handy 1994.
43. Holland 2005.
44. Ibid.
45. Handy 1994; Holland 2005.
46. Heidbrink 2020, 15.
47. Menjívar 2011.

48. Berger Cardoso et al. 2019; Yashar 2018.
49. Dudley 2020.
50. Terrio 2015, 20.
51. Massey 1990.
52. Yashar 2018, 17.
53. Suárez-Orozco 2019, 4.
54. Ibid., 13.
55. Ibid., 13–14.
56. Holguin and Schey 1986.
57. Terrio 2015, 10; Cordero, Feldman, and Keitner 2020.
58. Scallen 2019.
59. Terrio 2015, 56.
60. Aguilera 2019; Cordero, Feldman, and Keitner 2020.
61. InSightCrime 2021.
62. Castañeda 2018b; Massey 2018; Menjívar 2000.
63. Immigration and Ethnic History Society, n.d.-a.
64. Immigration and Ethnic History Society, n.d.-b.
65. Ward and Batalova 2023.
66. Mahé 2006; Sayad 2004.
67. Castañeda 2009.
68. Tilly 2007, 5; Zelizer and Tilly 2006.
69. Gil Martínez de Escobar 2006; Castellanos 2007b.
70. Yakshilikov 2022.
71. Sayad 2004.
72. DeParle 2019.
73. Suárez-Orozco, Todorova, and Louie 2002.
74. Terry and Wilson 2005.
75. Bryant 2005; Dreby 2006; Hondagneu-Sotelo 1994; Hondagneu-Sotelo and Avila 1997; Parreñas 2005.
76. Dreby 2006.
77. Parreñas 2005, 32.
78. Heymann 2006.
79. Sassen 1988, 2021; Wilson 1993.
80. Burawoy 1976.
81. Hondagneu-Sotelo and Avila 1997, 568.
82. Enríquez 2022, 20.
83. Burawoy 1976; Enríquez 2022, 22.
84. Foner 2009.
85. Mahler 2001, 120–21 (cited in Tilly 2007, 12).
86. Zelizer 1985, 2005.
87. Grinberg and Grinberg 1989.
88. World Bank 2006, 63.
89. Nazario 2006, xii.

90. Menjívar 2000.
91. Foxen 2020.
92. Heidbrink 2020, ix.
93. Ibid., 7.
94. Frank-Vitale 2021.

## Chapter 3: Reasons to Emigrate

1. Hondagneu-Sotelo 1994; Massey et al. 1987; Menjívar, Abrego, and Schmalzbauer 2016; Parreñas 2005; Rendón 2019; Schmalzbauer 2014.
2. Abrego 2014; Berger Cardoso et al. 2019.
3. Castañeda and Buck 2014, 178.
4. Abrego 2014.
5. Castañeda 2013; Castañeda and Buck 2011.
6. Castañeda and Buck 2011, 2014; Dreby 2010.
7. Luiselli 2017, 2019; Martínez 2014; Nazario 2006.
8. Villegas 2014.
9. Galli 2020; Rathod, Hershberg, and Stinchcomb 2017.
10. Menjívar and Abrego 2012.
11. Castañeda 2024.

## Chapter 4: Central Americans and Their Passage through Mexico to the United States

1. Stinchcomb and Hershberg 2014; U.S. Department of Health and Human Services 2020.
2. Part of chapter 4 was published in Spanish in *Ética, política, y migración* (Díaz Cepeda et al. 2021). Cristian Mendoza Gómez, Fernanda Pérez, Fernando Rocha, and Carina Cione helped prepare the Spanish chapter.
3. Abrego 2014; Berger Cardoso et al. 2019; De Jesus and Hernandes 2019; Menjívar 2011.
4. Canizales 2019; Menjívar and Perreira 2019; Teicher 2018.
5. We thank the first reviewer for this language and question.
6. Castañeda 2022b.
7. Castañeda and Schneider 2017, 282–85.
8. Flores and Schachter 2018.
9. Castañeda 2019, chap. 8.
10. Castañeda, Danielson, and Rathod 2023.
11. Ibid.; Gandini, Fernández de la Reguera, and Narváez Gutiérrez 2020.
12. Gandini, Fernández de la Reguera, and Narváez Gutiérrez 2020; Martínez 2014.
13. Villegas 2014.
14. Gandini, Fernández de la Reguera, and Narváez Gutiérrez 2020.
15. Vogt 2013.

16. Moreno Figueroa 2010.
17. Cortina 2022; Heidbrink 2020.
18. Gandini, Fernández de la Reguera, and Narváez Gutiérrez 2020.
19. Berger Cardoso et al. 2019; Donato and Sisk 2015; Zatz and Rodriguez 2015.
20. Berger Cardoso et al. 2019; Donato and Sisk 2015; Roth and Grace 2015; Soboroff 2020; Zatz and Rodriguez 2015.
21. Crea et al. 2017; Terrio 2015; Zatz and Rodriguez 2015.
22. Berger Cardoso et al. 2019, 276.
23. Callahan 2018.
24. Longazel and Hallett 2021.
25. Dennis Stinchcomb and Aida Romero helped with these analyzes and conclusions.
26. Gandini, Fernández de la Reguera, and Narváez Gutiérrez 2020, 31.
27. Castañeda 2022c.
28. Garip 2017; Massey, Durand, and Malone 2002.
29. Berger Cardoso et al. 2019; Castañeda and Buck 2014.

## Chapter 5: Legal Uncertainty, Family Reunification, and Learning a New Life

1. This chapter adapts a paper written with Cynthia Cristobal for a 2022 edited volume (Castañeda, Jenks, and Cristobal 2022).
2. Stinchcomb and Hershberg 2014; Terrasi and de Galarce 2017; Terrio 2015.
3. Castañeda 2013; Lakhani 2017; Sayad 2004; Schmalzbauer 2008.
4. Mahler 1995.
5. Gonzales 2016; Valdivia 2020.
6. Castro 2021.
7. Castañeda and Buck 2011, 2014.
8. Roth and Grace 2015.
9. Berger Cardoso et al. 2019; Lovato-Hermann 2017.
10. Berger Cardoso et al. 2019.
11. Castañeda and Buck 2011, 2014; Lovato-Hermann 2017.
12. McMichael, Gifford, and Correa-Velez 2011.
13. Berger Cardoso et al. 2019; Dreby 2007; Roth and Grace 2015; Rousseau et al. 2004; Suárez-Orozco, Bang, and Kim 2011.
14. Artico 2003. Other scholars have had similar results: see Berger Cardoso et al. 2019; Lovato-Hermann 2017; Rousseau et al. 2004; Suárez-Orozco, Bang, and Kim 2011.
15. Suárez-Orozco, Bang, and Kim 2011.
16. Boehm 2012.
17. Castañeda 2013; Gonzales 2016.
18. Lashley 2000.
19. Rousseau et al. 2004.
20. Nazario 2006.
21. Artico 2003.

22. Boss 2002.
23. Dreby 2015.
24. Abrego 2014; Castañeda and Buck 2011; Dreby 2007; Lovato-Hermann 2017.
25. Suárez-Orozco, Bang, and Kim 2011; Boehm 2012.
26. Dreby 2007.
27. Abrego 2014.
28. Perreira, Chapman, and Stein 2006.
29. McMichael, Gifford, and Correa-Velez 2011.
30. Boccagni 2017.
31. Castañeda 2018a.
32. Blumberg and Contreras 2015; Knapp 2015; Latin American Youth Center 2018.
33. Martinez Barahona 2020.
34. Castañeda and Buck 2011, 2014.
35. Lovato-Hermann 2017.
36. Berger Cardoso et al. 2019; Lovato-Hermann 2017.
37. Boss 2002; Castañeda and Buck 2011.
38. Castañeda et al. 2021.

## Chapter 6: Mental Health and Immigration: Symptoms of PTSD and Depression

1. Parts of the following chapter were published in Castañeda et al. 2021.
2. Castañeda and Buck 2011, 2014.
3. Walker, Venta, and Galicia 2021.
4. Ibid.
5. Ibid.
6. Castañeda and Buck 2011.
7. Castaneda and Buck 2011, 2014.
8. Castaneda and Buck 2014.
9. Centers for Disease Control and Prevention 2023.
10. Centers for Disease Control and Prevention 2023; Porche et al. 2011; Terrasi and de Galarce 2017.
11. Link and Phelan 1995.
12. Holmes et al. 2021.
13. Alegría et al. 2018; Hynie 2018.
14. Berger Cardoso et al. 2017; Chomsky 2014, 158; Semple 2019; Stinchcomb and Hershberg 2014.
15. Torres et al. 2018.
16. Castañeda 2013.
17. Dreby 2010; Parreñas 2005.
18. Dreby 2015.
19. Venta and Mercado 2019.

20. Breslau et al. 2011; Jamil et al. 2007; Park et al. 2019; Reavell and Fazil 2017.
21. Venta and Mercado 2019.
22. Perreira and Ornelas 2013.
23. Castaneda and Buck 2014.
24. Kaltman et al. 2011.
25. Chomsky 2022; Lovato 2020.
26. Suarez-Orozco 2019, 33.
27. Alegría et al. 2007; Cook et al. 2009; Hovey 2000.
28. Achotegui 2011; Moya et al. 2016.
29. Cook et al. 2009.
30. Finch, Kolody, and Vega 2000.
31. Szalacha et al. 2003.
32. Ibid.
33. Arbona et al. 2010; Leong, Park, and Kalibatseva 2013.
34. Hovey 2000.
35. Dunn and O'Brien 2009.
36. Castañeda 2019.
37. Androff et al. 2011.
38. Kaltman et al. 2011.
39. Ibid.
40. Castañeda 2019; Torres et al. 2018.
41. Escamilla García 2021.
42. Gandini, Fernández de la Reguera, and Narváez Gutiérrez 2020.
43. Mikolajczak, Petrides, and Hurry 2009; Zimmermann and Iwanski 2014.
44. Abramson 2018a; Walker, Venta, and Galicia 2021.
45. Castañeda 2019.
46. Abramson 2018b.
47. Kroenke and Spitzer 2002; Kroenke, Spitzer, and Williams 2001; Orange County Aging Services Collaborative 2005.
48. Diez-Quevedo et al. 2001; Serrano-Ibáñez, Ruiz-Párraga, and Esteve 2018.
49. Villarroel and Terlizzi 2020.
50. Geiger and Davis 2019.
51. Foa et al. 2001.
52. Center for Safe and Resilient Schools and Workplaces, n.d.
53. Foa et al. 2001.
54. Alisic et al. 2014.
55. Foa et al. 2001.
56. Lovato 2020.
57. Menjívar 2006; Patler, Hamilton, and Savinar 2021.
58. Walker, Venta, and Galicia 2021.
59. Castañeda and Buck 2011.
60. Ibid.
61. Haslam et al. 2020.

62. Rung 2020; Terrio 2015.
63. Bermúdez et al. 2010; Ciftci, Jones, and Corrigan 2012; Mendoza, Masuda, and Swartout 2015; Rastogi, Massey-Hastings, and Wieling 2012.
64. Drew et al. 2011.
65. Marshall, Schell, and Miles 2010; Millgram et al. 2019; van Winkel et al. 2015.
66. Castañeda, Smith, and Vetter 2020.
67. Torres et al. 2018.
68. Moya et al. 2016.

## Chapter 7: Immigrant Integration into School Environments

1. Abrego 2014; Berger Cardoso et al. 2019; Castaneda and Buck 2014.
2. Kao, Joyner, and Balistreri 2019.
3. Powers, Ressler, and Bradley 2009.
4. Alsarrani et al. 2022.
5. Gonzales 2011, 2016.
6. There was still a little gang activity in their new schools, but these gangs did not have the hold over neighborhoods and public spaces that they had in these youths' hometowns.
7. Castañeda and Jenks 2021a.

## Chapter 8: Family-Propelled Migration and Immigrant Integration

1. Castañeda and Jenks 2021a.
2. Cordero, Feldman, and Keitner 2020.
3. Immigration Policy Tracking Project 2018.
4. For a full list of policies, see Immigration Policy Tracking Project, n.d.
5. Androff et al. 2011; Torres et al. 2018.
6. Androff et al. 2011.
7. Ibid.
8. Romero 2011.
9. Luo and Escalante 2021.
10. Castañeda 2019.
11. Gandini, Fernández de la Reguera, and Narváez Gutiérrez 2020.
12. Soboroff 2020.
13. Harris 2021.
14. Castañeda and Jenks 2020.
15. Castañeda 2024.
16. We thank Dennis Stinchcomb and Aida Romero for an early draft of these findings.
17. Castañeda 2013; Castañeda and Buck 2011, 2014.
18. Perreira, Chapman, and Stein 2006.

19. Castañeda 2022b; Castañeda, Danielson, and Rathod 2023.
20. Babich and Batalova 2021; O'Connor, Batalova, and Bolte 2019.
21. Chishti and Hipsman 2016; Hipsman and Chishti 2015.
22. United Nations High Commissioner for Refugees 2014, 28–29.
23. *Frontline* 2021.
24. Hain 2021.
25. U.S. Department of Homeland Security 2021.
26. Castañeda and Rey 2023.
27. Kocher 2023.
28. Bó and Dukhovnov 2022; Calarco et al. 2020; Hsin and Felfe 2014.

# REFERENCES

Abramson, Ashley. 2018a. "Fear of Deportation Has Heartbreaking Mental Health Repercussions." Brit + Co, January 23. https://www.brit.co/fear-of-deportation-has-heartbreaking-mental-health-repercussions/.
———. 2018b. "U.S. Border Officials Are Creating Lifelong Trauma for Child Migrants by Separating Them from Their Families." Brit + Co, June 16. https://www.brit.co/us-border-officials-are-creating-lifelong-trauma-for-child-migrants-by-separating-them-from-their-families/.
Abrego, Leisy J. 2014. *Sacrificing Families: Navigating Laws, Labor, and Love across Borders.* Stanford, Calif.: Stanford University Press.
Abrego, Leisy J., Mat Coleman, Daniel E. Martínez, Cecilia Menjívar, and Jeremy Slack. 2017. "Making Immigrants into Criminals: Legal Processes of Criminalization in the Post-IIRIRA Era." *Journal on Migration and Human Security* 5(3): 694–715.
Achotegui, Joseba. 2011. *How to Assess Stress and Migratory Mourning: Scales of Risk Factors in Mental Health.* Llançà, Spain: Ediciones el Mundo de la Mente.
Aguilera, Jasmine. 2019. "Body Cavity Searches, Indefinite Detention, and No Visitations Allowed: What Conditions Were Like for Migrant Kids before the Flores Agreement." *Time*, August 21. https://time.com/5657538/flores-settlement-agreement-standards/ (accessed September 2, 2021).
Akhtar, Salman. 1995. "A Third Individuation: Immigration, Identity, and the Psychoanalytic Process." *Journal of Applied Psychoanalytic Studies* 43(4): 1051–84.
Alba, Richard, Tomás R. Jiménez, and Helen B. Marrow. 2014. "Mexican Americans as a Paradigm for Contemporary Intra-Group Heterogeneity." *Ethnic and Racial Studies* 37(3, February 23): 446–66. https://doi.org/10.1080/01419870.2013.786111.
Alba, Richard, Philip Kasinitz, and Mary C. Waters. 2011. "The Kids Are (Mostly) Alright: Second-Generation Assimilation: Comments on Haller, Portes and Lynch." *Social Forces* 89(3): 763–73. https://doi.org/10.1353/sof.2011.0024.

Alba, Richard D., and Victor Nee. 2003. *Remaking the American Mainstream: Assimilation and Contemporary Immigration.* Cambridge, Mass.: Harvard University Press.

Alegría, Margarita, Amanda NeMoyer, Irene Falgas, Ye Wang, and Kiara Alvarez. 2018. "Social Determinants of Mental Health: Where We Are and Where We Need to Go." *Current Psychiatry Reports* 20(11, September 17): 95. https://doi.org/10.1007/s11920-018-0969-9.

Alegría, Margarita, Patrick E. Shrout, Meghan Woo, Peter Guarnaccia, William Sribney, Doryliz Vila, Antonio Polo, et al. 2007. "Understanding Differences in Past Year Psychiatric Disorders for Latinos Living in the U.S." *Social Science and Medicine* 65(2, July): 214–30. https://doi.org/10.1016/j.socscimed.2007.03.026.

Alisic, Eva, Alyson K. Zalta, Floryt van Wesel, Sadie E. Larsen, Gertrud S. Hafstad, Katayun Hassanpour, and Geert E. Smid. 2014. "Rates of Post-Traumatic Stress Disorder in Trauma-Exposed Children and Adolescents: Meta-Analysis." *British Journal of Psychiatry* 204(5, May): 335–40. https://doi.org/10.1192/bjp.bp.113.131227.

Alsarrani, Abdullah, Ruth F. Hunter, Laura Dunne, and Leandro Garcia. 2022. "Association between Friendship Quality and Subjective Wellbeing among Adolescents: A Systematic Review." *BMC Public Health* 22(December 23): 2420. https://doi.org/10.1186/s12889-022-14776-4.

Anderson, Thomas P. 1992. *Matanza: The 1932 "Slaughter" That Traumatized a Nation, Shaping U.S.-Salvadoran Policy to This Day*, 2nd ed. Willimantic, Conn.: Curbstone Press.

Androff, David K., Cecilia Ayon, David Becerra, and Maria Gurrola. 2011. "U.S. Immigration Policy and Immigrant Children's Well-being: The Impact of Policy Shifts." *Journal of Sociology and Social Welfare* 38(1): 77–98.

Arbona, Consuelo, Norma Olvera, Nestor Rodriguez, Jacqueline Hagan, Adriana Linares, and Margit Wiesner. 2010. "Acculturative Stress among Documented and Undocumented Latino Immigrants in the United States." *Hispanic Journal of Behavioral Sciences* 32(3, August): 362–84. https://doi.org/10.1177/0739986310373210.

Artico, Ceres I. 2003. *Latino Families Broken by Immigration: The Adolescent's Perceptions.* New York: LFB Scholarly Publishing LLC.

Austermuhle, Martin. 2019. "Salvadorans Are D.C.'s Largest Immigrant Population. Now, Bowser Will Make an Official Visit to Their Home Country." dcist, August 9. https://dcist.com/story/18/08/09/mayor-bowser-is-taking-a-trip-to-el/.

Babich, Erin, and Jeanne Batalova. 2021. "Central American Immigrants in the United States." Migration Policy Institute, August 6. https://www.migrationpolicy.org/article/central-american-immigrants-united-states.

Bean, Frank D., and Gillian Stevens. 2003. *America's Newcomers and the Dynamics of Diversity.* New York: Russell Sage Foundation.

Berger Cardoso, Jodi, Kalina Brabeck, Dennis Stinchcomb, Lauren Heidbrink, Olga Acosta Price, Óscar F. Gil-García, Thomas M. Crea, and Luis H. Zayas. 2017. "Integration of Unaccompanied Migrant Youth in the United States: A Call for Research." *Journal of Ethnic and Migration Studies* 45(2, January 25): 273–92. https://doi.org/10.1080/1369183X.2017.1404261.

Bermúdez, J. Maria, Dwight R. Kirkpatrick, Lorna Hecker, and Carmen Torres-Robles. 2010. "Describing Latinos Families and Their Help-Seeking Attitudes: Challenging the Family Therapy Literature." *Contemporary Family Therapy: An International Journal* 32(2): 155–72. https://doi.org/10.1007/s10591-009-9110-x.

Blanchard, Sarah, Erin R. Hamilton, Nestor Rodríguez, and Hirotoshi Yoshioka. 2011. "Shifting Trends in Central American Migration: A Demographic Examination of Increasing Honduran-U.S. Immigration and Deportation." *The Latin Americanist* 55(4, December): 61–84. https://doi.org/10.1111/j.1557-203X.2011.01128.x.

Blumberg, Elliot, and Oliver Contreras. 2015. "They Made the Long, Rough Journey to Cross the U.S. Border Alone. Here Are Their Faces and Voices." *Washington Post*, October 14. https://www.washingtonpost.com/news/in-sight/wp/2015/10/14/they-made-the-long-rough-journey-to-cross-the-u-s-border-alone-here-are-their-faces-and-voices/ (accessed September 8, 2021).

Bó, Boróka B., and Denys Dukhovnov. 2022. "Tell Me Who's Your Neighbour and I'll Tell You How Much Time You've Got: The Spatiotemporal Consequences of Residential Segregation." *Population, Space, and Place* 28(7): e2561. https://doi.org/10.1002/psp.2561.

Boccagni, Paolo. 2012. "Practising Motherhood at a Distance: Retention and Loss in Ecuadorian Transnational Families." *Journal of Ethnic and Migration Studies* 38(2): 261–77. https://doi.org/10.1080/1369183X.2012.646421.

———. 2017. *Migration and the Search for Home: Mapping Domestic Space in Migrants' Everyday Lives*. New York: Palgrave Macmillan.

Boehm, Deborah A. 2012. *Intimate Migrations: Gender, Family, and Illegality among Transnational Mexicans*. New York: New York University Press.

———. 2016. *Returned: Going and Coming in an Age of Deportation*. Oakland: University of California Press.

Boehm, Deborah A., and Susan J. Terrio. 2019. *Illegal Encounters: The Effect of Detention and Deportation on Young People*. New York: New York University Press.

Bohrt, Marcelo A., and José Itzigsohn. 2015. "Class, Race, and the Incorporation of Latinos/as: Testing the Stratified Ethnoracial Incorporation Approach." *Sociology of Race and Ethnicity* 1(3, July 1): 360–77. https://doi.org/10.1177/2332649215570760.

Boss, Pauline. 2002. *Family Stress Management: A Contextual Approach*. Thousand Oaks, Calif.: SAGE Publications.

Brennan, Denise. 2010. "Key Issues in the Resettlement of Formerly Trafficked Persons in the United States." *University of Pennsylvania Law Review* 158: 28.

Breslau, Joshua, Guilherme Borges, Daniel Tancredi, Naomi Saito, Richard Kravitz, Ladson Hinton, William Vega, Maria Elena Medina-Mora, and Sergio Aguilar-Gaxiola. 2011. "Migration from Mexico to the United States and Subsequent Risk for Depressive and Anxiety Disorders: A Cross-National Study." *Archives of General Psychiatry* 68(4, April 4): 428–33. https://doi.org/10.1001/archgenpsychiatry.2011.21.

Brubaker, Rogers. 1992. *Citizenship and Nationhood in France and Germany.* Cambridge, Mass.: Harvard University Press.

Bryant, John. 2005. "Children of International Migrants in Indonesia, Thailand, and the Philippines: A Review of Evidence and Policies." Innocenti Working Paper 2005-05. Florence: UNICEF Innocenti Research Centre.

Bucerius, Sandra. 2014. *Unwanted: Muslim Immigrants, Dignity, and Drug Dealing.* New York: Oxford University Press.

Burawoy, Michael. 1976. "The Functions and Reproduction of Migrant Labor: Comparative Material from Southern Africa and the United States." *American Journal of Sociology* 82(5): 1050–87.

Calarco, Jessica McCrory, Emily Meanwell, Elizabeth Anderson, and Amelia Knopf. 2020. "'My Husband Thinks I'm Crazy': COVID-19-Related Conflict in Couples with Young Children." *SocArXiv* (October 9). https://doi.org/10.31235/osf.io/cpkj6.

Calhoun, Craig J. 2010. *Robert K. Merton: Sociology of Science and Sociology as Science.* New York: Columbia University Press,.

Callahan, Molly. 2018. "No, the Government Hasn't Lost 1,500 Children. What's Actually Happening Might Be Worse." *Northeastern Global News*, June 5. https://news.northeastern.edu/2018/06/05/no-the-government-hasnt-lost-1500-children-what-is-actually-happening-might-be-worse/.

Canizales, Stephanie. 2019. "The Uncontained Violence against Unaccompanied Central American Minor Migrants in the U.S." Los Angeles: University of Southern California, Center for the Study of Immigrant Integration (October). http://dornsifelive.usc.edu/csii/blog-violence-against-central-am-migrant-minors/.

———. 2022. "'*Si Mis Papas Estuvieran Aquí*': Unaccompanied Youth Workers' Emergent Frame of Reference and Health in the United States." *Journal of Health and Social Behavior* 64(1, September 9): 00221465221122831. https://doi.org/10.1177/00221465221122831.

Canizales, Stephanie L., and Daysi Diaz-Strong. 2021. "Undocumented Childhood Arrivals in the U.S.: Widening the Frame for Research and Policy." *Immigration Initiative at Harvard Issue Brief Series* 1(11, June). https://immigrationinitiative.harvard.edu/wp-content/uploads/2021/05/brief_11_eng.pdf.

Castañeda, Ernesto. 2009. "Remittances." In *The Palgrave Dictionary of Transnational History*, edited by Akira Iriye and Pierre-Yves Saunier. New York: Palgrave Macmillan.

———. 2013. "Living in Limbo: Transnational Households, Remittances, and Development." *International Migration* 51(s1, July): e13–e35. https://doi.org/10.1111/j.1468-2435.2012.00745.x.

———. 2014. "There Is No Immigration Security Threat That Reform with an Earned Path to Citizenship Cannot Address." Boston: Scholars Strategy Network (August 15). https://scholars.org/there-no-immigration-security-threat-reform-earned-path-citizenship-cannot-address.

———. 2018a. *A Place to Call Home: Immigrant Exclusion and Urban Belonging in New York, Paris, and Barcelona.* Stanford, Calif.: Stanford University Press.

———. 2018b. *Immigration and Categorical Inequality: Migration to the City and the Birth of Race and Ethnicity.* New York: Routledge.

———. 2019. *Building Walls: Excluding Latin People in the United States.* Lanham, Md.: Lexington Books.

———. 2020a. "Finding a Home in the City." *Sociological Forum* 35(3): 845–49. https://doi.org/10.1111/socf.12636.

———. 2020b. "Introduction to 'Reshaping the World: Rethinking Borders.'" *Social Sciences* 9(11, November): 214. https://doi.org/10.3390/socsci9110214.

———. 2021. "Mental Health Immigrant Youth Survey Instrument English & Spanish Castaneda et al." https://www.academia.edu/50307718/Mental_Health_Immigrant_Youth_Survey_Instrument_English_and_Spanish_Castaneda_et_al.

———. 2022a. "Immigrants Are Only 3.5% of People Worldwide—and Their Negative Impact Is Often Exaggerated, in the U.S. and around the World." *The Conversation*, June 13. http://theconversation.com/immigrants-are-only-3-5-of-people-worldwide-and-their-negative-impact-is-often-exaggerated-in-the-u-s-and-around-the-world-184522.

———. 2022b. "Expulsión de migrantes como oportunidad perdida y tarea para Sísifo." *Revista Mexicana de Sociología* 85(1, November 25): 229–38. https://doi.org/10.22201/iis.01882503p.2023.1.60420.

———. 2022c. "Why the Number of Encounters at the Southern U.S. Border Does Not Mean What the GOP Says It Means." *The Conversation*, November 8. http://theconversation.com/why-the-number-of-encounters-at-the-southern-u-s-border-does-not-mean-what-the-gop-says-it-means-191144.

———. 2024. "What Aids Immigrant Employment: Human or Cultural Capital? Education, Local Knowledge, and Employment." Working paper. Washington, D.C.: Center for Latin American and Latino Studies and the Immigration Lab.

Castañeda, Ernesto, and Lesley Buck. 2011. "Remittances, Transnational Parenting, and the Children Left Behind: Economic and Psychological Implications." *The Latin Americanist* 55(4): 85–110. https://doi.org/10.1111/j.1557-203X.2011.01136.x.

———. 2014. "A Family of Strangers: Transnational Parenting and the Consequences of Family Separation Due to Undocumented Migration." In *Hidden Lives and Human Rights in America: Understanding the Controversies and Tragedies of Undocumented Immigration*, edited by Lois Ann Lorentzen. Santa Barbara, Calif.: Praeger.

Castañeda, Ernesto, Michael Danielson, and Jayesh Rathod. 2023. "Fortress North America: Theorizing a Regional Approach to Migration Management." In *North American Regionalism: Stagnation, Decline, or Renewal?*, edited by Eric Hershberg and Tom Long. Albuquerque: University of New Mexico Press.

Castañeda, Ernesto, and Daniel Jenks. 2020. "What Could a Biden Presidency Mean for Immigrants?" Medium, November 28. https://ernestoc.medium.com/what-could-a-biden-presidency-mean-for-immigrants-8aade0ad7962.

———. 2021a. "How to Help Unaccompanied Children from Central America—Ideas from the Washington, D.C., Area." Boston: Scholars Strategy Network

(June 11). https://scholars.org/contribution/how-help-unaccompanied-children-central.

———. 2021b. "Supporting Unaccompanied Children from Central America in Arlington County Schools." Boston: Scholars Strategy Network (June 11). https://scholars.org/contribution/how-help-unaccompanied-children-central.

Castañeda, Ernesto, Daniel Jenks, Jessica Chaikof, Carina Cione, SteVon Felton, Isabella Goris, Lesley Buck, and Eric Hershberg. 2021. "Symptoms of PTSD and Depression among Central American Immigrant Youth." *Trauma Care* 1(2, September): 99–118. https://doi.org/10.3390/traumacare1020010.

Castañeda, Ernesto, Daniel Jenks, and Cynthia Cristobal. 2022. "Young Immigrants' Integration into a New Home: The Case of Central American Children and Youth Settling in Washington D.C." In *Children and Youths' Migration in a Global Landscape*, edited by Adrienne Lee Atterberry, Derrice Garfield McCallum, Siqi Tu, and Amy Lutz. Leeds, U.K.: Emerald Publishing Ltd.

Castañeda, Ernesto, Maria Cristina Morales, and Olga Ochoa. 2014. "Transnational Behavior in Comparative Perspective." *Comparative Migration Studies* 2(3, September 1): 305–33. https://doi.org/10.5117/CMS2014.3.CAST.

Castañeda, Ernesto, and Eva Rey. 2023. "The End of the Application of U.S. Code Title 42 at the Border." The Immigration Lab Blog, May 11. https://theimmigrationlab.org/blog/f/the-end-of-the-application-of-us-code-title-42-at-the-border.

Castañeda, Ernesto, and Cathy Lisa Schneider. 2017. *Collective Violence, Contentious Politics, and Social Change: A Charles Tilly Reader.* New York: Routledge.

Castañeda, Ernesto, Blaine Smith, and Emma Vetter. 2020. "Hispanic Health Disparities and Housing: Comparing Measured and Self-Reported Health Metrics among Housed and Homeless Latin Individuals." *Journal of Migration and Health* 1/2(December): 100008. https://doi.org/10.1016/j.jmh.2020.100008.

Castañeda, Ernesto, and Curtis Smith. 2022. "Conducting Research with Vulnerable Populations: Methodological and Ethical Implications of Interviewing People Experiencing Homelessness." *Journal of Applied Social Science* 17(1, March). https://doi.org/10.1177/19367244221141326.

Castañeda, Ernesto, Angelina Torres, Barbara Martinez, Madison Guare, and Emily Glover. 2019. "The Movement for Immigrant Rights." In Charles Tilly, Ernesto Castañeda, and Lesliy J. Wood, *Social Movements, 1768–2018.* New York: Routledge.

Castellanos, M. Bianet. 2007a. "Adolescent Migration to Cancun: Reconfiguring Maya Households and Gender Relations in Mexico's Yucatan Peninsula." *Frontiers* 28(3): 1–27.

———. 2007b. "Building Communities of Sentiments: Money, Emotions, and Decision-Making among Maya Migrants." University of California–Santa Barbara.

Castles, Stephen, and Alastair Davidson. 2000. *Citizenship and Migration: Globalization and the Politics of Belonging.* New York: Routledge.

Castro, Sandra. 2021. "Tears, Trauma and Transformation: Central American Mothers' Experiences of Violence, Migration, and Family Reunification."

PhD diss., City University of New York, The Graduate Center, Department of Social Welfare, June 1. https://academicworks.cuny.edu/gc_etds/4316.

Center for Safe and Resilient Schools and Workplaces. n.d. "Cognitive Behavioral Intervention for Trauma in Schools: About CBITS." https://cbitsprogram.org/forms.

Centers for Disease Control and Prevention (CDC). 2023. "Adverse Childhood Experiences (ACEs)." Last reviewed June 29, 2023. https://www.cdc.gov/violenceprevention/aces/index.html.

Chacón, Jennifer M. 2010. "Tensions and Trade-offs: Protecting Trafficking Victims in the Era of Immigration Enforcement." *University of Pennsylvania Law Review* 158(6): 1609–53.

Chaudhary, Ali R. 2018. "Organizing Transnationalism and Belonging among Pakistani Immigrants in London and New York." *Migration Studies* 6(3, November): 420–47.

Chauvin, Sébastien, and Blanca Garcés-Mascareñas. 2014. "Becoming Less Illegal: Deservingness Frames and Undocumented Migrant Incorporation." *Sociology Compass* 8(4): 422–32.

Cheatham, Amelia. 2021. "U.S. Detention of Child Migrants." Washington, D.C.: Council on Foreign Relations (May 4). https://www.cfr.org/backgrounder/us-detention-child-migrants.

Chiodo, John J., and Evette Meliza. 2014. "Orphan Trains: Teaching about an Early Twentieth-Century Social Experiment." *The Social Studies* 105(3, May 4): 145–57. https://doi.org/10.1080/00377996.2013.859119.

Chishti, Muzaffar, and Faye Hipsman. 2016. "Increased Central American Migration to the United States May Prove an Enduring Phenomenon." Washington, D.C.: Migration Policy Institute (February 18). https://www.migrationpolicy.org/article/increased-central-american-migration-united-states-may-prove-enduring-phenomenon.

Chomsky, Aviva. 2014. *Undocumented: How Immigration Became Illegal*. Boston: Beacon Press.

———. 2022. *Central America's Forgotten History: Revolution, Violence, and the Roots of Migration*. Boston: Beacon Press.

Ciftci, Ayse, Nev Jones, and Patrick W. Corrigan. 2012. "Mental Health Stigma in the Muslim Community." *Journal of Muslim Mental Health* 7(1): 17–32. https://doi.org/10.3998/jmmh.10381607.0007.102.

Coe, Michael D. 2012. *Breaking the Maya Code*, 3rd ed. London: Thames & Hudson.

Cohen, Jeffrey H. 2004. *The Culture of Migration in Southern Mexico*. Austin: University of Texas Press.

Cook, Benjamin, Margarita Alegría, Julia Y. Lin, and Jing Guo. 2009. "Pathways and Correlates Connecting Latinos' Mental Health with Exposure to the United States." *American Journal of Public Health* 99(12, December): 2247–54. https://doi.org/10.2105/AJPH.2008.137091.

Cordero, Carrie F., Heidi Li Feldman, and Chimène I. Keitner. 2020. "The Law against Family Separation." *Columbia Human Rights Law Review* 51(2): 430–506.

Cortina, Adela. 2022. *Aporophobia: Why We Reject the Poor Instead of Helping Them*. Princeton, N.J.: Princeton University Press.

Crea, Thomas M., Anayeli Lopez, Theresa Taylor, and Dawnya Underwood. 2017. "Unaccompanied Migrant Children in the United States: Predictors of Placement Stability in Long Term Foster Care." *Children and Youth Services Review* 73(C): 93–99.

Creswell, John W., and Vicki L. Clark-Plano. 2007. "Choosing a Mixed Methods Design." In Creswell and Clark-Plano, *Designing and Conducting: Mixed Methods Research*. Thousand Oaks, Calif.: Sage Publications.

Czaika, Mathias, and Hein de Haas. 2015. "The Globalization of Migration: Has the World Become More Migratory?" *International Migration Review* 48(2): 283–323.

De Jesus, Maria, and Carissa Hernandes. 2019. "Generalized Violence as a Threat to Health and Well-being: A Qualitative Study of Youth Living in Urban Settings in Central America's 'Northern Triangle.'" *International Journal of Environmental Research and Public Health* 16(18, September). https://doi.org/10.3390/ijerph16183465.

DeParle, Jason. 2019. *A Good Provider Is One Who Leaves: One Family and Migration in the 21st Century*. New York: Viking.

Díaz Cepeda, Luis Rubén, Roberto Sánchez Benítez, and Amy Reed-Sandoval, eds. 2021. *Ética, política, y migración*. Chihuahua: Universidad Autónoma de Ciudad Juárez.

Diaz-Strong, Daysi Ximena. 2021. "'When Did I Stop Being a Child?' The Subjective Feeling of Adulthood of Mexican and Central American Unaccompanied 1.25 Generation Immigrants." *Emerging Adulthood* (August 25): 2167696821992141. https://doi.org/10.1177/2167696821992141.

Diez-Quevedo, Crisanto, Teresa Rangil, Luis Sanchez-Planell, Kurt Kroenke, and Robert L. Spitzer. 2001. "Validation and Utility of the Patient Health Questionnaire in Diagnosing Mental Disorders in 1,003 General Hospital Spanish Inpatients." *Psychosomatic Medicine* 63(4). https://journals.lww.com/psychosomaticmedicine/Fulltext/2001/07000/Validation_and_Utility_of_the_Patient_Health.21.aspx.

Donato, Katharine M., and Blake Sisk. 2015. "Children's Migration to the United States from Mexico and Central America: Evidence from the Mexican and Latin American Migration Projects." *Journal on Migration and Human Security* 2(3): 58–79. https://doi.org/10.14240/jmhs.v3i1.43.

Dreby, Joanna. 2006. "Honor and Virtue: Mexican Parenting in the Transnational Context." *Gender and Society* 20(1): 32–59.

———. 2007. "Children and Power in Mexican Transnational Families." *Journal of Marriage and Family* 69(4): 1050–64. https://doi.org/10.1111/j.1741-3737.2007.00430.x.

———. 2010. *Divided by Borders: Mexican Migrants and Their Children*. Berkeley: University of California Press.

———. 2015. "U.S. Immigration Policy and Family Separation: The Consequences for Children's Well-being." *Social Science and Medicine* 132(May 1): 245–51. https://doi.org/10.1016/j.socscimed.2014.08.041.

Drew, Natalie, Michelle Funk, Stephen Tang, Jagannath Lamichhane, Elena Chávez, Sylvester Katontoka Dip, Soumitra Pathare, Oliver Lewis, Lawrence Gostin, and Benedetto Saraceno. 2011. "Human Rights Violations of People with Mental and Psychosocial Disabilities: An Unresolved Global Crisis." *The Lancet* 378(9803): 1664–75. https://doi.org/10.1016/S0140-6736(11)61458-X.

Dudley, Steven. 2020. *MS-13: The Making of America's Most Notorious Gang.* New York: Hanover Square Press.

Dunn, Marianne G., and Karen M. O'Brien. 2009. "Psychological Health and Meaning in Life: Stress, Social Support, and Religious Coping in Latina/Latino Immigrants." *Hispanic Journal of Behavioral Sciences* 31(2, May 1): 204–27. https://doi.org/10.1177/0739986309334799.

Durand, Jorge. 2007. "The Bracero Program (1942–1964): A Critical Appraisal." *Migración y Desarrollo* 9(2nd semester): 27–43.

Duruiz, Deniz. 2019. "Dispossession, Racialization, and Rural Kurdish Labor Migration in Turkey." PhD diss., Columbia University. https://doi.org/10.7916/d8-j7s1-5h58.

Duyvendak, Jan Willem. 2011. *The Politics of Home: Belonging and Nostalgia in Europe and the United States.* New York: Palgrave Macmillan.

Enríquez, Laura J. 2022. *Children of the Revolution: Violence, Inequality, and Hope in Nicaraguan Migration.* Stanford, Calif.: Stanford University Press.

Escamilla García, Angel Alfonso. 2021. "When Internal Migration Fails: A Case Study of Central American Youth Who Relocate Internally before Leaving Their Countries." *Journal on Migration and Human Security* 9(4, December 1): 297–310. https://doi.org/10.1177/23315024211042735.

Evans, Kerri, Jaime Perez-Aponte, and Ruth McRoy. 2020. "Without a Paddle: Barriers to School Enrollment Procedures for Immigrant Students and Families." *Education and Urban Society* 52(9): 1283–1304.

Falcke, Swantje, and Maarten Vink. 2020. "Closing a Backdoor to Dual Citizenship: The German Citizenship Law Reform of 2000 and the Abolishment of the 'Domestic Clause.'" *Frontiers in Sociology* 5(December 15). https://www.frontiersin.org/article/10.3389/fsoc.2020.536940.

Finch, Brian Karl, Bohdan Kolody, and William A. Vega. 2000. "Perceived Discrimination and Depression among Mexican-Origin Adults in California." *Journal of Health and Social Behavior* 41(3, September): 295. https://doi.org/10.2307/2676322.

Fish, Joe, and Cristina Sganga. 1988. *El Salvador: Testament of Terror.* London: Zed Books.

FitzGerald, David Scott. 2020. "Remote Control of Migration: Theorising Territoriality, Shared Coercion, and Deterrence." *Journal of Ethnic and Migration Studies* 46 (1, January 2): 4–22. https://doi.org/10.1080/1369183X.2020.1680115.

Flores, René D., and Ariela Schachter. 2018. "Who Are the 'Illegals'? The Social Construction of Illegality in the United States." *American Sociological Review* 83(5): 839–68. https://doi.org/10.1177/0003122418794635.

Foa, Edna B., Kelly M. Johnson, Norah C. Feeny, and Kimberli R. H. Treadwell. 2001. "The Child PTSD Symptom Scale: A Preliminary Examination of Its Psychometric Properties." *Journal of Clinical Child and Adolescent Psychology* 30(3, August): 376–84. https://doi.org/10.1207/S15374424JCCP3003_9.

Foner, Nancy. 2000. *From Ellis Island to JFK: New York's Two Great Waves of Immigration*. New Haven, Conn. and New York: Yale University Press and Russell Sage Foundation.

———. 2009. *Across Generations: Immigrant Families in America*. New York: New York University Press.

———. 2022. *One Quarter of the Nation: Immigration and the Transformation of America*. Princeton, N.J.: Princeton University Press.

Foner, Nancy, and Patrick Simon. 2015. *Fear, Anxiety, and National Identity: Immigration and Belonging in North America and Western Europe*. New York: Russell Sage Foundation.

Foxen, Patricia. 2020. *In Search of Providence: Transnational Mayan Identities*, updated ed. Nashville, Tenn.: Vanderbilt University Press.

Frank-Vitale, Amelia. 2021. "Leave if You're Able: Migration, Survival, and the Everydayness of Deportation in Honduras." PhD diss., University of Michigan, Department of Anthropology.

*Frontline*. 2021. *Trafficked in America* (documentary), produced by Daffodil Altan and Andrés Cediel. PBS, *Frontline*. https://www.youtube.com/watch?app=desktop&v=Mp9E5nkr-wQ.

Galli, Chiara. 2020. "Humanitarian Capital: How Lawyers Help Immigrants Use Suffering to Claim Membership in the Nation-State." *Journal of Ethnic and Migration Studies* 46(11, August 17): 2181–98. https://doi.org/10.1080/1369183X.2019.1582325.

———. 2023. *Precarious Protections: Unaccompanied Minors Seeking Asylum in the U.S.* Oakland: University of California Press.

Gandini, Luciana, Alethia Fernández de la Reguera, and Juan Carlos Narváez Gutiérrez. 2020. *Caravanas*. Mexico City: National Autonomous University of Mexico.

Gans, Herbert J. 1992. "Second-Generation Decline: Sceanrios for the Economic and Erhnic Futures of the Post-1965 American Immigrants." *Ethnic and Racial Studies* 15(2): 174–92.

Ganster, Paul. 2008. "Bracero." In *Encyclopedia of Latin American History and Culture*, 2nd ed., edited by Jay Kinsbruner and Erick D. Langer. Detroit: Charles Scribner's Sons.

García, Angela S. 2019. *Legal Passing: Navigating Undocumented Life and Local Immigration Law*. Oakland: University of California Press.

Garip, Filiz. 2017. *On the Move: Changing Mechanisms of Mexico-U.S. Migration*. Princeton, N.J.: Princeton University Press.

Garrard-Burnett, Virginia. 2008. "Indigo." In *Encyclopedia of Latin American History and Culture*, 2nd ed., edited by Jay Kinsbruner and Erick D. Langer. Detroit: Charles Scribner's Sons.

Geiger, A. W., and Leslie Davis. 2019. "A Growing Number of American Teenagers—Particularly Girls—Are Facing Depression." Washington, D.C.: Pew Research Center (July 12). https://www.pewresearch.org/fact-tank/2019/07/12/a-growing-number-of-american-teenagers-particularly-girls-are-facing-depression/ (accessed September 5, 2022).

Gil Martínez de Escobar, Rocío. 2006. *Fronteras de pertenencia: hacia la construcción del bienestar y el desarrollo comunitario transnacional de Santa María Tindú, Oaxaca*. Mexico City: Universidad Autónoma de México, Iztapalapa, Casa Juan Pablos.

Godlasky, Anne. 2022. "Don't Call Them 'Swarms.'" National Press Foundation, March 7. https://nationalpress.org/topic/dont-call-them-swarms/ (accessed October 7, 2023).

Gonzales, Roberto G. 2011. "Learning to Be Illegal: Undocumented Youth and Shifting Legal Contexts in the Transition to Adulthood." *American Sociological Review* 76(4): 602–19. https://doi.org/10.1177/0003122411411901.

———. 2016. *Lives in Limbo: Undocumented and Coming of Age in America*. Oakland: University of California Press.

Gonzales, Roberto G., Veronica Terriquez, and Stephen P. Ruszczyk. 2014. "Becoming DACAmented: Assessing the Short-Term Benefits of Deferred Action for Childhood Arrivals (DACA)." *American Behavioral Scientist* 58(14, December 1): 1852–72. https://doi.org/10.1177/0002764214550288.

Gonzalez-Barrera, Ana. 2015. "More Mexicans Leaving than Coming to the U.S." Washington, D.C.: Pew Research Center (November 19). https://www.pewresearch.org/hispanic/2015/11/19/more-mexicans-leaving-than-coming-to-the-u-s/.

Gonzalez-Barrera, Ana, and Jens Manuel Krogstad. 2019. "What We Know about Illegal Immigration from Mexico." Washington, D.C.: Pew Research Center (June 28). https://www.pewresearch.org/fact-tank/2019/06/28/what-we-know-about-illegal-immigration-from-mexico/.

Gowayed, Heba. 2022. *Refuge: How the State Shapes Human Potential*. Princeton, N.J.: Princeton University Press.

Grinberg, León, and Rebeca Grinberg. 1989. *Psychoanalytic Perspectives on Migration and Exile*. New Haven, Conn.: Yale University Press.

Groger, Jeff, and Stephen J. Trejo. 2002. *Falling Behind or Moving Up? The Intergenerational Progress of Mexican Americans*. Public Policy Institute of California. https://www.ppic.org/wp-content/uploads/content/pubs/report/R_502JGR.pdf.

Haggerty, Richard A. 1988. *El Salvador: A Country Study*. Washington, D.C.: Library of Congress, Federal Research Division. https://www.loc.gov/item/89048948/.

Hain, Tim. 2021. "DHS Sec. Mayorkas: 'The Border Is Closed,' but 'We Will Not Expel Young, Vulnerable Children.'" *RealClear Politics*, March 21.

https://www.realclearpolitics.com/video/2021/03/21/dhs_sec_mayorkas_we_will_not_expel_young_vulnerable_children_at_the_border.html.

Haller, William, Alejandro Portes, and Scott M. Lynch. 2011. "Dreams Fulfilled, Dreams Shattered: Determinants of Segmented Assimilation in the Second Generation." *Social Forces* 89(3): 733–62.

Hamlin, Rebecca. 2021. *Crossing: How We Label and React to People on the Move.* Stanford, Calif.: Stanford University Press.

Handy, Jim. 1994. *Revolution in the Countryside: Rural Conflict and Agrarian Reform in Guatemala, 1944–1954.* Chapel Hill: University of North Carolina Press.

Harris, Lindsay M. 2021. "Asylum under Attack: Restoring Asylum Protections in the United States." *Loyola Law Review* 67(2): 2–69.

Haslam, Nick, Brodie C. Dakin, Fabian Fabiano, Melanie J. McGrath, Joshua Rhee, Ekaterina Vylomova, Morgan Weaving, and Melissa A. Wheeler. 2020. "Harm Inflation: Making Sense of Concept Creep." *European Review of Social Psychology* 31(1, January 1): 254–86. https://doi.org/10.1080/10463283.2020.1796080.

Hayes, Terry. 2014. *I Am Pilgrim: A Thriller.* New York: Simon & Schuster.

Heidbrink, Lauren. 2014. "Unintended Consequences: Reverberations of Special Immigrant Juvenile Status." *Journal of Applied Research on Children* 5(2): 9.

———. 2020. *Migranthood: Youth in a New Era of Deportation.* Stanford, Calif.: Stanford University Press.

Hendriks, Martijn, and Martijn J. Burger. 2020. "Unsuccessful Subjective Well-being Assimilation among Immigrants: The Role of Faltering Perceptions of the Host Society." *Journal of Happiness Studies* 21(6): 1985–2006.

Heymann, Jody. 2006. *Forgotten Families: Ending the Growing Crisis Confronting Children and Working Parents in the Global Economy.* Oxford: Oxford University Press.

Hipsman, Faye, and Muzaffar Chishti. 2015. "The Child and Family Migration Surge of Summer 2014: A Short-Lived Crisis with a Lasting Impact." *Journal of International Affairs* 68(2, May 6). https://jia.sipa.columbia.edu/news/child-and-family-migration-surge-summer-2014-short-lived-crisis-lasting-impact.

Holguin, Carlos, and Peter A. Schey. 1986. "Challenging INS Detention of Minors." *In Defense of the Alien* 9: 152–64.

Holland, Max. 2005. "Private Sources of U.S. Foreign Policy: William Pawley and the 1954 Coup d'État in Guatemala." *Journal of Cold War Studies* 7(4): 36–73.

Holmes, Seth M., Ernesto Castañeda, Jeremy Geeraert, Heide Castañeda, Ursula Probst, Nina Zeldes, Sarah S. Willen, et al. 2021. "Deservingness: Migration and Health in Social Context." *BMJ Global Health* 6(suppl. 1, April 1): e005107. https://doi.org/10.1136/bmjgh-2021-005107.

Holmes, Seth M., and Heide Castañeda. 2016. "Representing the 'European Refugee Crisis' in Germany and Beyond: Deservingness and Difference, Life and Death." *American Ethnologist* 43(1): 12–24. https://doi.org/10.1111/amet.12259.

Hondagneu-Sotelo, Pierrette. 1994. *Gendered Transitions: Mexican Experiences of Immigration.* Berkeley: University of California Press.

Hondagneu-Sotelo, Pierrette, and Ernestine Avila. 1997. "I'm Here but I'm There: The Meanings of Transnational Motherhood." *Gender and Society* 11(5): 548–71.

Hovey, Joseph D. 2000. "Acculturative Stress, Depression, and Suicidal Ideation among Central American Immigrants." *Suicide and Life—Threatening Behavior* 30(2, Summer): 125–39.

Hsin, Amy, and Christina Felfe. 2014. "When Does Time Matter? Maternal Employment, Children's Time with Parents, and Child Development." *Demography* 51(5, October 4): 1867–94. https://doi.org/10.1007/s13524-014-0334-5.

Hynie, Michaela. 2018. "The Social Determinants of Refugee Mental Health in the Post-Migration Context: A Critical Review." *Canadian Journal of Psychiatry* 63(5): 297–303. https://doi.org/10.1177/0706743717746666.

Ignatiev, Noel. 1996. *How the Irish Became White*. New York: Routledge.

Immigration and Ethnic History Society (IEHS). n.d.-a. "American Baptist Churches (ABC) Settlement Agreement." Immigration History, a project of the IEHS. Austin: University of Texas, Department of History. https://immigrationhistory.org/item/abc-settlement-agreement/.

———. n.d.-b. "Nicaraguan Adjustment and Central American Relief Act." Immigration History, a project of the IEHS. Austin: University of Texas, Department of History. https://immigrationhistory.org/item/nicaraguan-adjustment-and-central-american-relief-act/.

Immigration Policy Tracking Project. 2018. "AG Sessions Issues Matter of A-B-, Restricting Asylum Claims Based on Domestic or Gang Violence." March 7. https://immpolicytracking.org/policies/ag-sessions-vacates-matter-of-a-b-/ (accessed July 29, 2023).

———. n.d. "1028 Policies." https://immpolicytracking.org/policies/.

InSightCrime. 2021. "MS13." InSight Crime, September 22. http://insightcrime.org/el-salvador-organized-crime-news/mara-salvatrucha-ms-13-profile/.

International Organization for Migration (IOM). 2022. "World Migration Report 2022." Geneva: IOM. https://worldmigrationreport.iom.int/wmr-2022-interactive/.

Itzigsohn, José. 2009. *Encountering American Faultlines: Race, Class, and the Dominican Experience in Providence*. New York: Russell Sage Foundation.

Jalongo, Mary Renck. 2010. "From Urban Homelessness to Rural Work: International Origins of the Orphan Trains." *Early Childhood Education Journal* 38(3, October 1): 165–70. https://doi.org/10.1007/s10643-010-0421-1.

Jamil, Hikmet, Mohamed Farrag, Julie Hakim-Larson, Talib Kafaji, Husam Abdulkhaleq, and Adnan Hammad. 2007. "Mental Health Symptoms in Iraqi Refugees: Posttraumatic Stress Disorder, Anxiety, and Depression." *Journal of Cultural Diversity* 14(1, Spring): 19–25.

Jiménez, Tomás R. 2010. *Replenished Ethnicity: Mexican Americans, Immigration, and Identity*. Berkeley: University of California Press.

Kaczmarczyk, Pawel, and Douglas S. Massey. 2019. "The Ethnosurvey Revisited: New Migrations, New Methodologies?" *Central and Eastern European Migration Review* 8(2): 9–38. https://doi.org/10.17467/ceemr.2019.15.

Kaltman, Stacey, Alejandra Hurtado de Mendoza, Felisa A. Gonzales, Adriana Serrano, and Peter J. Guarnaccia. 2011. "Contextualizing the Trauma Experience of Women Immigrants from Central America, South America, and Mexico." *Journal of Traumatic Stress* 24(6): 635–42. https://doi.org/10.1002/jts.20698.

Kao, Grace, Kara Joyner, and Kelly Stamper Balistreri. 2019. *The Company We Keep: Interracial Friendships and Romantic Relationships from Adolescence to Adulthood.* New York: Russell Sage Foundation.

Kasinitz, Philip, John H. Mollenkopf, and Mary C. Waters, eds. 2004. *Becoming New Yorkers: Ethnographies of the New Second Generation.* New York: Russell Sage Foundation.

Kasinitz, Philip, John H. Mollenkopf, Mary C. Waters, and Jennifer Holdaway. 2008. *Inheriting the City: The Children of Immigrants Come of Age.* New York and Cambridge, Mass.: Russell Sage Foundation and Harvard University Press.

Knapp, Jackson. 2015. "Local Photographer Takes Stunning Portraits of Young People Who Crossed into the U.S. Alone." *Washingtonian*, October 21. https://www.washingtonian.com/2015/10/21/oliver-contreras-unaccompanied-youth-seeking-refuge/.

Kocher, Austin. 2023. "Glitches in the Digitization of Asylum: How CBP One Turns Migrants' Smartphones into Mobile Borders." *Societies* 13(6, June): 149. https://doi.org/10.3390/soc13060149.

Kreisberg, A. Nicole, and Amy Hsin. 2021. "The Higher Educational Trajectories of Undocumented Youth in New York City." *Journal of Ethnic and Migration Studies* 47(17, December 13): 3822–45. https://doi.org/10.1080/1369183X.2020.1750947.

Kroc Institute for International Peace Studies. n.d. "Chapultepec Peace Agreement." Peace Accords Matrix. https://peaceaccords.nd.edu/accord/chapultepec-peace-agreement (accessed September 6, 2021).

Kroenke, Kurt, and Robert Spitzer. 2002. "The PHQ-9: A New Depression Diagnostic and Severity Measure." *Psychiatric Annals* 32(September 1): 509–21. https://doi.org/10.3928/0048-5713-20020901-06.

Kroenke, Kurt, Robert L. Spitzer, and Janet B. W. Williams. 2001. "The PHQ-9." *Journal of General Internal Medicine* 16(9, September): 606–13. https://doi.org/10.1046/j.1525-1497.2001.016009606.x.

LaFeber, Walter. 1993. *Inevitable Revolutions: The United States in Central America*, 2nd ed. New York: W. W. Norton.

Lakhani, Sarah M. 2017. "'Stranded': Asylum-Seeking in an Era of Humanitarian Decline." Research Brief 3. University of California Office of the President, California Immigration Research Initiative (Fall). https://escholarship.org/uc/item/1t28z68n.

Lashley, Myrna. 2000. "The Unrecognized Social Stressors of Migration and Reunification in Caribbean Families." *Transcultural Psychiatry* (June 1). https://doi.org/10.1177/136346150003700203.

Latin American Youth Center. 2018. *Voces Sin Fronteras: Our Stories, Our Truth.* Washington, D.C.: Shout Mouse Press.

LeoGrande, William M. 2008. *Our Own Backyard: The United States in Central America, 1977–1992*. Chapel Hill: University of North Carolina Press.

Leong, Frederick, Yong S. Park, and Zornitsa Kalibatseva. 2013. "Disentangling Immigrant Status in Mental Health: Psychological Protective and Risk Factors among Latino and Asian American Immigrants." *American Journal of Orthopsychiatry* 83(2/3): 361–71. https://doi.org/10.1111/ajop.12020.

Lilly López, Jane. 2021. *Unauthorized Love: Mixed-Citizenship Couples Negotiating Intimacy, Immigration, and the State*. Stanford, Calif.: Stanford University Press.

Lindo-Fuentes, Héctor, Erik Kristofer Ching, and Rafael Lara Martínez. 2007. *Remembering a Massacre in El Salvador: The Insurrection of 1932, Roque Dalton, and the Politics of Historical Memory*. Albuquerque: University of New Mexico Press.

Link, Bruce G., and Jo Phelan. 1995. "Social Conditions as Fundamental Causes of Disease." *Journal of Health and Social Behavior* (extra issue): 80–94.

Lokken, Paul. 2013. "From the 'Kingdoms of Angola' to Santiago de Guatemala: The Portuguese Asientos and Spanish Central America, 1595–1640." *Hispanic American Historical Review* 93(2, May 1): 171–203. https://doi.org/10.1215/00182168-2077126.

Longazel, Jamie, and Miranda Cady Hallett. 2021. *Migration and Mortality: Social Death, Dispossession, and Survival in the Americas*. Philadelphia: Temple University Press.

Lovato, Roberto. 2020. *Unforgetting: A Memoir of Family, Migration, Gangs, and Revolution in the Americas*. New York: HarperCollins. https://www.harpercollins.com/products/unforgetting-roberto-lovato.

Lovato-Hermann, Kristina. 2017. "Crossing the Border to Find Home: A Gendered Perspective on the Separation and Reunification Experiences of Mexican Immigrant Young Adults in the United States." *International Social Work* 60(2, March): 379–93. https://doi.org/10.1177/0020872815611197.

Luiselli, Valeria. 2017. *Tell Me How It Ends: An Essay in 40 Questions*. Minneapolis: Coffee House Press.

———. 2019. *Lost Children Archive*. New York: Knopf/Doubleday.

Luo, Tianyuan, and Cesar L. Escalante. 2021. "Stringent Immigration Enforcement and the Mental Health and Health-Risk Behaviors of Hispanic Adolescent Students in Arizona." *Health Economics* 30(1): 86–103. https://doi.org/10.1002/hec.4178.

Mahé, Alain. 2006. *Histoire de la Grande Kabylie: XIXe–XXe siècles: anthropologie historique du lien social dans les communautés villageoises*, 2nd. ed. Saint-Denis: Bouchène.

Mahler, Sarah J. 1995. *Salvadorans in Suburbia: Symbiosis and Conflict*. Boston: Allyn and Bacon.

———. 2001. "Suburban Transnational Migrants: Long Island's Salvadorans." In *Migration, Transnationalization, and Race in a Changing New York*, edited by Héctor R. Cordero-Guzmán, Robert C. Smith and Grosfoguel Ramón. Philadelphia: Temple University Press.

Mangual Figueroa, Ariana, and Wendy Barrales. 2021. "Testimonio and Counterstorytelling by Immigrant-Origin Children and Youth: Insights That

Amplify Immigrant Subjectivities." *Societies* 11(2, June): 38. https://doi.org/10.3390/soc11020038.

Marshall, Grant N., Terry L. Schell, and Jeremy N. V. Miles. 2010. "All PTSD Symptoms Are Highly Associated with General Distress: Ramifications for the Dysphoria Symptom Cluster." *Journal of Psychopathology and Clinical Science* 119(1): 126–35. https://dx.doi.org/10.1037%2Fa0018477.

Martínez, Óscar. 2014. *The Beast: Riding the Rails and Dodging Narcos on the Migrant Trail.* London: Verso Books.

Martinez Barahona, Selvyn. 2020. "The Usage of Voseo in Social Media: Hondurans and Salvadorans in the United States." *Macksey Journal* 1(1, September 30).

Massey, Douglas S. 1990. "Social Structure, Household Strategies, and the Cumulative Causation of Migration." *Population Index* 56(1): 3–26.

———. 2018. "Migration and Categorical Inequality." In *Immigration and Categorical Inequality: Migration to the City and the Birth of Race and Ethnicity*, edited by Ernesto Castañeda. New York: Routledge.

Massey, Douglas S., Rafael Alarcón, Jorge Durand, and Humberto González. 1987. *Return to Aztlan: The Social Process of International Migration from Western Mexico.* Berkeley: University of California Press.

Massey, Douglas S., Jorge Durand, and Nolan J. Malone. 2022. *Beyond Smoke and Mirrors: Mexican Immigration in an Era of Economic Integration.* New York: Russell Sage Foundation.

Massey, Douglas S., Jorge Durand, and Karen A. Pren. 2014. "Explaining Undocumented Migration to the U.S." *International Migration Review* 48(4): 1028–61.

Massey, Douglas S., Luin Goldring, and Jorge Durand. 1994. "Continuities in Transnational Migration: An Analysis of Nineteen Mexican Communities." *American Journal of Sociology* 99(6): 1492–1533.

McMichael, Celia, Sandra M. Gifford, and Ignacio Correa-Velez. 2011. "Negotiating Family, Navigating Resettlement: Family Connectedness amongst Resettled Youth with Refugee Backgrounds Living in Melbourne, Australia." *Journal of Youth Studies* 14(2, March): 179–95. https://doi.org/10.1080/13676261.2010.506529.

Mendoza, Hadrian, Akihiko Masuda, and Kevin M. Swartout. 2015. "Mental Health Stigma and Self-Concealment as Predictors of Help-Seeking Attitudes among Latina/o College Students in the United States." *International Journal for the Advancement of Counselling* 37: 207–22. https://doi.org/10.1007/s10447-015-9237-4.

Menjívar, Cecilia. 2000. *Fragmented Ties: Salvadoran Immigrant Networks in America.* Berkeley: University of California Press.

———. 2006. "Liminal Legality: Salvadoran and Guatemalan Immigrants' Lives in the United States." *American Journal of Sociology* 111(4): 999–1037.

———. 2011. *Enduring Violence: Ladina Women's Lives in Guatemala.* Berkeley: University of California Press.

———. 2017. "Temporary Protected Status in the United States: The Experiences of Honduran and Salvadoran Immigrants." Lawrence: University of Kansas,

Center for Migration Research (May). http://ipsr.ku.edu/migration/pdf/TPS_Report.pdf.
Menjívar, Cecilia, and Leisy Abrego. 2012. "Legal Violence: Immigration Law and the Lives of Central American Immigrants." *American Journal of Sociology* 117(5): 1380–1421.
Menjívar, Cecilia, Leisy J. Abrego, and Leah C. Schmalzbauer. 2016. *Immigrant Families*. Cambridge: Polity Press.
Menjívar, Cecilia, Victor Agadjanian, and Byeongdon Oh. 2022. "The Contradictions of Liminal Legality: Economic Attainment and Civic Engagement of Central American Immigrants on Temporary Protected Status." *Social Problems* 69(3, August 1): 678–98. https://doi.org/10.1093/socpro/spaa052.
Menjívar, Cecilia, and Krista M. Perreira. 2019. "Undocumented and Unaccompanied: Children of Migration in the European Union and the United States." *Journal of Ethnic and Migration Studies* 45(2, January 25): 197–217. https://doi.org/10.1080/1369183X.2017.1404255.
Mikolajczak, Moïra, K. M. Petrides, and Jane Hurry. 2009. "Adolescents Choosing Self-Harm as an Emotion Regulation Strategy: The Protective Role of Trait Emotional Intelligence." *British Journal of Clinical Psychology* 48(2): 181–93. https://doi.org/10.1348/014466508X386027.
Millgram, Yael, Jutta Joormann, Jonathan D. Huppert, Avital Lampert, and Maya Tamir. 2019. "Motivations to Experience Happiness or Sadness in Depression: Temporal Stability and Implications for Coping With Stress." *Clinical Psychological Science* 7(1): 143–61. https://doi.org/10.1177%2F2167702618797937.
Moffette, David. 2014. "Governing Immigration through Probation: The Displacement of Borderwork and the Assessment of Desirability in Spain." *Security Dialogue* 45(3, June 1): 262–78. https://doi.org/10.1177/0967010614530457.
Moore, Robert. 2023. "Man Who Killed 23 at El Paso Walmart Pleads Guilty to Hate Crimes." *Texas Tribune*, February 8. https://www.texastribune.org/2023/02/08/el-paso-walmart-shooting-pleads-guilty/.
Moreno Figueroa, Monica. 2010. "Distributed Intensities: Whiteness, Mestizaje, and the Logics of Mexican Racism." *Ethnicities* 10(3). https://journals.sagepub.com/doi/abs/10.1177/1468796810372305.
Moslimani, Mohamad, Luis Noe-Bustamante, and Sono Shah. 2023. "Facts on Hispanics of Salvadoran Origin in the United States, 2021." Washington, D.C.: Pew Research Center (August 16). https://www.pewresearch.org/hispanic/fact-sheet/u-s-hispanics-facts-on-salvadoran-origin-latinos/.
Moya, Eva M., Silvia María Chávez-Baray, Oscar A. Esparza, Leticia Calderón Chelius, Ernesto Castañeda, Griselda Villalobos, Itzel Eguiluz, et al. 2016. "Ulysses Syndrome in Economical and Political Migrants in Mexico and the United States." *EHQUIDAD Revista Internacional de Políticas de Bienestar y Trabajo Social* 5: 11–50.
Muchowiecka, Laura. 2013. "The End of Multiculturalism? Immigration and Integration in Germany and the United Kingdom." *Inquiries Journal* 5(6): 1–12. http://www.inquiriesjournal.com/articles/735/the-end-of-multiculturalism-immigration-and-integration-in-germany-and-the-united-kingdom.

Nazario, Sonia. 2006. *Enrique's Journey: The Story of a Boy's Dangerous Odyssey to Reunite with His Mother.* New York: Random House.

Nesterko, Yuriy, Michael Friedrich, Elmar Brähler, Andreas Hinz, and Heide Glaesmer. 2019. "Mental Health among Immigrants in Germany: The Impact of Self-Attribution and Attribution by Others as an Immigrant." *BMC Public Health* 19(1): 1–8.

Nevins, Joseph. 2016. "How U.S. Policy in Honduras Set the Stage for Today's Migration." *The Conversation,* October 31. http://theconversation.com/how-us-policy-in-honduras-set-the-stage-for-todays-migration-65935 (accessed September 5, 2021).

Ngai, Mae M. 2004. *Impossible Subjects: Illegal Aliens and the Making of Modern America.* Princeton, N.J.: Princeton University Press.

Nicholls, Walter J. 2013. *The DREAMers: How the Undocumented Youth Movement Transformed the Immigrant Rights Debate.* Stanford, Calif.: Stanford University Press.

O'Connor, Allison, Jeanne Batalova, and Jessica Bolter. 2019. "Central American Immigrants in the United States." Washington, D.C.: Migration Policy Institute (August 12). https://www.migrationpolicy.org/article/central-american-immigrants-united-states-2017.

Office of Refugee Resettlement (ORR). 2024a. "Fact Sheets and Data." https://www.acf.hhs.gov/orr/about/ucs/facts-and-data (accessed March 7, 2024).

———. 2024b. "Unaccompanied Alien Children Released to Sponsors by State." Updated March 7, 2024. https://www.acf.hhs.gov/orr/grant-funding/unaccompanied-children-released-sponsors-state (accessed March 7, 2024).

Okamoto, Dina G. 2003. "Toward a Theory of Panethnicity: Explaining Asian American Collective Action." *American Sociological Review* 68(6, December): 811–42. https://doi.org/10.2307/1519747.

———. 2006. "Institutional Panethnicity: Boundary Formation in Asian-American Organizing." *Social Forces* 85(1, September 1): 1–25. https://doi.org/10.1353/sof.2006.0136.

Olivares, Efrén C. 2022. *My Boy Will Die of Sorrow: A Memoir of Immigration from the Front Lines: Olivares.* New York: Hachette Books.

Oliveira, Gabrielle. 2018. *Motherhood across Borders: Immigrants and Their Children in Mexico and New York.* New York: New York University Press.

Orange County Aging Services Collaborative. 2005. "Cuestionario Sobre La Salud Del Paciente-9." Pfizer. https://www.ons.org/sites/default/files/PatientHealthQuestionnaire9_Spanish.pdf.

Osuji, Chinyere K. 2019. *Boundaries of Love: Interracial Marriage and the Meaning of Race.* New York: New York University Press.

Park, Jinme, Thomas Elbert, Seog Ju Kim, and Jinah Park. 2019. "The Contribution of Posttraumatic Stress Disorder and Depression to Insomnia in North Korean Refugee Youth." *Frontiers in Psychiatry* 10(April 8): 211. https://doi.org/10.3389/fpsyt.2019.00211.

Parreñas, Rhacel Salazar. 2005. *Children of Global Migration: Transnational Families and Gendered Woes.* Stanford, Calif.: Stanford University Press.

Patler, Caitlin, Erin R. Hamilton, and Robin L. Savinar. 2021. "The Limits of Gaining Rights While Remaining Marginalized: The Deferred Action for Childhood Arrivals (DACA) Program and the Psychological Well-being of Latina/o Undocumented Youth." *Social Forces* 100(1, September 1): 246–72. https://doi.org/10.1093/sf/soaa099.

Perlmann, Joel, and Roger Waldinger. 1997. "Second Generation Decline? Children of Immigrants, Past and Present—A Reconsideration." *International Migration Review* 31(4, December 1): 893–922. https://doi.org/10.1177/019791839703100405.

Perreira, Krista M., Mimi V. Chapman, and Gabriela L. Stein. 2006. "Becoming an American Parent: Overcoming Challenges and Finding Strength in a New Immigrant Latino Community." *Journal of Family Issues* 27(10, October): 1383–1414. https://doi.org/10.1177/0192513X06290041.

Perreira, Krista M., and India Ornelas. 2013. "Painful Passages: Traumatic Experiences and Post-Traumatic Stress among U.S. Immigrant Latino Adolescents and Their Primary Caregivers." *International Migration Review* 47(4, December 1): 976–1005. https://doi.org/10.1111/imre.12050.

Porche, Michelle V., Lisa R. Fortuna, Julia Lin, and Margarita Alegría. 2011. "Childhood Trauma and Psychiatric Disorders as Correlates of School Dropout in a National Sample of Young Adults." *Child Development* 82(3, June): 982–98. https://doi.org/10.1111/j.1467-8624.2010.01534.x.

Portes, Alejandro, and Rubén G. Rumbaut. 2014. *Immigrant America: A Portrait*, 4th ed. Berkeley: University of California Press.

Portes, Alejandro, and Min Zhou. 1993. "The New Second Generation: Segmented Assimilation and Its Variants." *The Annals of the American Academy of Political and Social Science* 530(1, November): 74–96.

Powers, Abigail, Kerry J. Ressler, and Rebekah G. Bradley. 2009. "The Protective Role of Friendship on the Effects of Childhood Abuse and Depression." *Depression and Anxiety* 26(1): 46–53. https://doi.org/10.1002/da.20534.

Rastogi, Mudita, Nicole Massey-Hastings, and Elizabeth Wieling. 2012. "Barriers to Seeking Mental Health Services in the Latino/a Community: A Qualitative Analysis." *Journal of Systemic Therapies* 31(4): 1–17. https://doi.org/10.1521/jsyt.2012.31.4.1.

Rathod, Jayesh, Eri Hershberg, and Dennis Stinchcomb. 2017. "Country Conditions in Central America and Asylum Decision-Making: Report from a January 2017 Workshop." 15 vols. Working Paper 15. Washington, D.C.: American University, Center for Latin American and Latino Studies (April 1). https://ssrn.com/abstract=2954216.

Reavell, James, and Qulsom Fazil. 2017. "The Epidemiology of PTSD and Depression in Refugee Minors Who Have Resettled in Developed Countries." *Journal of Mental Health* 26(1, January 2): 74–83. https://doi.org/10.1080/09638237.2016.1222065.

Rendón, María G. 2019. *Stagnant Dreamers: How the Inner City Shapes the Integration of the Second Generation.* New York: Russell Sage Foundation.

Rivera, Gerardo. 2015. "Honduras Chapter: Childhood and Migration in Central and North America: Causes, Policies, Practices, and Challenges." February. https://www.academia.edu/12384314/Honduras_Chapter_Childhood_and_Migration_in_Central_and_North_America_Causes_Policies_Practices_and_Challenges.

Romero, Mary. 2011. "'Are Your Papers in Order?' Racial Profiling, Vigilantes, and 'America's Toughest Sheriff.'" *Harvard Latin America Law Review* 14: 337.

Rose, Steve. 2022. "A Deadly Ideology: How the 'Great Replacement Theory' Went Mainstream." *Guardian*, June 8. https://www.theguardian.com/world/2022/jun/08/a-deadly-ideology-how-the-great-replacement-theory-went-mainstream.

Roth, Benjamin J., and Breanne L. Grace. 2015. "Falling through the Cracks: The Paradox of Post-Release Services for Unaccompanied Child Migrants." *Children and Youth Services Review* 58(November): 244–52. https://doi.org/10.1016/j.childyouth.2015.10.007.

Rousseau, Cécile, Marie-Claire Rufagari, Déogratias Bagilishya, and Toby Measham. 2004. "Remaking Family Life: Strategies for Re-establishing Continuity among Congolese Refugees during the Family Reunification Process." *Social Science and Medicine* 59(5, September): 1095–1108. https://doi.org/10.1016/j.socscimed.2003.12.011.

Ruehs-Navarro, Emily. 2022. *Unaccompanied: The Plight of Immigrant Youth at the Border.* New York: New York University Press.

Rumbaut, Rubén G. 2005. "Sites of Belonging: Acculturation, Discrimination, and Ethnic Identity among Children of Immigrants." In *Discovering Successful Pathways in Children's Development: Mixed Methods in the Study of Childhood and Family Life*, edited by Thomas S. Weisner. Chicago: University of Chicago Press.

Rung, Daile Lynn. 2020. "Processes of Sub-Citizenship: Neoliberal Statecrafting 'Citizens,' 'Non-Citizens,' and Detainable 'Others.'" *Social Sciences* 9(1, January): 5. https://doi.org/10.3390/socsci9010005.

Ruoxi, Liu. 2020. "Achieving Better Structural Integration? Evidence from the Career Pathways of Second-Generation Chinese Immigrants in France." In *Chinese Immigrants in Europe: Image, Identity, and Social Participation*, edited by Yue Liu and Simeng Wang. Berlin: De Gruyter.

Ruszczyk, Stephen P. 2019. "Inclusion in the Nation via the City: Assessing Immigrant Claims of Belonging." *Sociological Forum* 34(3): 786–90. https://doi.org/10.1111/socf.12527.

Sajjad, Tazreena. 2022. "Strategic Cruelty: Legitimizing Violence in the European Union's Border Regime." *Global Studies Quarterly* 2(2, April 1): ksac008. https://doi.org/10.1093/isagsq/ksac008.

Sassen, Saskia. 1988. *The Mobility of Labor and Capital: A Study in International Investment and Labor Flow.* Cambridge: Cambridge University Press.

———. 2001. *The Global City: New York, London, Tokyo,* 2nd ed. Princeton, N.J.: Princeton University Press.

Sayad, Abdelmalek. 2006. *L'immigration ou les paradoxes de l'altérité: L'illusion du provisoire*, vol. 1 of 3 vols. Montreal: Éditions Liber.
———. 2004. *The Suffering of the Immigrant*, translated by David Macey. Cambridge: Polity Press.
Scallen, Patrick. 2019. "'The Bombs That Drop in El Salvador Explode in Mount Pleasant': From Cold War Conflagration to Immigrant Struggles in Washington, D.C., 1970–1995." PhD diss., Georgetown University, Graduate School of Arts and Sciences. https://repository.library.georgetown.edu/handle/10822/1057308.
Schmalzbauer, Leah. 2004. "Searching for Wages and Mothering from Afar: The Case of Honduran Transnational Families." *Journal of Marriage and Family* 66(December 1): 1317–31. https://doi.org/10.1111/j.0022-2445.2004.00095.x.
———. 2008. "Family Divided: The Class Formation of Honduran Transnational Families." *Global Networks* 8(3): 329–46.
———. 2014. *The Last Best Place? Gender, Family, and Migration in the New West*. Redwood City, Calif.: Stanford University Press.
Scholtes, Jennifer, and Emily Ethridge. 2014. "Alone, Illegal, and Underage: The Child Migrant Crisis." *Roll Call*, May 28. https://www.rollcall.com/2014/05/28/alone-illegal-and-underage-the-child-migrant-crisis/.
Sedgewick, Augustine. 2021. *Coffeeland: One Man's Dark Empire and the Making of Our Favorite Drug*. New York: Penguin Press.
Segovia, Alexander. 2021. *El gran fracaso: 150 años de capitalismo ineficiente, concentrador y excluyente en Centroamérica*. Guatemala City: F&G Editores.
Semple, Kirk. 2019. "Migrants in Mexico Face Kidnappings and Violence While Awaiting Immigration Hearings in U.S." *New York Times*, July 12. https://www.nytimes.com/2019/07/12/world/americas/mexico-migrants.html.
Serrano-Ibáñez, Elena R., Gema T. Ruiz-Párraga, and Rosa Esteve. 2018. "Validation of the Child PTSD Symptom Scale (CPSS) in Spanish Adolescents." *Psicothema* 30(1, February): 130–35. https://doi.org/10.7334/psicothema2017.144.
Small, Mario Luis. 2011. "How to Conduct a Mixed Methods Study: Recent Trends in a Rapidly Growing Literature." *Annual Review of Sociology* 37(1, August 11): 57–86. https://doi.org/10.1146/annurev.soc.012809.102657.
Smith, Robert C. 2006. *Mexican New York: Transnational Lives of New Immigrants*. Berkeley: University of California Press.
Soboroff, Jacob. 2020. *Separated: Inside an American Tragedy*. New York: HarperCollins.
Solari, Cinzia D. 2017. *On the Shoulders of Grandmothers: Gender, Migration, and Post-Soviet Nation-State Building*. New York: Routledge.
Spitzer, Robert L., Janet B. W. Williams, Kurt Kroenke, et al. 2010. Patient Health Questionnaire Modified for Teens (PHQ-9). https://www.aacap.org/App_Themes/AACAP/docs/member_resources/toolbox_for_clinical_practice_and_outcomes/symptoms/GLAD-PC_PHQ-9.pdf.
Stepick, Alex, and Carol Dutton Stepick. 2009. "Diverse Contexts of Reception and Feelings of Belonging." *Forum Qualitative Sozialforschung* (*Forum: Qualitative Social Research*) 10(3). https://doi.org/10.17169/fqs-10.3.1366.
Stinchcomb, Dennis. 2020. "In Children's Best Interests: Charting a Child-Sensitive Approach to U.S. Immigration Policy." Working Paper 28. Washington, D.C.:

American University, Center for Latin American and Latino Studies (July 1). https://doi.org/10.2139/ssrn.3644399.

Stinchcomb, Dennis, and Jodi Berger Cardoso. 2018. "Newcomer Central American Immigrants' Access to Legal Services." Working Paper 19. Washington, D.C.: American University, Center for Latin American and Latino Studies (September). https://ssrn.com/abstract=3254133.

Stinchcomb, Dennis, and Eric Hershberg. 2014. "Unaccompanied Migrant Children from Central America: Context, Causes, and Responses." Working Paper 7. Washington, D.C.: American University, Center for Latin American and Latino Studies (November). https://doi.org/10.2139/ssrn.2524001.

Stokes, Lauren. 2022. *Fear of the Family: Guest Workers and Family Migration in the Federal Republic of Germany.* Oxford: Oxford University Press.

Stone, John, and Kelsey Harris. 2017. "Symbolic Ethnicity and Herbert Gans: Race, Religion, and Politics in the Twenty-First Century." *Ethnic and Racial Studies* 40(9, July 15): 1397–1409. https://doi.org/10.1080/01419870.2017.1300295.

Streib, Jessi. 2020. *Privilege Lost: Who Leaves the Upper Middle Class and How They Fall.* Oxford: Oxford University Press.

Suárez-Orozco, Carola, Hee Jin Bang, and Ha Yeon Kim. 2011. "I Felt Like My Heart Was Staying Behind: Psychological Implications of Family Separations and Reunifications for Immigrant Youth." *Journal of Adolescent Research* 26(2, March): 222–57. https://doi.org/10.1177/0743558410376830.

Suárez-Orozco, Carola, Francisco X. Gaytán, Hee Jin Bang, Juliana Pakes, Erin O'Connor, and Jean Rhodes. 2010. "Academic Trajectories of Newcomer Immigrant Youth." *Developmental Psychology* 46(3): 602–18. https://doi.org/10.1037/a0018201.

Suárez-Orozco, Carola, Irina L. G. Todorova, and Josephine Louie. 2002. "Making Up for Lost Time: The Experience of Separation and Reunification among Immigrant Families." *Family Process* 41(4, Winter): 625–43.

Suárez-Orozco, Marcelo. 2019. "Catastrophic Migrations." In *Humanitarianism and Mass Migrations: Confronting the World Crisis*, edited by Marcelo Suárez-Orozco. Oakland: University of California Press.

Szalacha, Laura A., Sumru Erkut, Cynthia García Coll, Odette Alarcón, Jacqueline P. Fields, and Ineke Ceder. 2003. "Discrimination and Puerto Rican Children's and Adolescents' Mental Health." *Cultural Diversity and Ethnic Minority Psychology* 9(2): 141–55. https://doi.org/10.1037/1099-9809.9.2.141.

Teicher, Martin H. 2018. "Childhood Trauma and the Enduring Consequences of Forcibly Separating Children from Parents at the United States Border." *BMC Medicine* 16(1, December): 146. https://doi.org/10.1186/s12916-018-1147-y.

Telles, Edward Eric, and Vilma Ortiz. 2008. *Generations of Exclusion: Mexican Americans, Assimilation, and Race.* New York: Russell Sage Foundation.

Telles, Edward, and Christina A. Sue. 2019. *Durable Ethnicity: Mexican Americans and the Ethnic Core.* New York: Oxford University Press.

Terrasi, Salvatore, and Patricia Crain de Galarce. 2017. "Trauma and Learning in America's Classrooms." *Phi Delta Kappan* 98(6). https://doi.org/10.1177/0031721717696476.

Terrio, Susan J. 2015. *Whose Child Am I? Unaccompanied, Undocumented Children in U.S. Immigration Custody*. Oakland: University of California Press.

Terry, Donald F., and Steven R. Wilson, eds. 2005. *Beyond Small Change: Making Migrant Remittances Count*. Washington, D.C: Inter-American Development Bank.

Ticktin, Miriam Iris. 2011. *Casualties of Care: Immigration and the Politics of Humanitarianism in France*. Berkeley: University of California Press.

Tilly, Charles. 1998. *Durable Inequality*. Berkeley: University of California Press.

———. 2005. "Chain Migration and Opportunity Hoarding." In Tilly, *Identities, Boundaries, and Social Ties*. Boulder, Colo.: Paradigm Press.

———. 2007. "Trust Networks in Transnational Migration." *Sociological Forum* 22(1, March): 1–25.

———. 2010. "Mechanisms of the Middle Range." In *Robert K. Merton: Sociology of Science and Sociology as Science*, edited by Craig Calhoun. New York: Columbia University Press.

Tilly, Charles, and Harold C. Brown. 1967. "On Uprooting, Kinship, and the Auspices of Migration." *International Journal of Comparative Sociology* 8(2): 139–64.

Torres, Rebecca Maria, Sarah Blue, Caroline Faria, Tamara Segura, and Kate Swanson. 2022. "'Asylum Is Not for Mexicans': Unaccompanied Youth and Racio-Governance at the U.S. Border." *Geopolitics* (July 18): 1–30. https://doi.org/10.1080/14650045.2022.2086459.

Torres, Stephanie A., Catherine DeCarlo Santiago, Katherine Kaufka Walts, and Maryse H. Richards. 2018. "Immigration Policy, Practices, and Procedures: The Impact on the Mental Health of Mexican and Central American Youth and Families." *American Psychologist* 73(7, October): 843–54. https://doi.org/10.1037/amp0000184.

UNICEF Mexico. n.d. "Niñez Migrante en la Frontera Norte: Legislación y Procesos." México DF, México. https://www.unicef.org/mexico/migraci%C3%B3n-de-ni%C3%B1as-ni%C3%B1os-y-adolescentes.

United Nations High Commissioner for Refugees (UNHCR). 2014. "Children on the Run." Washington, D.C.: UNHCR. https://www.unhcr.org/us/media/children-run-full-report.

U.S. Customs and Border Protection (CBP). 2016. "United States Border Patrol Southwest Family Unit Subject and Unaccompanied Alien Children Apprehensions: Fiscal Year 2016." https://www.cbp.gov/newsroom/stats/southwest-border-unaccompanied-children/fy-2016 (accessed June 30, 2018).

———. 2018. "U.S. Border Patrol Southwest Border Apprehensions by Sector: FY2018." https://www.cbp.gov/newsroom/stats/usbp-sw-border-apprehensions.

———. 2023. "Southwest Land Border Encounters | U.S. Customs and Border Protection," Last modified October 21, 2023. https://www.cbp.gov/newsroom/stats/southwest-land-border-encounters.

U.S. Department of Health and Human Services. 2020. "Unaccompanied Children Released to Sponsors by State—December 2019." https://www.hhs.gov

/programs/social-services/unaccompanied-children-released-to-sponsors-by-state-december-2019.html (accessed October 14, 2020).

U.S. Department of Homeland Security (DHS). 2021. "Statement by Homeland Security Secretary Alejandro N. Mayorkas Regarding the Situation at the Southwest Border." Washington: DHS (March 16). https://www.dhs.gov/news/2021/03/16/statement-homeland-security-secretary-alejandro-n-mayorkas-regarding-situation.

Valdivia, Carolina. 2020. "Undocumented Young Adults' Heightened Vulnerability in the Trump Era." In *We Are Not Dreamers: Undocumented Scholars Theorize Undocumented Life in the United States*, edited by Leisy J. Abrego and Genevieve Negrón-Gonzales. Durham, N.C.: Duke University Press.

Venta, Amanda C., and Alfonso Mercado. 2019. "Trauma Screening in Recently Immigrated Youth: Data from Two Spanish-Speaking Samples." *Journal of Child and Family Studies* 28(1, January 1): 84–90. https://doi.org/10.1007/s10826-018-1252-8.

Veytskin, Yuriy, Claire Lockerb, and Steven McMullen. 2009. "The Soccer War." Soccer Politics. https://sites.duke.edu/wcwp/research-projects/the-soccer-war/.

Villarroel, Maria A., and Emily P. Terlizzi. 2020. "Symptoms of Depression among Adults: United States, 2019." Data Brief 379. Washington, D.C.: National Center for Health Statistics (September). https://www.cdc.gov/nchs/products/databriefs/db379.htm.

Villegas, Rodrigo Dominguez. 2014. "Central American Migrants and 'La Bestia': The Route, Dangers, and Government Responses." Washington, D.C.: Migration Policy Institute (September 10). https://www.migrationpolicy.org/article/central-american-migrants-and-%E2%80%9Cla-bestia%E2%80%9D-route-dangers-and-government-responses.

Vine, David. 2021. "175 Years of Border Invasions: The Anniversary of the U.S. War on Mexico and the Roots of Northward Migration." Washington, D.C.: Council on Hemispheric Affairs (April 22). https://www.coha.org/175-years-of-border-invasions-the-anniversary-of-the-u-s-war-on-mexico-and-the-roots-of-northward-migration/.

Vogt, Wendy A. 2013. "Crossing Mexico: Structural Violence and the Commodification of Undocumented Central American Migrants: Migration, Violence, and Commodification." *American Ethnologist* 40(4, November): 764–80. https://doi.org/10.1111/amet.12053.

Wacquant, Loïc. 2022. *The Invention of the "Underclass": A Study in the Politics of Knowledge*. Cambridge: Polity Press.

Walker, Jesse, Amanda Venta, and Betsy Galicia. 2021. "Who Is Taking Care of Central American Immigrant Youth? Preliminary Data on Caregiving Arrangements and Emotional-Behavioral Symptoms Post-Migration." *Child Psychiatry and Human Development* 52: 217–24. https://doi.org/10.1007/s10578-020-01002-8.

Ward, Nicole, and Jeanne Batalova. 2023. "Central American Immigrants in the United States." Washington, D.C.: Migration Policy Institute (May 10). https://www.migrationpolicy.org/article/central-american-immigrants-united-states.

Wassink, Joshua, and Douglas S. Massey. 2022. "The New System of Mexican Migration: The Role of Entry Mode–Specific Human and Social Capital." *Demography* 59(3, (June 1): 1071–92. https://doi.org/10.1215/00703370-9938548.

Wikipedia. 2022. "List of North American Settlements by Year of Foundation." Revised August 8, 2022. https://en.wikipedia.org/w/index.php?title=List_of_North_American_settlements_by_year_of_foundation&oldid=1103104604.

Wilson, Eli Revelle Yano. 2020. *Front of the House, Back of the House: Race and Inequality in the Lives of Restaurant Workers.* New York: New York University Press.

Wilson, Tamar Diana. 1993. "Theoretical Approaches to Mexican Wage Labor Migration." *Latin American Perspectives* 20(3, Summer): 98–129.

Winkel, Mark van, Nancy A. Nicolson, Marieke Wichers, Wolfgang Viechtbauer, Inez Myin-Germeys, and Frenk P.M.L. Peeters. 2015. "Daily Life Stress Reactivity in Remitted versus Non-Remitted Depressed Individuals." *European Psychiatry* 30(4): 441–47. https://doi.org/10.1016/j.eurpsy.2015.02.011.

World Bank. 2006. "Global Economic Prospects 2006: Economic Implications of Remittances and Migration." Washington, D.C.: World Bank Group. http://documents.worldbank.org/curated/en/507301468142196936/Global-economic-prospects-2006-economic-implications-of-remittances-and-migration.

Xiang, Biao, and Johan Lindquist. 2014. "Migration Infrastructure." *International Migration Review* 48(1, suppl., September 1): 122–48. https://doi.org/10.1111/imre.12141.

Yakshilikov, Yorbol. 2022. "The Unexpected Rise in Remittances to Central America and Mexico during the Pandemic." International Monetary Fund, September 21. https://www.imf.org/en/News/Articles/2022/09/19/cf-the-unexpected-rise-in-remittances.

Yashar, Deborah J. 2018. *Homicidal Ecologies: Illicit Economies and Complicit States in Latin America.* Cambridge: University of Cambridge Press.

Yuval-Davis, Nira. 2006. "Belonging and the Politics of Belonging." *Patterns of Prejudice* 40(3, July 1): 197–214. https://doi.org/10.1080/00313220600769331.

Zamora, Javier. 2022. *Solito.* New York: Simon & Schuster.

Zamora-Kapoor, Anna, and Ernesto Castañeda. 2014. *Using Mixed Methods in Comparative Research: A Cross-Regional Analysis of Anti-Immigrant Sentiment in Belgium and Spain.* London: Sage Publications, Ltd.

Zapata-Barrero, Ricard. 2015. *Interculturalism in Cities: Concept, Policy, and Implementation.* Cheltenham, U.K.: Edward Elgar Publishing.

Zatz, Marjorie S., and Nancy Rodriguez. 2015. *Dreams and Nightmares: Immigration Policy, Youth, and Families.* Berkeley: University of California Press.

Zelizer, Viviana A. 1985. *Pricing the Priceless Child: The Changing Social Value of Children.* New York: Basic Books.

———. 2005. *The Purchase of Intimacy.* Princeton, N.J.: Princeton University Press.

Zelizer, Viviana A., and Charles Tilly. 2006. "Relations and Categories." In *The Psychology of Learning and Motivation,* edited by Arthur Markman and Brian Ross. San Diego, Calif.: Elsevier.

Zimmermann, Peter, and Alexandra Iwanski. 2014. "Emotion Regulation from Early Adolescence to Emerging Adulthood and Middle Adulthood: Age Differences, Gender Differences, and Emotion-Specific Developmental Variations." *International Journal of Behavioral Development* 28(2): 182–94. https://doi.org/10.1177%2F0165025413515405.

# INDEX

Tables and figures are listed in **boldface**.

ABC Settlement Agreement of 1991, 68
abuse by parents or relatives, XXIII, XXVII–XXVIII, 146, 200–201
acculturation, selective, 8
acculturation stress, 144
adverse childhood experiences (ACEs), XI, 141, 142, 143
*American Baptist Churches v. Thornburgh* (1991), 68
anti-immigrant sentiment, 31
Arizona law targeting undocumented, 189
assimilation: race and, 5–9; required, as racist and xenophobic, 5, 18
assimilation theories, 6–9
asylum: ABC Settlement Agreement and, 68; applicants' inability to visit home country, 27; asylum seekers *vs.* migrants or refugees, 36–37; for children, legal requirements for, 37; claims of violence and, 201; deportations without hearing, 205; interviews for, XX; needed reforms in, 31, 205

belonging: students reporting feeling of, 174; as subjective feeling of integration, 7
La Bestia, XI, 90, 104–5, 114
Biden Administration, 188, 203, 205, 206

Black immigrants, racialization of, 6, 7
border, migrant's arrival at, 109–13. *See also* travel to U.S. border
border security: effect on migrants, 15, 104; proponents' false arguments for, 15
Bracero Program. *See* Mexican Farm Labor (Bracero) Program

capitalism: global, 30; racial, 9
caravans of migrants: advantages for migrants, 105; alarm caused by, 15, 105, 204; Mexican protests against, 106
caregivers at home, 21–22; child's sadness at leaving, 126, 180; death of, and trauma, 145–46; grandparents as, xxvi, 24–25, 93, 138–39, 146, 192, 198, 201; lack of, in some cases, 24; loss of, and migration, 198
CBP. *See* U.S. Customs and Border Protection
Central America: most residents' lack of interest in migration, 93; natural disasters and emotional trauma, 143; precolonial period, 55; restrictions on emigration, 103–4; turmoil in, as fault of U.S., 54, 62–63. *See also* gangs in Central America

# 270    INDEX

Central America, immigrants from: caravans of, 15, 105, 106, 204; countries of origin for UAMs, 15, 39, **40**, 68; as deserving of respect, 10, 30; difficulty of deporting, 15; number of, 14, 39; temporary protective status (TPS) and, 41; traumatic experiences of, 140; U.S. destinations, 41, **42**, **43**. See also reasons for migration to U.S.

Central American Minor (CAM) program, 187

Chicago School of Sociology, 5

childcare, affordable, U.S. lack of, 24

childhood experiences, effects of, 23, 24

child migrants: agency of, 11, 14, 36; connection to home via social media, 200; lack of services for, 16–17; need for supportive environment, 12; number referred to ORR, 39; numbers of, 39–44; scholarship on, 11. See also unaccompanied minors (UAMs)

Child PTSD Symptom Scale (CPSS), 164–66, **165**, 168

children left behind by migrants: longing for parents, 23–24; mental health of, 23, 69–71, 73–74, 78–79, 140–41, 142, 161, 167. See also caregivers at home; family separation; transnational families

climate change, 85, 143, 203–4

Clinton administration, 67

Cold War: migration to U.S. in, 63–64; U.S. in Central America and, 58, 60, 63–66, 203

contributions of this study: research contributions, 30–32, 34; theoretical contributions, 10–14

country of origin: migrants' plan to return to, 93, 100, 200; migrants' ties to, 99–100

COVID-19, 16, 169, 194, 197, 203

*coyotes*: child migrants' reluctance to discuss, 97–98; cost of, XXIV, 131; crackdowns on migration and, 90–91, 105, 115; definition of, XI–XII; limited food provided by, 108; marketing of services, 199; migrants' temporary work as, 26; organized crime and, 90, 107; protection provided by, XX, 90–91, 114; as quick approach to family reunion, 14; sophistication of, 116; threats against migrants with unpaid fee, 97; transport of unaccompanied minors, 90–91; turnover of migrants to CBP, 97, 110

CPSS. See Child PTSD Symptom Scale

cultural capital accumulated in schools, 177

cultural humility, as preferred ideal, 18

DACA. See Deferred Action for Childhood Arrivals

decision to migrate, 87–89; emotions surrounding, 88–89, 93–97, 102, 103; family circumstances and, 78–82, 128; as often sudden, 123–24; time frames for, 78, 82, 89–90; without parents' knowledge, 90

dedemocratization, and migration, 85

Deferred Action for Childhood Arrivals (DACA), 187, 199

deportation: ABC Settlement Agreement and, 68; dangers at home and, 76; family separation and, 27, 128; mental health and, 161

discrimination: migrants' awareness of, 144; self-esteem and, 144

drug cartels, 63, 104, 116

education: interruption in migrant children, 80, 196; as reason for migration, 77–78, 81, 84–86. See also schools

El Salvador: civil war, 41, 57–59, 65; Cold War and, 58; conflict with Honduras, 57; development of gangs in, 62–63, 67; humanitarian crisis in, 203; inequality in, 56; *La matanza* massacre, 56–57; plantation economy, impact of, 54, 56; precolonial and colonial period, 55, 56; unrest of masses in, 56–57; U.S. intervention in, 60

El Salvadoran migrants to U.S.: downward social mobility, 59; educational deficits, 196; history of migration by UAMs, 21; incentives for undocumented entry, 59, 65; number of documented migrants, 198; number of UAMs, 15, 39, **40**, 65; as product of U.S. policies, 65; reasons for migration, XXIV, XXV–XXVI, 41, 58–59, 195; remittances and, 69; temporary protected status (TPS) and, 59

ethnicity, durable, and integration, 6

family members in U.S., and migration, 11–12, 196–97, 202

family-propelled migration, XII, 11–12. *See also* reunification of families

family reunification. *See* reunification of families

family separation: caregiver problems and, 86–87; causes of, XIX, 35, 70; chronic uncertainty and, 79; emotional and economic factors in, 73; enforced, and creation of UAMs, 26–27; estrangement between family members and, XXII, XXVI, XXVIII–XXIX, 16, 20, 86–87, 126–28; family roles and, 22; forced, history of, 17–20, 26; impact on children, 23, 34, 69–71, 73–74, 78–79, 127, 128, 140–41, 142, 161, 167; Mexican families and, 82; scholarship on, 37–39; separated siblings, 79–80; separation of labor and labor reproduction and, 71; structural, definition of, XIV; tensions created by, 72; through deportation, 27, 128; typical length of, 71; by U.S. border officials, 153–54, 156, 157; U.S. immigration law and, 3, 12, 14, 16, 18–19, 28, 35–36, 128; varying experiences of, 78–79, 142; wealthy-nation migrants and, 19; workers'

migration to U.S. and, 67–68. *See also* transnational families; Trump administration immigration policies

family unity, as right, 12, 79

Filipinos, as temporary laborers in U.S., 17, 20

Flores Settlement Agreement, XII, 66, 187, 190

France, African migration to, 13, 18, 68–69

gangs in Central America: aggressive recruitment by, XXV, XXVII, 82–83; association of immigrants with, 15; inability to attend school and, 80, 82–83; as reason for migration to U.S., XXI–XXII, XXIV, XXV–XXVI, XXVII–XXVIII, 10, 36, 77, 82–84, 148, 150–51, 176–77; U.S. role in growth of, 54, 62–63, 66–67; violence from, and trauma, 147–51

gender roles, and migration, 22

Global North, and cheap labor, 34, 35, 72

Great Replacement theory, XXI, 31

Guatemala: civil war, 62; development of gangs in, 67; friendliness toward migrants, 106; humanitarian crisis in, 203; inequality in, 64; mistreatment of Indigenous people, 75; ongoing violence in, 62; plantation economy, impact of, 54; precolonial and colonial period, 55; U.S. intervention in, 60, 61–62

Guatemalan migrants to U.S.: educational deficits, 196; history of migration by UAMs, 21; incentives for undocumented entry, 65; Indigenous people as, 75–76; number of UAMs, 15, 39, **40**; reasons for migration, 195; remittances and, 69

guest workers: family separation and, 17–20, 25; return home of most, 19

health, social determinants of, 141. *See also* mental health of child migrants

*hielera* (freezer), detention in, XXIV, 91, 110–11, 112, 151, 153–54
Hispanic paradox, 141
Honduran migrants to U.S.: areas of high emigration, 76; educational deficits, 196; history of migration by UAMs, 21; number of, 60; number of UAMs, 15, 39, **40**; reasons for migration, XXI–XXII, 60, 61, 195; remittances and, 69
Honduras: Cold War and, 60; conflict with El Salvador, 57; development of gangs in, 67; inequality in, 64; plantation economy, impact of, 54; precolonial and colonial period, 55; U.S. intervention in, 60; violence and instability in, 60–61, 64, 203; Walker's invasion of, 60
households: factors creating instability in, 38; migration as economic decision by, 20–21
human trafficking laws, 26
Hurricane Mitch, 60, 143

immigrant, definition of, XII
Immigration and Nationality 1952 (INA), 18–19
imperialism, impact of, 30
Indigenous people, 55, 56, 75
inequality: categorical, 9; in Central America, 64; family separation and, 35, 70; global, need to address, 207
integration, structural, 4–9; age of migrant and, 172, 175; *vs.* assimilation, 5; barriers to, 185, **186**; as currently-preferred concept, 5; de facto White status and, 5–6; definition of, XII; durable ethnicity and, 6; education to counter xenophobia, 30–31; effect of trauma exposure on, 158; facilitators of, **186**; factors affecting, 7–8, 183; general well being and, 172; helping with, 30, 31, 138, 202–9; immigrants' assessment of environment and, 13; in immigrants *vs.* African Americans, 230n25; initial problems with, 179, 184; language and, 174, 175, 176, 179–80, 181–82, 184, 193; legal status and, 52; migration experience and, 100, 116–17; multicultural approach of, 7; obstacles to, 12, 39; selective acculturation and, 8; signs of, 10; social safety net and, 30; success of, 13; symbolic ethnicity and, 5–6; unaccompanied status and, 47–48; by wealthy and well-educated, 9
internal migration: as alternative, 202; for labor, children and, 19, 25; of workers to migrant-sending towns, 73
interviewees, 45; characteristics of, XX, 119, 167–68; demographics of, 47–49, **48**, **50–51**; documentation status of, 52, 197–98; mental health evaluations of, 45, 46; randomized sample and, 169; service providers interviewed, 45, 49; sponsors interviewed, 45; subsequent deportation of some, 11, 192; unique experiences of, 10–11

labor protections, benefits of, 31
language of child migrants: integration and, 174–76, 179–80, 181–82, 184, 193; programs to improve, 193; service providers and, 17
Latin, as term, XIII
Latin America, U.S. interventions in, 59–60
Latin immigrants, racialization of, 7
law enforcement, profiling of Hispanics, 31
legal migration: benefits of increased avenues for, 92; relative ease of, 91–92
legal representation for UAMs, 119–20, 121, 122
legal status, as pointless distinction, XIII
legal status, obtaining: emotional toll on minors, 122, 123, 125; minors' reliance on others for, 119–20, 122
legal status, unclear: mental health and, 161; as obstacle, XXII, 14, 119, 120, 122–23

Mary's Center, 178, 180
media coverage of migrants, 1, 13, 14, 113, 114
Medicaid coverage for D.C. students, 178
mental health of child migrants, 169–70; abusive caretakers and, 143; Child PTSD Symptom Scale (CPSS) on, 164–66, **165**, 168; deportation fears and, 161; factors affecting, 140, 142; family separation and, 140–41, 142, 161, 167; family support and, 166; findings, 167–69; hostile environment and, 144; integration and, 171; limitations of data, 160–61, 168–69; loneliness and, 167; loss of stand-in parents and, 24, 79, 129, 130, 138; Mary's Center program and, 178, 180; measurements used, 158–59; multigenerational trauma in Central America and, 143–44; need for support programs, 194; Patient Health Questionnaire modified for children (PHQ-8) on, 163–64, **164**; peer relationships and, 174; PTSD and, 142, 143; self-reported, before and after migration, **159**, 159–61, **162**; self-reported stressors, 161–63, **162**, 166–67; self-reported traumatic experiences, 145–51; social determinants of, 141–43, 169–70; stressors for new arrivals, 144, 161; trauma exposure checklist and, 169, 222–25; traumatic detention experiences and, 153–58; traumatic life experiences in Central America, 140; travel to U.S. and, 145, 151–54; unclear legal status and, 161; unique stressors of migration and, 141, 142; U.S. immigration policies and, 144–45, 188, 189. *See also* adverse childhood experiences (ACEs)
methodology, 45–47; interviewers, 46; interview guide for officials, 211; interviews, 46–47; *vs.* large data-driven studies, 233n37; limitations, 49–52; Patient Health Questionnaire modified for children (PHQ-8), 220–22; sampling methods, 45–46, 51; Survey Guide for Sponsors, 226–28; survey of UAMs, 212–20; trauma exposure checklist, 222–25. *See also* contributions of this study; interviewees
Mexican Farm Labor (Bracero) Program, 17, 25
Mexico: accounts of detention in, 151–52; anti-immigrant sentiment in, 106; crackdown on migration, XX, 103–4, 106, 114–15; decline in immigration from, 14–15; difficulty of crossing, XXIII; enforcement of U.S. immigration policies, 197; history of migration by UAMs, 21; Mexican family separations, 82; migrants' bribing of authorities, XXIII; temporary labor in U.S. and, 17, 25; transit visas for migrants, 103; U.S. policies causing migration from, 68
migrant protection protocols (MPPs), XIII, XX, 16, 187, 188, 190
migrants: *vs.* asylum seekers or refugees, 36–37; importance of feeling at home, 129; reasons for recent increase in, 202–3, 204; types of, XIII; U.S. stigma against, 103
migration theory, 11–12
migration to U.S.: benefits to U.S. from, XXI, 203; in Cold War, 63–64; equity in opportunities and outcomes and, 7; factors promoting, 105; family separation and, 67–68; internal migration of workers to migrant-sending towns and, 73; as masculine right of passage, 22; migration pathways, factors in, 4; migration stream diversification, 21; obstacles in, XX, 104, 122; as often family decision, 77; psychological impact of, 22–23; reasons for, 85; reproduction across generations, 72–73; statistics on, and repeat migrants, 115–16; success in, as relatively rare, 76;

U.S. policies as root cause of, 68; vignettes of, XXI–XXVIII; volume of, in 2022, 21
minimum wage, 208
Monroe Doctrine, 55, 64
MPPs. *See* migrant protection protocols
MS-13, 54, 66–67, 189
multiculturalism, as preferred ideal, 18

National Security Doctrine (NSD), 60, 64
neocolonial extraction, 35
neoliberalism, and wages, 72
New York Second Generation Study, 7–8
Nicaragua, history of, 54, 60, 61

Obama administration, 35, 199
opportunity: equity for immigrants as goal, 7; as reason for migration, 77–78, 81, 84–86, 100; settled migrants and, 124–25
ORR. *See* U.S. Office of Refugee Resettlement

parents working in U.S.: fear of failure, 130–31; isolation, impact of, 79. *See also* family separation; transnational families
Patient Health Questionnaire modified for children (PHQ-8), 163–64, **164**, 220–22
*perrera* (dog pound), detention in, 151, 155–56
Personal Responsibility and Work Opportunity Reconciliation Act of 1996 (PRWORA), 188
PHQ-8. *See* Patient Health Questionnaire modified for children (PHQ-8)
post-traumatic stress disorder (PTSD) in child migrants, 16, 142, 143, 164–70, **165**, 168

race, assimilation and, 5–9
racial capitalism, 9
racism: education to counter, 30–31; opposition to migrants as, 106
Reagan, Ronald W., 60, 67

reasons for migration to U.S., 36–37; changing circumstances as, 36; country of origin as predictor of, 195–96; economic desperation as, 20, 68–69; flight from violence as, 9–10; imperialism and global capitalism as, 30; instability as, 39, 53–54; loss of caregiver as, 198; need for remittances as, 69, 199; opportunity as, 77–78, 81, 84–86, 100; reunification of family as, XXII, XXVIII, 16, 74–75, 77–78, 82, 84–87, 89, 93, 116, 124, 196, 199–200, 203, 204; as similar in all regions, 68, 100; structural reasons, XX, 1–2, 4; theory on, 3–4; three main reasons, 77, 93; in UAMs, 21; U.S.-created problems as, 62–63; various types of, 180, 195–96. *See also* gangs in Central America, as reason for migration to U.S.
refugee house (*casa hogar*), accounts of, 151, 153–54, 156
refugees, *vs.* migrants or asylum seekers, 36–37
Remain in Mexico program. *See* migrant protection protocols (MPPs)
remittances: definition of, 69; economic desperation and, 69; economic importance of, XXV, XXVIII, 23, 69, 70, 81–82; family separation and, 23–24, 70; need for, as motive for migration, 69, 199; pressure on others to migrate and, 69; separation of labor and labor reproduction and, 71
reunification of families: adjustment to new life and, XXII, XXIV, 29, 124–26, 127, 129–31; benefits for children, 28–29; changes in family and, 16, 124, 126, 135, 136, 137–38; children's views on, 38; child's relationship with mother and, 133–36; counseling services for, 180; as difficult but worthwhile, 184, 192; estrangement over time and, XXVI, 16, 20, 86–87, 126–28, 129–31, 132; factors shaping

process, 35, 126, 128–29; joy of family members, 27, 28; legal obstacles to, 14, 38–39, 119–24; mental health of child migrants and, 139, 166; mothers as sponsors and, 136–37; mutual respect, importance of, 136–38; parents' rules and, 129–31, 132, 137; as process, 126; range of experiences in, 125; as reason for migration, XXII, XXVIII, 16, 74–75, 77–78, 82, 84–87, 89, 93, 116, 124, 196, 199–200, 203, 204; reforms needed to support, 31, 192–93; sponsor's commitment and, 138; stress of, 161; through legal migration, 91–92; transformation of receiving nations and, 19; trauma at loss of stand-in parents and, 24, 79, 129, 130, 138

sanctuary movement in U.S., 41
schools: demographic change in, 179; federally funded programs for, 178–79; Medicaid for students, 178; migrants' trauma and, 180; *vs.* schools in Central America, 181; separate, for interrupted formal education (SIFE) students, 180–81; social justice classes, 181
schools, integration and: bullying and, 176; caring relationships with adults, **172**, 172–73; cultural sensitivity in staff and, 179; identity formation and, 177; language as barrier, 174, 175, 176, 179–80, 181–82, 184, 193; migrants' mental health and, 171; officials' views on, 177–80; positive educational experiences and, 175; programs to improve migrant English ability, 193; relationships with peers, **173**, 173–77; school officials' views on, 177–80; services for immigrant students, 171, 178, 181, 182, 183–84; social and cultural capital and, 177; support networks, benefits of, 184
SIJ. *See* special immigrant juvenile

social networks/social capital: accumulation in schools, 177; definition of, XIV, 177; ease of migration and, 20–21; migrants' development of, XXII; transnational, facilitation of migration, 35, 85; in Washington, D.C., 42
social safety net, needed reforms, 30, 203
special immigrant juveniles (SIJs), XIV, 26, 120
sponsors: interviews of, 45, 226–28; legal responsibilities of, XIV; release of UAMs to, 205; undocumented, risk of, XIV
students with interrupted formal education (SIFE), programs for, 180–81
support programs: migrants' failure to access, 178–79; need to increase awareness of, 194–95; staff's lack of training, 16–17

temporary protected status (TPS), 41, 59
Title 8, XX, 191–92
Title 42, XIV, XX, 16, 188, 191
Trafficking Victims Protection Reauthorization Act (TVPRA), XIV, 109, 191
transnational families: benefits *vs.* costs, 27; degrees of success, 24–26; different types of, 37–38; effect on children, 38; history of, 25; immigration policy and, 27–28; parenting at a distance and, 24; undocumented workers and, 25–26. *See also* parents working in U.S.
trauma of migration, 23, 34, 194. *See also* mental health of child migrants
travel to U.S. border, XXII, XXIII–XXIV, XXVIII, 113–16; child migrants' silence on, 97–98, 102–3; cost of, XXIV, 99; dangers of, XX, 74–75, 88, 91, 97–98, 104–5, 113–14; extortion by gangs and, 107–8; fear of Mexican

authorities, 104, 108; freight trains, illicit riding of, XX, 74–75, 90, 104–5, 114; groups providing aid, 108–9; as "illegal," implications of, 103; mental health and, 145, 151–54; Mexico, danger in, 106–7; Mexico's anti-immigration push and, 103–4, 106, 114–15; repeat migration, 115–16; time required for, 105–6. *See also coyotes*; visas

Trump administration immigration policies, 186–92; demonization of migrants, 52, 189; family separation and, 15, 26, 34, 35, 36, 187, 190; immigrants' rights and, 66, 188–89, 190, 192; impact on migrants, 189–90; timeline of, 187–88; "zero tolerance" policy, 15, 26, 187, 190. *See also* migrant protection protocols (MPPs); Title 42

Turkey, seasonal workers in, 20

T-visas, XV, 26, 120

unaccompanied alien child/children (UAC), as term, XV, 41, 89

unaccompanied alien minors (UAMs), as term, 89

"unaccompanied," as term, 27

unaccompanied child(ren) (UC), as term, 89

unaccompanied minors (UAMs): alarmism about, 34; from Central America, history of, 3, 21; from Central America, U.S. destinations, 41, **42**, **43**; countries of origin, 15, 39, **40**, 68; *coyotes* and, 90–91; danger and, 90; family separation and, 14, 26–27; first person accounts by, 44–45; good behavior of, 121; history of migration by, 1–2, 34; legal responsibility to protect, 2, 15; from Mexico, history of, 21; number of, 1, 2, 3, 14, 185; release to family or sponsors, 205; stigmatization of, 2; travel with friends or extended family, 74–75, 89–90; treatment by U.S. legal system, 65–66; variation in needs and experiences, 44

unaccompanied refugee minor (URM), XV, 109

undocumented migrants: amnesty and, 199, 206, 207; as artificial category, 188; benefits of work in U.S. and, 120; as caregivers, 140; criminalization of, 26; fear of reporting crimes, 145; inability to bring family members, 35, 100, 205; inability to return home, 25–26; increased U.S. scrutiny on, 144–45; recent increases in, 188; in this study's sample, 197–98

UN Refugee Agency (UNHCR), 200

URM. *See* unaccompanied refugee minor

U.S. Customs and Border Protection (CBP): detention by, XXIV, XXVIII, 36, 91, 98–99, 106, 110–12, 156; migrant surge of 2014 and, 1; treatment of child migrants, 97–98; turnover of children to ORR, 109; undocumented migrants and, XXIV

U.S. immigration system: as burden on transnational families, 27–28; as confusing and bureaucratic, 121–22, 123, 197, 205; COVID-19 and, 16, 169; family separation and, 3, 12, 14, 16, 18–19, 28, 35–36, 128; fears about relaxing, XXI; focus on individuals, 18–19; hard-line, problems with, 31; help in integration and, 30, 31; legal violence and, 99; migrant safety and, XXI, 208; migrants' health and, 34, 144–45, 188, 189; migrants' limited knowledge about, 198–99; processing of UAMs, 120; racial profiling and, 189; recommendations for, 205, 206–9; reforms, imperfect, 26; restrictions on immigrants' rights, 188–89, 190; restrictions on return visits, 35–36, 128; state laws targeting migrants, 189; undocumented migrants and, 144–45; unintended consequences of, 31. *See also* Trump administration immigration policies

U.S. intervention in Latin America, 59–60; problems in Central America and, 34, 52, 54–55, 63–65, 203; U.S. responsibility for migrants and, 204

U.S. Office of Refugee Resettlement (ORR): access to federal programs and, 178–79; migrant integration and, 177–80; number of UAMs referred to, 2012-2021, 39; processing of UAMs, 120; shelters, described, 111–13; treatment of UAMs, 109, 121; on UAMs released in D.C. area, 41–42

U-visas, XV, 26, 120

violence: in Central America, trauma from, 146–51; as motive for migration, 9–10, 201; in Washington, DC, XXIV–XXV. *See also* gangs in Central America

visas: ease of travel and, XXVI; types of, 26, 120

war on drugs, immigration and, 62–63, 68, 85, 203

Washington D.C. area: Central American population in, 41, 44; child immigrants settled in, 42, **43**, **44**, 185; immigrant businesses in, 44; Latin-majority neighborhoods, 41, 42; residents' aid to migrants, 40–41; Salvadoran migration to, 41, 59; social services in, 174

well-being of migrants, 172, 183

West Germany, guest workers in, 17–18

William Wilberforce Trafficking Victims Protection Reauthorization Act of 2008 (TVPRA), XIV, 109, 191

women in workforce, neoliberalism and, 72

xenophobia, 5, 18, 30–31, 144